Social Business

FONS VAN DER VELDEN (ED.)

Social Business

Transformational approach to a fair and just society

RAWAT PUBLICATIONS

Jaipur • New Delhi • Bangalore • Guwahati • Kolkata

ISBN 978-81-316-1016-9

Indian Reprint, 2019

First published in 2018 by
LM Publishers, Parallelweg 37, 1131 DM Volendam, The Netherlands
info@impublishers.nl
www.impublishers.nl

Editor Fons van der Velden
Text editor Hilde Bakker
Design and layout Ad van Helmond

Published by
Prem Rawat for **Rawat Publications**
Satyam Apts., Sector 3, Jawahar Nagar, Jaipur - 302 004 (India)
Phone: 0141 265 1748 / 7006 Fax: 0141 265 1748
E-mail : info@rawatbooks.com
Website: rawatbooks.com

New Delhi Office
4858/24, Ansari Road, Daryaganj, New Delhi 110 002
Phone: 011-23263290

Also at *Bangalore, Guwahati* and *Kolkata*

Printed at Nice Printing Press, New Delhi.

'While we do our good works let us not forget that the real solution lies in a world in which charity will have become unnecessary'.

CHINUA ACHEBE[1]

1 Achebe, C. (1988), *Anthills of the Savannah*, London, Heinemann Educational Books Ltd, page 155.

Contents

List of Diagrams, boxes and tables

Diagrams

Boxes

Tables

Introduction: Take back the economy

Fons van der Velden

The Isle of Jura and the Wizard of Oz

In the summer of 2017, my wife and I visited family members on the Isle of Jura, one of the Hebridean islands off the west coast of Scotland. Our relatives have both been trained in organic farming and worked with great pleasure for the owners of the Ardfin estate on Jura for more than 40 years. They developed an internationally acclaimed public garden that became the main tourist attraction of the island, and they looked after visitors of the estate. This was our last visit to them on Jura, as our relatives had decided to leave the beautiful and peaceful island and move to England.

They lost their appetite for staying on Jura as the Ardfin estate and a major part of the island had been bought by a 41-year-old retired hedge fund manager, Mr Greg Coffey, who changed the rules of the game on the island. The Guardian reports: 'The 12,000-acre Ardfin estate is said to offer superb views across the Irish Sea and on a clear day it is said that you can see Northern Ireland. Not that Coffey would know: according to locals he has only visited twice since snapping it up for £3.5 million in 2010. Nevertheless, he has still managed to incur the wrath of islanders by closing the estate's previously public gardens and attempting to build a nine-hole golf course and shooting range'.[1] The author is unfortunately not well informed: the view from the estate of the Irish Sea is really superb, but is now blocked to the general public on account of a prestigious nineteen-hole golf course. And yes, hunting appears to be a hobby of the new owner, as his employees are now rearing ducks for shooting parties.

Who is this man, this Greg Coffey, who brings so much disturbance to this beautiful island? According to The Guardian he is a 'hedge fund maestro' with a 'glittering career'. The Telegraph writes that 'Mr Coffey, 41, made his name – and the bulk of his $700m fortune – at GLG Partners where he racked up a seemingly invincible track record. He then sent the firm into a tailspin by abruptly quitting in 2008, having reportedly turned down a $250m "golden handcuffs" deal to stay at GLG'.[1] His new employer, Mr Bacon of Moore Capital, praised him – as per various sources – as 'one of the most impressive traders in the world'. 'He had reportedly generated annual returns of 22 percent a year since 2004'.[2] This track record earned him the nickname 'The Wizard of Oz'. Coffey is not afraid of spending his vast wealth. He owns houses across the world, including a

1 Armistead, 2012.
2 Ibid.

West London mansion, a 'handful of Scottish islands' and the Ardfin estate on Jura.[3] Mark Dampier, head of the Hargreaves Lansdown, remarks in the same article in The Guardian that people like Coffey 'start to think that they can walk on water'.

Walk on water: Finance capitalism

So that is what it is: 'Coffey made his money with trading' and starts to believe 'that he can walk on water'. Greg Coffey is not alone in this. He is a representative of what can be called finance capitalism, which is characterised by 'a predominance of the pursuit of profit from the purchase and sale of, or investment in, currencies and financial products such as bonds, stocks, futures and other derivatives'.[4] For approximately half a century finance capitalism – in which basically nothing is really being produced – has gained importance over older forms of capitalism. Commodities are now financial products (such as shares and derivatives of which the value fluctuates constantly), which are not related to production or even profit.[5] (As per the London-based Financial Times there have been days that Greg Coffey revamped his entire investment portfolio 22 times.) This is basically a betting and gambling process ('casino capitalism') with winners – such as Greg Coffey and his colleagues – and many, many losers as the recent financial crisis in Europe and the United States has made clear.[6]

Global Inequality: Thomas Piketty's Capital

Mr Coffey's wealth is still quite modest compared with that of some other men: Oxfam International reports that eight men own as much as the poorest 50% of the world. Thomas Piketty's international bestseller *Capital in the Twenty-First Century* and the related annual *World Inequality Report* provide detailed empirical data about inequality in the contemporary world. Piketty's research indicates that since the 1970s income inequality has increased significantly in the Unites States, but not only in the US.[7] He reports further that global inequality ranges from the regions where the per capita income is in the order of €150 to €200 per month (sub-Saharan Africa, India) to regions where it is €2,500 to €3,000 per month (Western Europe, America and Japan), that is, 10 to 20 times higher.[8] In this context it should be noted that '... the rich countries are doubly wealthy: they produce more at home and invest more abroad, so that their income per head is greater than their output per head. The opposite is true for poor countries'.[9] Piketty does not only pay attention to the income distribution between countries but also within countries and notes e.g. that inequality in countries such as India and China is rising rapidly.[10] The World Bank reports that a marked concentration of wealth at the top end of the income-distribution scale, particularly in the United

3 Neville, 2012.
4 Ref. Wilson, 2013. See e.g. also https://en.wikipedia.org/wiki/Finance_capitalism
5 Berardi, 2015.
6 Varoufakis, 2016.
7 Piketty, 2014: 19.
8 Piketty, 2014: 81.
9 Ibid: 86.
10 Ibid: 416.

States and other English-speaking countries, India, and China, is increasing and a long-term and continuous increase in the within-country component of global inequality is taking place. 'And if the benefits of economic growth are unevenly distributed within countries, upcoming technological changes and urbanization are likely to intensify these divisions further.'[11] It is reported that income inequality is typically higher in developing and emerging economies than in advanced economies. In most major emerging economies, income inequality rose over the past three decades. The largest increases in these economies that are G-20 members, as measured by the Gini coefficient of disposable income, were in China, Russia, and South Africa, with India also experiencing a notable increase. The picture is more broadly mixed in the developing world.[12]

One of the main messages of Piketty's study is that the resurgence of inequality after 1980 is largely due to political shifts, especially with regard to taxation and finance.[13] The second main conclusion of his book is that 'the dynamics of wealth distribution reveal powerful mechanisms pushing alternatively to convergence and divergence. Furthermore, there is no natural spontaneous process to prevent destabilizing inegalitarian forces from prevailing permanently.'[14]

Implications of inequality: Equality is better for everyone

The Italian activist, philosopher and writer, Franco Berardi, links this process to what he calls 'deterritorialization' of production and exchange: finance capitalists are no longer connected to a specific physical environment or state (nor are they accountable to states, fellow investors and civil society) but enjoy almost complete deregulation as global legal control of their activities is virtually impossible. Berardi argues that this form of capitalism has far-reaching implications not only at systemic level, but at the level of individuals as well: according to the World Health Organisation (WHO), depression, shootings and suicides are on the increase.[15] In the recent (2018) *World Inequality Report* it is stated that '… if rising inequality is not properly monitored and addressed, it can lead to various sorts of political, economic, and social catastrophes.'[16]

In a monumental study *The Spirit Level: Why Equality is Better for Everyone*, Wilkinson (economic historian) and Pickett (health researcher) have explored the validity of the intuitive belief that inequality is socially corrosive and that materialism beyond a certain level of fundamental needs actually inhibits the satisfaction of social needs. They conclude that while economic growth has benefited humanity by providing better health, increased longevity and higher measures of well-being and happiness, there

11 Verbeek, 2015.
12 Dervis & Qureshi, 2016.
13 Piketty, 2014: 27.
14 Piketty, 2014: 28.
15 Berardi, 2015.
16 Alvaredo et al, (*World Inequality Report*, research team) 2018: 4.

is now evidence that developed societies have got close to the end of what economic growth can do in social terms. In fact, as affluent societies grow richer, there have been long-term rises in rates of anxiety, depression and numerous other social problems.[17]

In the first part of their book, these authors reinforce the point that in poorer countries economic growth increases health, longevity and social well-being. These increases cannot be underestimated and it points to the importance of economic assistance for poorer countries.

Wilkinson and Pickett also make clear, however, that the benefits of economic growth drop off beyond a certain point, so for those countries that have achieved a certain level of development wealth is no longer a good predictor of any of the indicators of social happiness and well-being.

This leads to the second part of the book in which they demonstrate on the basis of abundant empirical data that the level of equity in a country is a strong and accurate predictor of social well-being. That is, countries that have lower economic standing but are relatively more equitable will do better on almost everything. One of their main conclusions is that even though rich people tend, on average, to be healthier and happier than poor people in the same society, it is important to note that in more equitable societies both richer and poorer will do better. In other words, inequality is not only bad for the poorer half of society, but for everyone.[18] In countries with higher equality, everybody is healthier, including the rich.[19]

'Take back the economy': Social and solidarity economy

If the story of the Greg Coffeys of this world and the research of Piketty and Wilkinson make one thing clear, it is this: the time has come to take back the economy.[20] This publication takes as an entry point the subject of social business, i.e. organisations that use business principles to create 'blended value'[21] in a (financially) sustainable manner in order to contribute to systemic societal change. It should especially be noted that in a social business, the social and financial purposes are intertwined. In this publication the concept of social business is not defined within the technocratic a-political tradition, which is currently followed by many so-called social enterprises, but conceptualised as a political project, as a radical (read 'transformative') element in a transformation process towards a social and solidarity economy (SSE). The social

17 Wilkinson & Pickett, 2009. See also Edgar, 2010.

18 https://www.ted.com/talks/richard_wilkinson
and e.g. http://edition.cnn.com/2011/11/06/opinion/wilkinson-inequality-harm/index.html

19 Wilkinson & Pickett provide in their book a detailed account of the costs of inequality for: Community life and social relations; Mental health and drug abuse; Physical health and life expectancy; Obesity; Educational performance; Teenage births; Violence; Imprisonment and punishment; Social mobility.

20 Gibson-Graham et al, 2013.

21 With components such as reducing inequality, contributing to global social justice, improved environment and enhanced democracy.

and solidarity economy sector 'aims to replace fundamentally unjust or unequal social, economic and power relations with democratically run institutions providing sustainable livelihoods, in order to bring democratically run, economically just, socially inclusive and environmentally sustainable futures.'[22]

Hence, in this book, the concept of a social business will be regarded as a strategic approach towards a much broader political-economic discourse that aims at fundamentally transforming the neo-liberal development model through a combined strategy of interrelated local and global action. It is an approach whereby alternative business models are positioned with the broader macro-economic systemic change processes. Among traditional (neo- Marxist) leftists thinkers and organisations there is generally quite a bit of scepticism about development of social, political and economic alternatives in a 'hostile' (predominantly neo-liberal) external environment.[23] José Luis Coraggio puts this debate in a Polanyian perspective, that argues that the SSE is an attempt by society 'to take back and democratise the economy to prevent capitalism destroying society – or, we might say, the planet as a whole.'[24] Hence, SSE should be seen as part of a Polanyian counter-movement to a neo-liberalism that, 'left unchecked, would destroy society'.[25]

Utting and others are rightly raising the question whether SSE can be scaled up in ways that are consistent with the core values and objectives of such an approach.[26] He and his co-authors of the UNRISD publication[27] basically arrive at the conclusion that while SSE has a considerable potential in relation to inclusive, sustainable development, '... the scope of realising this potential is heavily constrained by structural contexts, relations with external actors and institutions, trade-offs between different objectives, and internal dynamics within SSE organisations, enterprises and networks', but they contend that under certain conditions some of these constraints and tensions can be mitigated. They conclude that the entire issue is still 'work in progress'. At the same time, it may already be concluded that SSE as an approach needs to be enabled through public policy.[28]

22 North & Scott Cato, 2017: 6 -7.

23 In the leftists, (neo-) Marxist discourse working on alternatives is not uncontested and often labelled as reformist and as a social democratic approach. The argument here is that poor and marginalised communities cannot wait for Godot to come; that it is worthwhile to state experimenting with alternatives at local, regional and national level; that interrelated transformative political activities that are carried out at different levels simultaneously contribute to systemic change.

24 North & Scott Cato, 2017: 9.

25 North, 2017: 89. See also Coraggio, 2017.

26 He calls this integrative scaling up. Utting, 2015: 3.

27 Ref. also: www.unrisd.org/sse

28 Utting: 2015:5 and various chapters in the book.

The present volume: Outcome of co-creation

The present volume has emerged from the work that we have carried out over the last ten years at Context, international cooperation (Utrecht, The Netherlands).[29] We have had the privilege of working with activists, social entrepreneurs (including those aspiring to be such), social investors and development organisations on four continents: Africa, Asia, Europe and Latin America. With many of our client organisations we have engaged in collaborative action research; we have provided often very practical business development support; and we have analysed, documented and disseminated our learnings through master classes, articles, blogs, books and brochures. This volume is a follow-up of the two Social Return on Investment (SROI) guides that we published in 2008 and 2011; the volume about social business as an innovative approach to change processes (2011) and a publication about leadership and social business (2013). SOS Children's Villages International was so kind as to support us with the documentation of our experiences with social business as a transformational approach.

A lot of what is being presented here has emerged in interactive, co-creation sessions with staff members of client organisations from across the globe: from milk farmers in Bolivia and women in the jungle in Suriname (a former Dutch colony in Latin America), to Maasai men and women in Kenya and Tanzania. From apple farmers in the Himalayas (India), to young enthusiastic social entrepreneurs in Cambodia and a community centre in the Netherlands, to aspiring social business leaders in Africa, Asia and Latin America.

The book is meant for practitioners who are interested in learning from other experiences and reflecting upon their own work; for trainers; business developers; policy-makers and researchers. There is no need to read the book from cover to cover: all chapters can be read as stand-alone texts and have references (in footnotes and a reference list at the end of each chapter).

The book consists of three types of contributions: case descriptions of social businesses; outcomes of collaborative action research; and more theoretical conceptual chapters. The case descriptions are presented in Chapter I (a social business managed by apple farmers in the Himalayas, India), Chapter III (a self-financing health scheme in Nepal) and Chapter VII (provision of internet facilities in Uganda). In order to broaden the scope of the debate, a case description about shared value creation (SVC) is also included (Chapter V about Pactics in Cambodia). In Chapter IX a description is provided of what it takes to foster a more entrepreneurial approach within an International Non-Governmental Development Organisation (INGDO).

29 www.contextinternationalcooperation.org

Outcomes of collaborative action research are presented in Chapter IV (detailed description and analysis of a leadership development and support programme for leaders of social businesses), Chapter VI (business performance measurement) and Chapter VIII (mentoring of social entrepreneurs).

More conceptual reflections are offered in this introduction with a focus on the implications of casino capitalism; Chapter II, which deals with the *why*, *what* and *how* of a social business approach to change processes; Chapter X, which deals with the extent to which social business can be regarded as an emerging new mode of production and as an entry point for the materialisation of a social and solidarity economy.

The main messages of this book are that social business is a radical transformative approach to fostering the development of a social and solidarity economy; that it is useful to come up with very practical experiments and examples that provide insights into the fundamental transition processes; and that such an approach needs to be enabled through combined and interrelated local and global action.

Acknowledgements

As indicated in the previous section, this book is the product of intensive dialogue and co-creation. I hereby want to acknowledge the contribution of the members of our informal social business community, which consists of leaders of social businesses, social investors, action researchers and business development providers with whom we collaborated during the past decade: Worku Behonegne, Pradeep Esteves, Alan Fowler, Sathyasree Goswami, Pol De Greve, Marleen Hasselerharm, Martin Kariongi Ole Sanago, Zunaid Moolla, Manase Owade, Malla Reddy, Laxmi Prakash Semwal, Titus van der Spek, and Meidert Witvliet.

Laila Bouallouch, Carmen Curvers, Elja van Diemen, Margherita Scazza and Titus van der Spek provided research assistance during various stages of the collaborative action research process.

Many people were so kind as to review one or more chapters of this book before publication. They are all acknowledged and named in the chapters they contributed to.

Hilde Bakker did not only accept the responsibility for the editing of the book, but also acted as advisor and sounding board during the final stages of the writing process.

I want to acknowledge the contribution of my business partner Pol De Greve; together we explored many of the issues that are being dealt with in this volume. I would furthermore like to express my gratitude for their direct or indirect contributions and encouragement, to Ben Boerkamp, Jessie Bokhoven, Betteke de Gaay Fortman, Johan van de Gronden, Sharad Joshi, David Katzlinger, Mary Njuguna, Ntombi Nyathi, Tom Olila, Munya Saruchera, James Taylor, Rob van Tulder and Marieke de Wal, and to SOS

Children's Villages as an institution for their support with regard to documenting our experiences. Chantel Sharon Kennedy was so kind as to allow me to include her rap text in this volume.

Last but not least a special word of thanks is due to my life partner Karin Baumans who had to bear the stories of the ups and downs of the emergence of this volume.

References

Alvaredo, F. et al, (World Inequality Report, research team), *World Inequality Report* 2018, World Inequality Lab 2018.

Armistead, L. (2012), Greg Coffey, the Wizard of Oz, quits hedge fund industry, in: *The Telegraph*, October 18. (https://www.telegraph.co.uk/finance/newsbysector/banksandfinance/9617223/Greg-Coffey-the-Wizard-of-Oz-quits-hedge-fund-industry.html)

Berardi, F. (2015), *Heroes: Mass murder and suicide*, Brooklyn, Verso Books.

Coraggio, J.L. (2017), Towards a new economics: concepts and experiences from Latin America, in: North, P. & Scott Cato, M. (eds.) (2017*), Towards just and sustainable economies; The social and solidarity economy North and South*, Bristol, Policy Press, pp. 15 – 35.

Dervis, K. & Qureshi, Z. (2016), *Income distribution within countries: rising inequality*, Washington, Brookings Institution, August. (https://www.brookings.edu/wp-content/uploads/2016/08/income-inequality-within-countries_august-2016-003.pdf)

Edgar, B. (2010), Review Wilkinson, R. & Pickett, K. (2009), The spirit level; Why equality is better for everyone, in: *Crucible*, Vol. 3, no.1 (November).

Gibson-Graham, J., Cameron, J. & Healy, S. (2013), *Take back the economy; An ethical guide for transforming our, communities*, Minneapolis, University of Minnesota Press.

Neville, S (2012), Have super star traders lost their magic, in: *The Guardian*, October 12. (https://www.theguardian.com/business/2012/oct/21/superstar-traders-lost-magic)

North, P. (2017), Transitioning towards low carbon solidarity economies, in: North, P. & Scott Cato, M. (eds.) (2017*), Towards just and sustainable economies; The social and solidarity economy North and South*, Bristol, Policy Press, pp. 73 – 95.

Piketty, T. (2017), *Capital in the Twenty-First Century*, Cambridge, The Belknap Press of Harvard University Press.

Utting, P. (ed.) (2015), *Social and solidarity economy; Beyond the fringe*, London, Zed Press.

Varoufakis, Y. (2016), *And the weak suffer what they must?*, London, The Bodley Head.

Verbeek, J. (2015), *Increasingly, inequality within, not across, countries is rising.* (http://blogs.worldbank.org/developmenttalk/increasingly-inequality-within-not-across-countries-rising), February 10.

Wilkinson, R. & Pickett, K. (2009), *The spirit level; Why equality is better for everyone*, London, Penguin Books.

Wilson, L. (2013), Finance capital: a tumour on the capitalist system or a fundamental part of it?, *In Defence of Marxism*, April, 2. (http://www.marxist.com/finance-capital-a-tumor-on-the-capitalist-system-or-a-fundamental-part-of-it.htm)

CHAPTER I

A case of apples in the Himalayas

The story of a successful social business

Laxmi Prakash Semwal[1]

Position of small and marginal farmers in India

Small farmers in India continue to be among the poorest in the world. Yet, their importance in ensuring sustainable economic development and food security cannot be underestimated. Indian agriculture is largely characterised by small and marginal holdings, accounting for 83% of the operational land. Despite their collectively high number, individual farmers face many challenges which limit their options. While growing perishables would in principle be a profitable undertaking, a large number of small farmers grow low-value crops such as wheat, sugarcane and rice. Their 'choice' is based on several factors, including: no guarantee of minimum support price for fresh produce, the risk of crop failure due to unpredictable climatic conditions, lack of storage facilities, price volatility, and low price realisation due to spoilage. In general, small farmers lack integration into value chains.

Marginal and small apple farmers in India are often dependent on and unable to escape the powerful grip of middlemen, informal lenders and other intermediaries. Financial institutions are hesitant to develop financial products that consider the entire value chain. This means existing loan and grant schemes tend to be patching solutions rather than structural ones. So, the position of small and marginal apple farmers in India remains dire. Two things that often contribute directly to the poverty of small apple producers in India are the absence of collective efforts for marketable volumes in order to reach economies of scale; and limited bargaining power in competitive markets due to insufficient storage facilities and therefore holding capacities.

Main challenges for apple growers in the Himalayas

Due to its bio-sphere, the Himalayan region in South Asia is blessed with unique, healthy and organically grown fresh as well as dry products, such as fruits, vegetables, special grains, spices, herbs, and medicinal plants. These precious (and often rare)

1 The author wants to express his gratitude to Hilde Bakker, Pradeep Esteves, Pol De Greve and Uday Thakkar who were so kind to peer review this chapter.

products are in high demand, both nationally and internationally. However, farmers are not able to optimally benefit from this situation for several interrelated reasons:

- *Slow delivery to consumers*: In India, the traditional practice of production, storage, transportation and distribution of apples is fragmented, which results in poor-quality supply to consumers who then prefer to buy imported apples. For example, an apple farmer starts to harvest apples on his farm on a Monday and continues until the weekend. With family support he is able to pick less than half a truck-load on the hilly terrain. From the farm, the harvest is transported on a donkey or human back to the road, where the other half truck-load will arrive from nearby farmers. After a week the truck (owned by a transporter) carries the apples to an auction place in a city, where a broker will settle the auction price and sell the truck-load to various buyers who deliver the produce to retailers. The produce will reach consumers only two weeks after picking.
- *Absence of infrastructure*: Farmers have small, fragmented pieces of land on the slopes of hills. After retaining produce for their own family consumption, very little remains for sale on the market. Dry commodities can be stored, but for the proper storage of fresh produce cash crops there is insufficient knowledge – and a lack of cold storage supply chain facilities – among government, businesses and consumers. Not enough has been invested in infrastructure and technologies for quality grading, storage, processing and distribution chains.
- *Absence of a professional value chain*: A professionally managed value chain of these fresh products is completely absent. Multiple layers of middlemen and processing parties control the process of produce reaching the market, which is run purely on commission basis. In this business model, many issues are not taken into account, including the risks that are taken by apple farmers, product development, and quality control.
- *Improper handling affects quality*: The unique qualities of the products are severely affected by improper handling and packaging, inadequate transportation, humidity, eating by animals such as rats, infestations of insects, (anaerobic) micro-organisms like fungi, and oxidation. The fact that products are often sorted and transported along with other commodities, that affect their flavour and fragrances, also negatively affects them.
- *Absence of technical assistance*: Individual small farmers do not receive any technical assistance on how to improve the quality and quantity of their produce.
- *Dependency on intermediaries*: The individual small and marginal apple farmers do not have direct access to the market, but are dependent on intermediaries such as transporters, input suppliers and auctioneers.
- *Absence of farmers' organisations*: There are some attempts to organise farmers in collectives. However, organisations that focus on the common good and on social cooperative spirits are rarely seen in remote villages and mountain habitations, due to prevailing individual interests and divisions influenced by middlemen.

The Apple Project

In view of the above-mentioned challenges, the Non-Governmental Development Organisation (NGDO) Shri Jagdamba Samiti (SJS) – an organisation with vast experience in working with marginal and small apple farmers in the Indian Himalayas – and Stichting Het Groene Woudt (SHGW) – a social investor[2] from the Netherlands – decided to start working together. They formed a social business consortium in 2007, aiming to support small and marginal apple farmers in the Himalayas to escape their dependence on middlemen, informal lenders and other intermediaries. SJS and SHGW invited Fresh Food Technology (FFT, a Dutch technology provider with offices in the Netherlands, India and Poland) and Context, international cooperation (a social business based in Utrecht, the Netherlands) to join as partners in the consortium.[3] The consortium has become commonly known as the Apple Project.

The consortium partners

Realising that poverty and indebtedness hinder social development of small and marginal apple growers in the Himalayas, SJS had already implemented some projects in cooperative-based agricultural value chains. The projects were all founded on the understanding that, for small farmers, collectives are crucial in order to generate enough marketable volume. However, these small-farmer collectives have generally had limited success in the scaling up of business, multiple commodity trading and distribution, and branding in consumer-led marketplaces. As a result, the cooperatives have remained dependent on external aid and finances, which has led to political interferences with management and control, to the detriment of the farmers.

The Dutch social investor SHGW was – according to the then director – looking for opportunities to invest in agricultural value chains with producers. This social investment is intended to lead to eventual ownership transfer to the farmers involved in the value chain, based on easy terms of repayment. SHGW understood that most of the existing investment schemes in India are designed by government departments as quick financial relief measures in order to secure farmers' votes for incumbent political parties. These schemes offer no options for structural or rigorous reforms in agricultural production, value-chain development or distribution networks, and hence do not structurally support the small and marginal apple farmers.

FFT is a Dutch technology provider specialised in building controlled atmosphere storage and cold chain infrastructure. The company conducted a survey of apple marketing in India, in order to examine the possibility of selling their long-term storage technology to farmers (as they do in Europe to big farmers). In traditional practices, fruit traders only come into the picture when farmers bring their produce to the market. FFT realised that working with small farmers would not be possible without an

2 A Dutch family foundation that acts as the social investor in this particular case.

3 Ref: http://sjsindia.org/; http://www.fftcompany.com/; www.contextinternational cooperation.org

intermediary business venture (i.e. farmers collectives such as those being organised by SJS) to take the risks of collecting, sorting and procuring the storage-quality apples.

Context, international cooperation, is a social business specialised in providing business development support to social entrepreneurs. The organisation facilitated a social entrepreneurship mapping exercise of the above three partners in New Delhi in 2007. Subsequently, the consortium members jointly identified the challenges and frameworks for social business development for an apple value chain with farmers collectives in the Indian Himalayas. Based upon the principles of civic driven change and Social Return on Investment, stakeholder deliberations were organised with the support of Context, international cooperation in the period 2008 to 2015.[4]

Background: By-passing the power of *mandis*

Since the start of the Apple Project in 2007, SJS, SHGW and FFT have been working together with other local and international consortium partners to improve the well-being of small and marginal apple farmers in the states of Himachal Pradesh and Uttarakhand. The Apple project in Uttarakhand was and remains based on the realisation that the main reason for marginalisation of small apple farmers in a market-oriented agribusiness is the dominance of *mandis*. Mandis are chains of well-organised intermediaries, who control the entire process from regulatory aspects, credit supply for farm inputs, transportation and marketing of produce, to the auction of produce brought by individual farmers. The Apple Project focused on an alternative marketing strategy to replace the *mandis*. It strives to create a model of business-driven, decentralised, independent and small-scale production with coordinated arrangements for sorting, grading, storage and marketing. This is done by providing technical, managerial and investment support. A crucial factor is the organisation of the small and marginal famers into collectives, which enable them to jointly improve their position and collectively move up in the apple value chain. This collective feature of the business model saves individual farmers time, distributes risk, maintains price assurance, pursues damage control and saves on handling costs such as storage and transportation. The principle of collectiveness is taken one step further in the Apple Project, by working towards ownership of businesses by the farmers.

With this new approach, the Apple Project attempts to advance the involvement of small and marginal farmers as business partners in value-addition businesses. These businesses add value in several ways: setting up ultimately farmer-owned joint venture companies for sorting, grading and timely picking and supplying of fresh apples in the farmers' areas; and setting up storage, grading and packing facilities at a centralised place. In so doing, the Apple Project – supported by (social) investors

4 Context, international cooperation, provided support with regard to these two subjects. Regarding civic driven change reference may be made to Fowler & Biekart, 2008 and Fowler & Biekart 2013; with regard to SROI reference can be made to De Greve et al., 2013.

– seeks to address the shortcomings in the traditional supply chain. These include disenfranchised growers, low productivity, poor quality of produce, the omnipotence of intermediaries, lack of proper storage facilities, and absence of trust and synergy between the different players in the value chain. The Project creates a robust ecosystem that brings together five key aspects of the apple value chain – the product, the farmers, the investor, the market and the entrepreneur. The key difference between the Apple Project's value chain and other farmer-led value chains lies in the partnership between the newly created producer (farmer) collectives and the entrepreneurs in the management of the value chain. While the producers manage the supplier base, food business entrepreneurs manage the necessary value additions to the product. This business-based model of a consortium balances two schools of thought: maximisation of producer's income which leads to enhanced family incomes leading to improved welfare in terms of habitat, food security, health and educational opportunities for children; and maximisation of fair profit for ultimately farmer-owned companies.

In short, the Apple Project aims to increase and strengthen the bargaining capacity of small apple farmers in India and to increase their income level substantially, by:

- *Organising*: Creating formal farmer organisations that will jointly handle, sell and/or process their apples;
- *Providing*: Supplying these farmer organisations with appropriate financial means and equipment to allow them to collect, sort, pack, pre-cool and handle the apples in a professional manner;
- *Marketing*: Arranging that premium apples can be sold to the long-term storage company, whereas medium grade apples go directly to the market and inferior grades (and other fruits) are used for producing juice;
- *Owning*: Using the profits generated through the legally registered companies to make premium payments to the supplying farmer groups; repay the investors in the companies; and gradually transfer the full economic ownership of the companies to the farmers.

The main socio-political purpose of this intervention is essentially to change the local power balance in the apple value chain in favour of small and marginal apple farmers.

Organisational set-up

First tier: Collection points

By December 2008, SJS was entrusted to coordinate the Apple Project. To date, SJS has set up six collection centres in six different locations of Uttrakhand,[5] which are functioning as joint venture companies of Annamrit farmers and participating farmer trusts (which are self-organisations of farmers). Each of the trusts consists of between 300 and 500 farmers from 10 to 30 villages; and each trust is in a single location based on

5 In Dhari, Pissaon, Purola, Chausal, Jhala and Dharali.

Box I.1: The four tiers system of the Apple Project

Level	Entities
First tier	(1) *Farmer trusts* at six collection points. These are organisations that are fully owned and managed by apple farmers themselves. These farmer trusts are the co-owners of (2) *farmer joint venture companies* (that are set up at collection point level) together with *Annamrit* (the farmers-owned investment company) (see further on).
Second tier	(3) *Central controlled atmosphere storage facility company* (4) *Processing units* such as the apple juice processing factory. These are joint ventures of the farmer trusts and Annamrit, but managed by professionals.
Third tier	(5) *Marketing, sales and branding company* for forward and backward linkages, which is also a joint venture of the six farmer joint venture companies (first tier) and Annamrit. This company is also managed by professionals.
Fourth tier	(6) *Annamrit* which is the farmer-owned investment company that is to replace the social investor from the Netherlands (SHGW) and to attract social capital. Annamrit is owned by the farmer trusts (at the first tier), the central controlled storage company and processing units at the second tier.

the watershed, and on culture and connectivity. These trusts function as mutual benefit entities. Members supply their entire yearly harvest to their joint venture company at the prevailing market prices. The area-specific and value chain-based farmer trusts are formed to experiment with a hybrid business model in agricultural value chains. All joint venture companies collect the participating farmers' produce from their farm gate. All are equipped with a production extension and quality advisor (who is a full-time field staff member), a grading and pre-cooling facility and a refrigerated van for transportation of quality fresh fruits to markets and storage facilities.

Thus far, 4,200 farmers have been registered as primary suppliers, partners and eventual owners of the businesses of the joint venture companies. The collection centres' facilities to sort and pre-cool apples have a capacity of 500 metric tons (MT) in one harvesting season (August to October). As indicated earlier, in the beginning, 100% of the investment required for infrastructure creation, transport and quality improvement was made by the social investor from the Netherlands (SHGW). It was projected that the farmers would in due course fully repay this investment upon sufficient profit generation by the joint venture companies. Based on these expected repayments, it was promised that proportionate ownership would be transferred to the farmer trusts.

Second tier: Central storage company and processing units

In addition to the storage and sorting facilities at collection-point level, one central controlled atmosphere storage facility has been constructed at a central place.[6] This

6 In the village Nogaon.

has a capacity of 1,200 MT and can store apples for a longer time, so they can fetch better prices by selling them off-season. All collection-point centres sell their storable apples to the central controlled atmosphere storage company. Non-storable quality apples are sold directly to the market, as well as to the juice processing unit. The apple juice processing unit has been created as an employment opportunity for female farmers. In this unit 1,200 women are organised in a women trust for processing the fruits into fresh juice and other processed items.

Third tier: Marketing, sales and branding company

As indicated in Box I.1, at the next (third) level a marketing, sales and branding company has been set up. The companies at the second and third tiers are managed by professionals, in order to secure full economic benefit in competitive market situations.

Fourth tier: Investment company (Annamrit)

Initially SHGW – which has the risk-taking capacity – was sole owner of the business in order to secure the long-term business interests. Following the idea of promoting ultimately farmer-owned agricultural value chain businesses, the entity Annamrit was launched in January 2015. Annamrit is a farmer-owned investment vehicle that will gradually take over the role of SHGW. The goal of Annamrit is to build a strong partnership between producers (farmers, the growers of *Annam* (food)), entrepreneurs (for collection, packing, distribution and value addition businesses to food supply chain), development cooperation organisers (coordinators and co-operators in the food value chain) and investors (financers for storage, packing, quality control and handling of foods). The main role of Annamrit is to attract social investors to build the food value chain with a focused approach of producing, storing, collecting and distributing the pure and healthy food which should be as beneficial as *Amrit* (nectar).

Diagram I.1: Relationships between main actors in the Apple Project

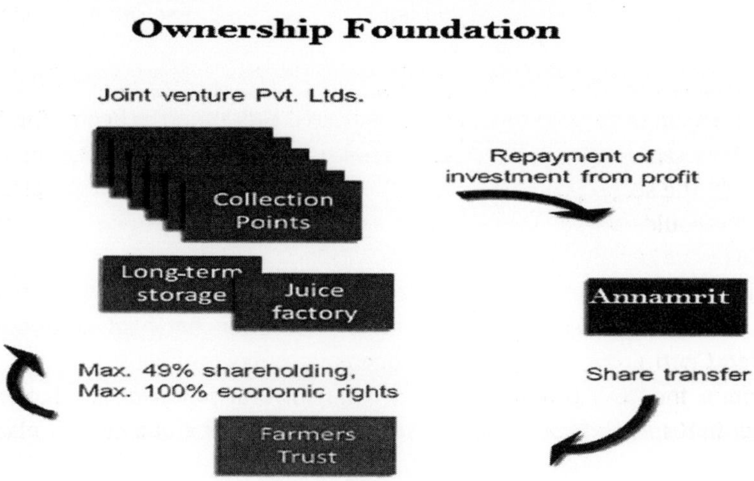

Source: Semwal.

The main purpose: Systemic change through partnership model

The vision behind the Apple Project is to set in motion a self-perpetuating model that can be applied throughout India, for the benefit of small-scale farmers. An important aspect of the model is furthermore that the costs of the technical assistance, the bridging funds and equipment that are being provided under the project, are to be recovered from the additional income that farmer companies are able to generate, alongside regular government subsidies for commercial companies managed by professional managers. The second important aspect is that apple farmers themselves become the legal owners of companies within the Apple Project. Both aspects are drivers towards systemic change.

Schematically the differences between a cooperative model, private sector model and partnership (hybrid) model can be summarised as follows (see Diagram I.2).

Diagram I.2: Differences in cooperative, private sector and partnership (hybrid) models

	Cooperate model	Private sector model	Partnership model
Main aim	Sustain production and improvement farmer income	Optimise profit, secure continuity at minimum cost	Optimise benefits (blended value) for farmers, secure continuity and growth through increased production
Value drivers	Farmer income maximisation	Profit maximisation for shareholders	Blended value for farmers, customers and society at large
Daily control	Farmers have direct control over appointed management	Investors have direct control appointed management	Farmers together with investor/ private sector party oversee daily management
Strength	Backward linkages with farmers Economic benefits go to farmers Focus on increased production Financial risks (partly) covered by government programmes Few successful examples to replicate	Strong drive for innovation and leading in market Strong drive for diversification Ability to diversify Focus on quality and reliability Well organised consumer linkages through market outreach	Farmers treated as equal partners Strong linkages with farmers as suppliers Value creation for multiple stakeholders (farmers, investors and customers) No political or government interference
Weakness	Limited forward linkages to the market Limited competition in open market Limited diversification Little investment in product development and R&D Political interference	Weak linkages with farmers Limited concerns for social and environmental sustainability and development Rely on suppliers in any stage of the value/supply chain	Potential conflict among partners Balancing financial and social objectives Risk of partners falling back to their old values and practices Finding social investors

Source: Semwal.

The partnership business models – with collaboration between corporate-sector agencies and non-profit sector actors – opens up opportunities to finance the cold storage chain for fresh produce and other agricultural produce. The partners that collaborate in the Apple Project can be categorised into four groups:

- *Producers collectives* – particularly the farmer groups organised in farmer trusts or any other legal form at the six different locations;
- *Inclusive development actors* – particularly knowledge/training institutions, government and (international) development agencies;
- *Business partners* – experienced and socially conscious entrepreneurs to manage and operate the business activities in a competitive market;
- *Financial supporters* – social investors/banks and government agencies to invest in ventures with a focus on economic profits as well as social impact.

The actors involved are mutually supportive and complementary in terms of expertise, experience, networks and access to external resources. These actors, collectively referred to in this chapter as the 'social business management consortium', should obviously have a shared vision on social, political and economic objectives as the prime driver to participate in this approach.

The interdependent structure of the model aligns all these entities and the stakeholders to work towards a single mutually beneficial goal.

The business principles of the Apple Project

To overcome the problems mentioned in the beginning of this chapter, the Apple Project initiators conducted a quick assessment of the commodity availability and market potential, appropriate technology requirements for value addition, and added value products' market demands, and designed a business model for the Apple Project with the following characteristics:

i *Apple collection points*: Logistics, collection, sorting/grading, packaging, storage and processing units are centrally located in the production areas. The apple collection points market and sell their products directly to the centrally located long-term storage company set up for further collective value addition by all the farmer trusts, to the juice processing facilities and to retail chains and/or consumers. To save the individual farmers time, and to avoid transportation costs and exploitation by intermediaries, they only sell their produce to collection point companies (which are jointly owned by their collectives) based on a transparent price build-up formula. According to this business model, the value addition (profits) made will be used to strengthen the businesses, repay the investment and pay premiums to the supplying farmers. The local apple collection points thus form the backbone of the Apple Project.

ii *Adhere to food quality standards*: To protect the unique quality of the products and avoid losses (in terms of quantity and quality) the products are handled (at collection point) according to accepted food quality standards. In this manner, the products are optimally conserved and protected against humidity, insects, development of micro-organisms and animal attacks. Moreover, the shelf life of the products is markedly extended, as optimum humidity levels are observed, so no oxidation will occur and qualities like flavour and fragrance are preserved.

iii *Internet-based tracking system*: A cloud-based farmer database has been installed that enables tracking of apples from trees to consumers, right from the flowering days till final harvest, storage and distribution. This system helps all participants along the entire value chain to establish themselves as producers and suppliers of good-quality apple brands in the market. It also assists in a transparent multi-stakeholder consultative process for fair distribution of returns with shared risk.

iv *Branding*: A separate marketing and public relations strategy has been developed in order to brand and market the products as coming 'directly from the Himalayas'.

v *Link with research institutions*: Farmers have been connected to and trained by research organisations and technical support programmes in order to improve the yield, so consumers can experience the conserved, original flavour and fragrances of these special products.

vi *Market information:* The farmer trusts are providing the farmers with information[7] to get fair prices for their produce and to connect them to existing schemes and facilities for more socio-political benefits for the member farmers and grower communities. The additional income generated by the farmer's family is then used to access better health and education facilities, for improved habitat, et cetera.

vii *Collective action*: The joint activities of the farmers and their families and communities within the apple value chain enhance more collective action in other spheres of life as well, to establish social, economic and political changes, such as political attention; shared ideas for enhanced income; better utilisation of additional income for children's education, women's health and cultural festivals.

viii *Controlling external influences*: Since the inception of the idea to organise the farmers collectives as mutual benefit trusts of participating farmers (instead of as self-help groups and producer cooperatives), the partnership approach worked with cooperative contribution of all the actors. This means that external influences are kept out and farmers are getting the economic returns as premiums and dividends.

ix *Win-win farmers and social investor*: Once the farmers showed their ability to form mutual collectives with enough produce to gain better bargaining positions in the market, they were invited to join the mutual benefit trusts of producers and joint venture companies formed with the investors to add value to the produce and to share the added value mutually between the investors and farmers. The practice soon highlighted the win-win situation for all the partners and allowed them to move further up into the value chain, to storage and distribution networks.

x *Governance*: All the partners agree on the price build-up of produce (which should not be lower than the prevailing market price) at the beginning of the harvest. This is done in order to ensure reasonable prices to participating farmers; increments and minimum salary payments of operational staff and management team; service charges for organising and supporting institutions such as SJS and Context,

7 The farmer database (maintained in cloud-based ICT software) provides information about land holding, family income, number of trees, input application data, harvest of crops as per quality and quantity to the government development schemes, research institutions, development cooperation organisations and local bodies.

international cooperation; to run the business in competitive markets. They further discuss the outputs and returns in an Annual General Body Meeting at the end of the harvest season and at the half-yearly consultation after sales of apples from the central storage facility, to decide on the additional premium payments to farmers, bonus remuneration to employees and/or repayment of investors' money based on the added value to the produce in the entire chain.

xi *When returns are lower than expected*: In case a year falls below the expectation of financial return, the investor is firstly requested to postpone the repayment, then employees' additional bonus and premium payments to farmers are not taken into consideration. The minimum salaries or prevailing prices of produce are paid as a priority to ensure the family income for the farmers, so they can better prepare for the next harvest and maintain their quality of life with dignity.

The above process creates sufficient trust and risk-sharing abilities among the stakeholders to understand their own gains and dues, either economic or social, in achieving a shared vision of their social business. So far, it has been practiced as a concept of co-creation of blended value[8] (multiple values) for all partners in Annamrit.

Box I.2: Value addition by the Apple Project

Gaps in the traditional supply chain	Value added by the Apple Project
Small and marginal producers with poor quality and low yield.	Farmer associations and farmer trusts are set up to collectivise individual apple producers at village and area level to: organise access to knowledge institutions and social business support organisations such as SJS and Context, international cooperation which mentor and advise the farmers throughout the cultivation process and season to increase yield and understanding of the multi-stakeholder role in a social business; Organise access to seeds, fertilisers and technology to increase quality of yield.
Exploitative intermediaries who buy produce from growers at arbitrary prices.	Joint venture companies are set up to procure from individual growers, with: a participative process with producers to determine fair market prices to purchase commodities; collection centres to procure all farmers' produce from individual growers; a marketing company to connect farmers to distant markets.
Foods being sold locally in distress by farmers and in season when prices are low because of poor storage facilities.	Decentralised and central storage facilities are set up to cater for the demand for food throughout the year with regular supplies at consistently good quality at fair prices.
Poor transport infrastructure resulting in wastage.	Chilled transportation facilities owned by the farmer joint venture companies.

8 The concept of blended value is further explained in Chapter II of this volume.

The major activities and their rationale can be summarised as seen in Box I.2.

Diagram I.3: Distribution of revenue

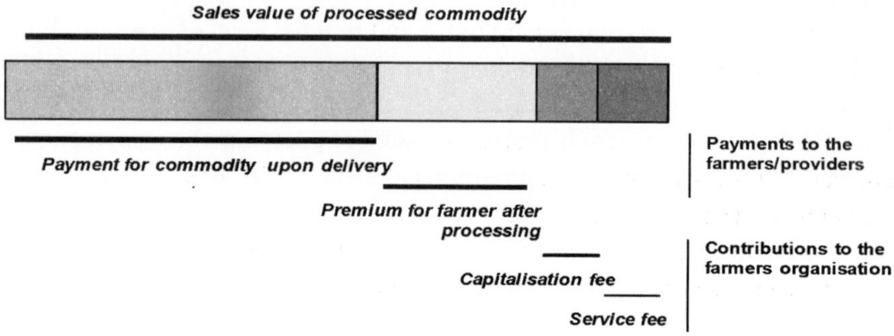

Source: Semwal.

The profit that the business makes is allocated for three purposes:

a. repayment of the investment to the social investor (i.e. SHGW);
b. capitalisation of the company for further growth;
c. premiums to supplying farmers, in addition to purchase prices, which may be used for enhanced family welfare.

Major outcomes and impact of the Apple Project

Box I.3: Outcomes and impact in four interrelated areas

The Apple Project achieves results in four interrelated areas:

- *Financial capital* – the ability of participating farmers and operational team to save money, enhance liquidity and investment in expansion and replication.
- *Social capital* – the expansion of networks of participating farmers and relationships that support them to improve their bargaining capacities for better prices of produce and to obtain a dignified position for producers in the buyers' market. Moreover, the enhanced economic position of the participating farmers improves the socio-economic position of the famers and their families in general very considerably.
- *Knowledge capital* – the access to information and technical/technological know-how that is necessary to succeed in the markets and grow quality crops.
- *Material capital* – the capacity to build assets that generate wealth and welfare in the long term throughout the apple value chain.

Financial capital

The financial capital of the supplying farmers, operational team and social investors has increased as the farmers are getting advance payments for inputs and farm labour from their own joint companies. This is possible, because they have committed themselves to supply their produce to the joint companies at prevailing market prices. Hence, their access to financial resources has increased. Additional premium payments from the added value of produce provide the involved farmers with an opportunity to invest in the joint companies with the perspective of co-owning them. The joint companies have also locally created employment opportunities for the full-time techno-managerial staff and part-time packing labourers. This saves the staff and labourers from having to search for employment opportunities in faraway places (such as New Delhi) and having to migrate. It also enables them to save on costs of living, so they can start new businesses in their own (green and less-populated) areas. This enables many farmers to diversify their sources of income.

Social capital

The main social goal of the above described business model is that it serves the interests of small and marginal apple growers through a democratic member-controlled entity, which delinks votes from shareholders from political and religious interests. As a result, larger numbers of apple farmers are joining the Apple Project. Since the inception of the project in 2007, it has grown more than tenfold. The project began with 300 farmers and is now working with 4,200. The number of villages involved has increased from 12 to 140. Having a collective voice helps the farmers to represent themselves when key decisions are being made by policy makers and politicians. The employees of the trust and joint companies (who come from local villages) and the farmers established a team spirit with business rigour. This has enabled them to explore opportunities, both for positioning themselves more favourably, and for moving up the apple value chain; and it contributes to the broader objective of import substitution.[9]

In general, the self-respect of individuals in entities that are collectively run and owned has increased substantially through peer learning. Particularly women groups have shown this through their participation in groups and village meetings by raising issues for the benefit of their children, themselves and the community at large. This shows that, apart from the economic benefits, the bargaining power has increased step by step both socially and politically.

Knowledge capital

The technical knowledge of the producers has increased through participation in trainings, exposure visits, conferences, et cetera. Farmers have strengthened their knowledge regarding better farming practices such as picking at the right time, quality improvement of produce, and how to control supplies in response to market demand. This extended reach and infrastructure availability improved their bargaining power, market positioning and decision-making in the price build-up. The joint venture companies understand the value of having the farmers on board for regular and sufficient supply of produce, and to establish themselves in the market as trusted and consistent quality suppliers. The co-creation increased the self-confidence of the employees and the farmers at the same time, and enhanced their learning about

9 No longer need to import high quality apples from abroad.

produce supply, value addition through multiple utilities and building brands as producers of good quality produce. This has improved the farmer's risk-taking capacity and has minimised external influences on their investment decisions.

Material capital

The participating partners in the Apple Project have shared ownership in the six joint venture companies at collection point level. Each unit at local level has a grading and pre-cooling shed, pre-sorting machine, refrigerated truck and primary testing equipment. At secondary level, three other joint venture companies own the central controlled atmosphere storage, a juice processing unit and copyrights on the tracking software of the apple value chain.

The hybrid model is structured in such a way that the farmer trusts eventually own the joint venture companies at the second and third tier. The farmers will co-own the assets that will continue to generate wealth in the long-term. The farmers collectives already own the majority shares in the collection point companies. They also fully own the controlled atmosphere storage company, by having generated sufficient profit in the business to repay the investment by the social investor (SHGW).

The Apple Project has been invited by planners and policy-makers in government to replicate the concept for government, IFAD and World Bank supported projects in other regions of Uttrakhand. It is important to understand here that previous government interventions with a cooperative concept also created an asset base for value addition, but the ownership always remained with the administrators appointed from the top. The farmers consider those structures as 'outsider businesses' rather than their own and these cooperatives become dependent on aid and subsidies, rather than realisation of surplus from the market. For example, in the sugar cooperatives in India the farmers are dependent on government and politicians, leading to unpaid debt of both the producers and cooperatives. This resulted in an unrealistic market-oriented business, ultimately leading to many farmer suicides and closure of cooperatives.

Major lessons from the Apple Project

Step 1: Analysis and feasibility

As a first step, those who initiated the Apple Project needed to understand what potential and interest the farmers had to move up in the value chain, based on the commodities or resources they have. Several questions then need to be asked: What forms of processing of produce can add value to the final product and how viable are these options? How much value can be added based on the prevailing local market rates? What technologies are available and how can the ultimately famer-led company distinguish itself in the market with this technology? How much (capital) investment is required? Are all the various levels of processing (primary, secondary, et cetera), likely to be economically viable by themselves? And, most of all, what is the willingness of

Box I.4: Social Return on Investment of the Apple Project

As part of the regular business performance measurement, in 2014 a Social Return on Investment (SROI) analysis was carried out by staff members of SJS, together with apple farmers and other relevant stakeholders. Staff members of Context, international cooperation provided support with regard to this analysis.

The essence of this SROI exercise can be captured as follows:[1] '*Before introduction of the project, farmers picked their apples and sold directly to the market through middlemen. Now farmers collect their apples and bring them to a collection point, where apples are cleaned, graded and stored. In the new constellation, farmers receive more money for their apples immediately as well as a share of the profit later on. They do not need to purchase packing material anymore as this is provided by the collection point. In the present situation, the farmer has more options than before. Earlier they were dependent on the middlemen only. The risk of the farmers is reduced in the process. People get more employment even in the off-season. Now farmers feel motivated and start investing in apple production again.*'

Women added the following elements: '*Earlier we did not know about the use of the apricot. Before we produced oil from the stone of the apricot. Now we are trained and have started to produce juice, jam and pickle of the apricot, so that we have got better social life, schooling for our children and better health. We got good employment. Now we are self-dependent and feel more confident*'.

In conclusion the SROI study says: '*In view of the above, and based on informal interviews and interactions with farmers the key elements of Theory of Change of the Apple Project can be summarised as follows. Before the apple farmers did not receive a good price for their apples due to indebtedness to middleman and money lenders, who provide a certain risk reduction for the farmer but at the same time the farmers were bound to sell their apples to them at prices which were not always competitive. The present programme tries to change this vicious circle of poverty by implementing the overall strategies of purchasing of apples at collection point (A, B and C grade) from the farmers at the prevailing market price. B grade apples are sold directly to the market; C grade apples are (will be) sold to the juice factory. Grade apples are transferred (sold) to the Long Term Cold Storage which is owned by the farmers and located at a central point. Technical assistance (trainings, fertilisers, hand-on support) is provided by collection point and associated companies to the apple farmers.*

Moreover, the centre manager and extension officers support farmers (men and women) to organise themselves in groups such as Farmer Committees, Farmer Trust Joint Venture Company (collection point), Women Committees, and Women Trust. The emergence and functioning of these bodies is being supported by SJS and has strengthened the resilience and bargaining capacity of the small and marginal apple growers and their families considerably. By increase of their income the households of the apple farmers are (in principle) better positioned to spend money on basic social services such as health and education. The programme does not provide any systematic support with regard to resource utilisation at household level but has an indirect impact on the social welfare of farmers and their households.'

individual farmers and farmer groups to participate in collective action by organising themselves – and how can they be supported and guided in this?

This kind of quick scan should give good insights into the potential of the various value-addition options that can be explored jointly by the organising team and the farmers. For these options, a more thorough assessment of the practical and socio-economic feasibility needs to be made. Given the amount of uncertainty and the potential threats that typically surround these initiatives (often in remote, underdeveloped areas), this is not an easy exercise and needs to be undertaken with practical knowledge about the local circumstances, as well as a good understanding of the value addition chain of the commodity involved.

In this context, it is important that *all* assumptions and choices that form the basis for the feasibility study, are well substantiated with source references (preferably based on verifiable historical data). In this manner, the feasibility study can also be a good management tool during implementation (among other purposes to update and actualise assumptions to the prevailing [expected] circumstances).

In addition, the assumptions in the feasibility study should at least be assessed for a 'worst', 'best', 'realistic', and 'conservative' scenario. Based on this feasibility study, an overall risk analysis can be made to gain insights into the financial consequences of these scenarios. Apart from the financial risks, a thorough assessment of other factors that may in due course jeopardise the anticipated business (e.g. openness of the market, subsidies, price inflation, harvest losses, farmers' continued participation and involvement), should complete the risk assessment. By categorising these factors according to the influence the operational management of the farmer-led company may have on them,[10] the risk assessment can be used as a management tool during operation as well. The traditional practices can also be assessed for economic feasibilities, however, to assess social and political realities and make assumptions based on them is always difficult. Moreover, there is always a chance to fall into the trap of resorting to patching solutions, populism and attractive announcements without providing empirical evidence and a long-term vision.

At its start, the Apple Project was not labelled as a development-sector project, or a hard core financial investors' business, or a politically-influenced local area development. Based on time allowed for the partners to engage in mature discussions and analyses through SROI studies, regular stakeholder consultations and learning from CDC workshops, it evolved into a process. Achievement of feasibility developed into a balancing act between social and economic returns for all the four partners. They contributed their best within the limits of their knowledge and expertise for a common good for all (including themselves).

Step 2: Securing financial, entrepreneurial and material resources through sound investment plans

Based on the above feasibility study, a team of entrepreneurs developed an investment plan for the social investor(s) and banks, in order to secure sufficient capital investment. Besides the social investor and the banks, other funding options were explored, e.g. subsidies related to promotion of rural development or relevant clusters; export/ import subsidies; grant support from development organisations; soft-loans from

10 Whereby a distinction may be made in issues that are under the control of the farmers; where farmers have direct or indirect influence; where farmers have an interest but no direct control or interest.

development banks. Important to include in the investment plan is the working capital requirements during the operational phase, including costs involved for community organisation of farmers. Particularly for new companies without a financial track record, it may prove difficult to secure regular loans from (local) banks.

The farmers collectives should be an integral part of investment plans to secure sufficient produce for future business and risk management in case of low yield, and of plans to address the challenge of securing the livelihood of all participants while waiting for the next harvest.

A socially conscious investor is generally the most difficult partner to find and involve. In a social business, such as the Apple Project, the main challenge is to combine two different financing approaches: conventional business financing and a grant-making welfare project approach. These are two different approaches to investment, i.e. maximising shareholders' money and the safeguarding and securing of financial needs and rights of people at the bottom (the farmers). Within the Project both were taken into account. In this particular case the investment in assets is owned by investors, who receive a suitable interest until full transfer of ownership to the farmers-owned entities can take place. The businesses' goodwill or brands are owned by the farmers or producers from the start to ensure co-ownership. The business management team and organising Non-Governmental Development Organisation (i.e. SJS) will stay on to build bridges.

Step 3: (Legal) organisation: To register the entity (farmers) under legal institution
Once it is clear which business is feasible and capital can be secured, the legal organisation of the initiative is to be arranged. The legal organisation should well integrate the key principles on which the initiative operates. In the Apple Project attention was and is being paid to:

- *Legal representation farmers*: Anchoring the farmer interests as the prime objective through legal representation;
- *Safeguarding business rigour*: Business rigour is achieved through professional management and oversight; a board of directors (BoD) is to reflect the professional disciplines alongside (minority) farmer representatives. A BoD is to appoint the company's management, which is to report to the BoD;
- *Institutional coherence*: Alignment of the Articles of Association of the farmer trusts with the Articles of Association of the joint venture companies;
- *Ownership*: Long-term, gradual ownership transfer arrangement from the social investor to the farmer-owned companies is to be anchored in shareholder agreement;
- *Interests of the social investor*: The interests of the (social) investors are to be guaranteed, e.g. through representation on the BoD;
- *Continuity*: Make provisions in case one or more groups of farmers are to discontinue (e.g. when not supplying enough produce or some other malfunction): the continuity of the company should not be jeopardised;

- *Allocation of profit*: Profit of the company is to be allocated for repayment of the investment to the social investor, capitalisation of the company and premiums to supplying farmers in order to enhance their families' welfare;
- *Incentives*: Sharing of the economic benefits with the farmers (like premium payments) is to stimulate sufficient supply of good-quality produce.

Organisational and institutional development has to be well taken care of within the existing legal framework. The above presented four-tier system needs to be adopted towards eventual farmer ownership through mutual benefit trusts of producers (farmer trusts). As a business entity, the joint venture companies are operated and managed by business professionals and co-owned by investors and producers as an investment vehicle to secure the repayments and re-investment in a perpetual way. The social organisers and knowledge partners like SJS and Context, international cooperation play a facilitating, supportive and bridging role as and where required.

Step 4: Design, construction, team-building and start-up

In the design and construction phase, when the emphasis is on creating the necessary infrastructure, the best available technologies and suppliers are to be sourced. This is preferably done under supervision of a single responsible party with a proven and verified track record. Clear contractual agreements and payment conditions should secure efficient construction of the infrastructure, to be realised within the allocated budget and timelines.

At the same time, a professional team of qualified staff is to be recruited (from management, finance, quality control to operational staff) which is able to run the company upon completion of the infrastructure building. This team is not only expected to operate the business in a professional and profitable manner, but also to understand (and cope with) the complexity of a *social* business that is focused on the creation of blended value. Challenges include achieving both financial and socio-political objectives and involving and reporting to all stakeholders concerned: from farmers to the (social) investors.

The key points to be addressed are:
- *Role of farmers*: The role of the farmers should be clear and the management should make optimum use of (the leaders within) these groups;
- *Win-win approach*: Look for solutions that work for all partners, not just the company;
- *Operational manager*: The operational manager cum director is responsible to the board of directors at all times;
- *Board of directors*: The board is to have a pro-active supportive role to the company, particularly in the start-up phase: the experience, expertise and networks of board members should be utilised optimally;
- *Procedures and protocols*: Robust procedures and protocols are to be in place for all critical work flows of the company. Particularly on the financial side, sufficient

safeguards should be in place for maximum transparency, control and reporting to all stakeholders, including the farmers;
- *Mission drift*: Mechanisms should be in place to avoid so-called 'mission drift', i.e. bias towards either the financial or social purpose of the social business.

Conclusion

Over the past few decades, India has liberalised its markets to take advantage of the benefits of a globalising economy. However, the benefits have not accrued equally to all citizens of the country and have largely remained restricted to certain sections of the population. In fact, the consequences of a globalising economy worked against the interests of a large number of poor and marginalised people, such as small and marginal apple growers in the Himalayas. In an agrarian economy like India's, any assessment of the transfer of benefits at the grassroots level must focus on the change brought about in the socio-economic conditions of small and marginal farmers. In remote rural areas of the country, the situation is particularly grim for these farmers. Local power structures, born out of asymmetric socio-cultural and economic arrangements and concomitant politics, play a major role in determining economic activities in rural areas where farmers are heavily dependent on, as well as exploited and misled by money lenders and middlemen. Although India is positioning itself as a worldwide leading economic power, it is still home to one-third of the world's poorest people, concentrated mostly in its rural areas. The growth potential of rural India however, is enormous with an increasing concern about food security and increasing food prices.

Despite the fact that significant efforts are made by the central and state governments to help small and marginal farmers in the country, numerous problems continue to exist that bind farmers to a cycle of poverty and deprivation. While agricultural production has been on the rise in India, it has not translated into enhanced income for the producers of food grains. Critical factors in this have been lack of organised access to markets; absence of appropriate technologies; dearth of awareness about actual prices in the market; lack of financial support; dominance and exploitative behaviour of middlemen and other intermediaries; limited access to capital due to lending policies that are not in favour of small and marginal farmers. The recent increase in farmer suicides in India also indicates that agriculture is a challenging livelihood option for many people in rural India. With a large proportion of India's rural population engaged in agricultural activities, it is important to strengthen the socio-economic position and bargaining capacity of small and marginal farmers through innovative models of development.

The vision behind the Apple Project - as described in this chapter - is to set in motion a self-perpetuating model that can be applied throughout India, for the benefit of small-scale farmers. An important aspect of this model is that the cost of technical assistance, bridging funds and equipment provided under the project are to be recovered from the additional income that farmers' companies are able to generate, alongside regular government subsidies for commercial companies. The Apple Project India in Uttarakhand is changing the mindsets of farmers and protecting them from the exploitation of middlemen and other intermediaries. It has not only organised farmers into organisations or joint venture companies, but has provided them with infrastructural, technological and storage options for their produce. Moreover, it has supported them with an innovative solution through which they can sell their produce in an organised way directly to the consumers and at better prices. The outreach of the project has steadily been increasing and has been augmented by enhanced infrastructure. Joint venture farmer companies make important contributions to employment and income generation in states like Uttarakhand. They have key roles in the production, processing and distribution of fruits and vegetables and are central actors in developing sustainable agricultural value chains.

The main difference in this new approach is that the farmers, along with socially conscious corporate partners and investors, become equal business partners. There is no external governance or political influence. Instead, the company is run by a professional management and professional board to secure business rigour, profitability and continued focus on socio-political objectives and hence the long-term interest of the company is secured. Similar to the cooperative model, the farmers have full rights to the economic gains of the company, though they have no direct control over the daily management, which is in the hand of professionals who report to the board of directors of the joint venture companies. It is a win-win situation for both investors and farmers. The economic benefits of the company are ploughed back to the participating farmers, mostly in the form of premiums over their supply (based on quantity and quality), while the investments made by the social investor are fully repaid on commercial terms, for reinvestments in new social ventures. The new social business approach, which is outlined in this and other chapters of this book, could well capitalise on the immense potential of rural India and break through the inefficiencies of the current rural production-trade relations.

Box I.5: Farmer speak

- 'We are not mere farmers; we are respected as real business partners'.
- 'We can produce anything, but we need farmers as owners to sell it for us'.
- 'We do not want to work together for only two or three years: we want to be part of this forever'.
- 'Working together saves us time, money and a lot of work. Most importantly, we do not have the stress of negotiating with middlemen anymore'.
- 'Farmers as owners have brought stability and progress to our village. The cooperation is crucial for the future of this place'.

References

De Greve, P., Lont, H. & Van der Velden F. (2013), *Narrative numeracy: social impact assessment; A brief guide to Social Return on Investment*, Utrecht, Context, international cooperation (Contextual No. 10).

Fowler, A. & Biekart, K. (2008), *Civic Driven Change; Citizen's imagination in action*, The Hague, Institute of Social Studies.

Fowler, A. & Biekart, K. (2013), Relocating Civil Society in a Politics of Civic-Driven Change, *Development Policy Review*, 2013, 31 (4), pp. 463 – 483.

Pundir, S. et al. (2013), *Report Social Return on Investment analysis of the apple collection point at Chausal*, Rishikesh/Utrecht, SJS/Context, international cooperation.

Semwal, L.P. & Willemsen, E. (2011), Fostering farmer organisations with business rigour: experiences from the Himalayas, in: Van der Velden, F. (2011), Social business, a novel approach to socio-political change, in: Velden, F. van der (red.), *New approaches to international development cooperation – a tribute to Meindert Witvliet*, Utrecht, Context, international cooperation: pp. 153 - 160.

Websites

www.annamrit.com

www.contextinternational cooperation.org

http://sjsindia.org/;

http://www.fftcompany.com/

CHAPTER II
Social business as an approach to transformational change

'To paraphrase Albert Einstein, what is needed is simple – but that doesn't mean it is easy; what is needed is a re-visioning of our personal and professional understanding of the notion of the value we create over the trajectory of our lives. With this new understanding of value in place we may then – each one of us – be in the best possible position to change our organizations, our investment practices and the legacy of the life we have lived'.[1]

Fons van der Velden[2]

Introduction
In the introduction to this volume, the concept of social business was positioned as a strategic approach to a much broader political-economic discourse. This discourse aims at fundamentally transforming the neo-liberal economic model towards a social and solidarity economy (SSE) through a combined strategy of interrelated local and global action. The present chapter looks at the rationale for the emergence of social business as an approach to transformational change, and at characteristics and challenges of a social business. The chapter's main purpose is to provide deeper insights into characteristics of social businesses.

Crisis in capitalism and the end of the traditional golden triangle

Capitalism under siege
In recent years, business has increasingly been viewed as a major cause of social, environmental, and economic problems. In their article in the Harvard Business Review about shared value creation, the Harvard Professors Porter and Kramer observed that 'capitalism is under siege'.[3]

---

1 Jed Emerson, http://www.blendedvalue.org/framework/.

2 The author wants to express his sincere gratitude for the peer review of this chapter by Laila Bouallouch, Pol De Greve, David Sogge and Karol E. Soltan.

3 Porter and Kramer, 2011.

Box II.1: Some data about inequality in the world[4]

- Since 2015, the richest 1% have owned more wealth than the rest of the planet.
- Over the next 20 years, 500 people will hand over $2.1 trillion to their heirs – a sum larger than the GDP of India, a country of 1.3 billion people.
- The incomes of the poorest 10% of the world's population increased by less than $3 a year between 1988 and 2011, while the incomes of the richest 1% increased 182 times as much.
- A chief executive on the Financial Times Stock Exchange-100 earns as much in a year as 10,000 people working in garment factories in Bangladesh.
- New research by economist Thomas Piketty shows that in the US, over the last 30 years the growth in incomes of the bottom 50% has been zero, whereas incomes of the top 1% have grown 300%.
- In Vietnam, the country's richest person earns more in a day than the poorest person earns in 10 years.

Despite the fact that over the past two decades poverty has been reduced substantially, the world is being confronted with three interrelated systemic problems: there is growing inequality; the limits of the carrying capacity of the earth have been reached (climate change as part of the general ecological crisis is another major challenge); the functioning of political institutions is being eroded. Many countries are faced with a crisis in democracy and space for civil society organisations is shrinking.[5] There is a clear link between capitalism and these systemic, life-threatening problems.

Box II.2: Limits to growth: Environmental crisis[6]

Mainstream businesses operating within the neo-liberal development model tend to ignore the more than significant costs they pass on to the wider world. Sukhdev argues that due to the sheer size these 'negative externalities' make an 'invisible' footprint, (see Adam Smith's concept of the 'invisible hand') which is 'recognizable through its very large visible "footprint"'.[7] The primary and most pervasive category of externalities consists of those that relate to damage to the environmental and ecological commons through unrestrained greenhouse-gas emissions, waste generation, and excessive use of energy, land and fresh water. The bottom line is that for almost half a century the ecological footprint has been bigger than the carrying capacity of the earth (see Diagram II.1).

A vast body of scientific literature points to the fact that the dominant development model (based on unlimited growth) is not in line with the carrying capacity of the earth: the planet is an ecosystem with limited biophysical resources. The present economic model does not respect these boundaries, resulting in climate change and reduced biodiversity. Environmental impact of economic activities has to be reduced by a factor 10 by 2050.[8] These observations are not new. Way back in 1972 the Systems Dynamics Group of the Massachusetts Institute of Technology (MIT) published - at the request of the Club of Rome - the report 'Limits to Growth'. This report stated that the global growth trends in terms industrialisation, population, pollution, food production and management of natural resources were no longer feasible and therefore no longer desirable.[9] After Limits to Growth several similar studies followed, including 'Our

4 Hardoon, 2017. Ref. also: www.oxfam.org

5 Barrez, 2016. Reference is also made to the text boxes about inequality, environmental challenges and the crisis of democracy.

6 Johan van de Gronden was so kind to share resource material for this section.

7 Sukhdev, 2012:4.

8 Barrez, 2016: 11.

9 Ibid, page 19.

Common Future' (1987)[10] (which introduced the concept of sustainability). In 1992 The United Nations Conference on Environment and Development was held which led to the Rio Declaration on Environment and Development, followed by no less than 23 Convention of Parties (COP) of the United Nations Convention of Climate Change.[11]

The Kyoto Protocol was adopted at COP3 on December 11, 1997. It has become a beacon of climate action and an inspiring precursor to the 2015 Paris Climate Change Agreement.[12] Academics, policy makers, representatives of the corporate sector and civil society organisations debate to what extent these international climate change agreements actually work. However, it is a fact that the world is not yet on track to meet the central goal of the 2015 Paris Agreement: to limit the global average temperature rise to well below 2 degrees Celsius and as close as possible to 1.5 degrees.[13]

The limited progress with regard to environmental issues may be linked to the dominant development paradigm with a hegemony of the economic system of capitalism, the free market approach: the environmental challenges are perceived as a technical, a-political problem that may be solved by experts. There is a bias towards influencing consumer behaviour (end of the pipeline) and less attention is being paid to primary producers, processors, traders, manufacturers and retailers.

Diagram II.1: Global ecological footprint[14]

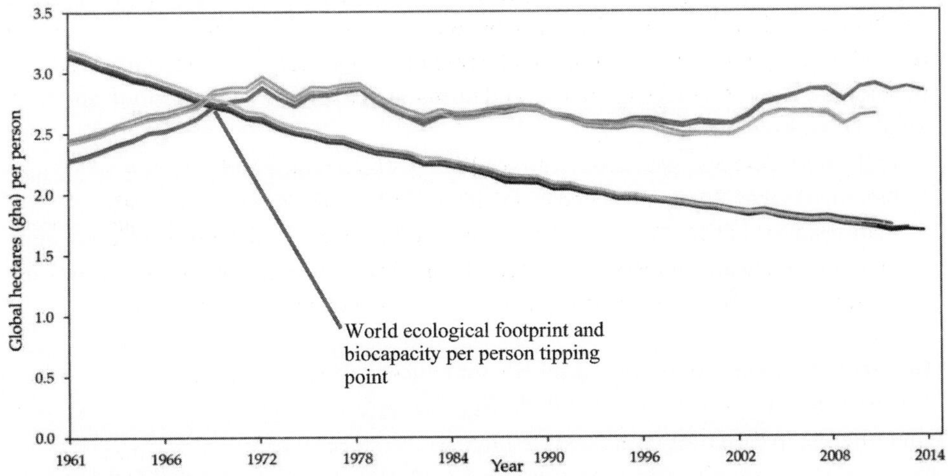

10 Also known as the Brundtland-report.

11 http://unfccc.int/bodies/body/6383.php

12 See: https://cop23.unfccc.int/news/un-guterres-hails-kyoto-success-celebrate-the-20th-anniversary-with-un-climate-change.

13 UN Secretary General Gutteres on November 15, 2017 at COP 23.

14 http://www.footprintnetwork.org/our-work/

Box II.3: Some data about the environmental crisis

Think-tanks and thought leaders on the environmental crisis make the following observations[15]:

- If current population and consumption trends continue, we will soon require the equivalent of two planets to provide the natural resources and services humanity consumes in a year.[16]
- The Living Planet Index shows a decline of 58% between 1970 and 2012, with the greatest losses in freshwater environments.
- If current trends continue, then for the period 1970 to 2020, there may be an average decline of 67% among vertebrate populations.
- Increased human pressure threatens the natural resources that humanity depends upon, increasing the risk of water and food insecurity and competition over natural resources.
- Wildlife populations have already shown a concerning decline of an average of 58% since 1970 and this is likely to reach 67% by the end of the decade.

From the 10 Science 'Must Knows' on Climate Change:[17]

- Evidence shows that Earth has entered a new geological epoch – the Anthropocene – with profound implications for humanity and the relative stability of the earth system.
- Earth is approaching tipping points due to human pressure.
- Risks of extreme weather are increasing.
- Human health is at risk from air pollutants that alter the climate and from the impacts of a changing climate, which are decreasing food security and increasing the risks of disease and heat stress.[18]
- Climate change is likely to exacerbate the risk of large-scale migration and civil unrest.

For a long time now, the functioning of the capitalist, neo-liberal development model has been questioned by several actors from within and outside of the 'system'. A number of academics, politicians and representatives of civil society organisations argue that poverty is a violation of social justice and human rights. The Buddhist monk and writer Sulak Sivaraksa puts it bluntly:

> In the post-Cold war, capitalist triumphalism has bred hubris and delusion. Free-market capitalism preached by neoliberal school of economics is a stark manifestation of this. Tolerance for socioeconomic diversity and alternative models of development are almost non-existent. Formerly diverse ways of life worldwide continue to be eroded by consumerism and the implementation of neoliberal policies.

He argues that 'Free-trade advocates do not concern themselves with which groups in society prosper and which ones fall behind'. Countering this notion, Sivaraksa states that interest in the commons needs to be re-established. [19]

Those who argue from an ethical humanitarian perspective are not alone; many contemporary political economists have joined them. In 1960, the American economic historian Walt Rostow asserted that countries follow five stages of economic development, from 'traditional society' to 'high mass consumption'.[20] Almost 60 years

15 WWF, 2016.

16 www.oneplanetthinking.org

17 Future Earth, 2017.

18 Ibid.

19 Sivaraksa, 2009: 43. See also his earlier book 'Seeds of peace; A Buddhist vision of renewing society' (1992).

20 Rostow, 1960.

later, it is clear that this modernisation theory and its successors are no longer valid. While modernisation has brought about greater efficiency in production and increased the standard of living for some, in North and South, East and West large segments of the population continue to live in abject poverty. A causal relationship between economic growth – measured in GDP (Gross Domestic Product) – and human development and well-being can no longer be assumed.

Not everybody might agree with the observation of Michael Welton[21] that:

> We, the citizenry of the world, have been forced to live in an absurd and totally insecure world with a criminal economy run by gangrenous gangsters and military monsters who do not think twice about invading a country to destroy its state structures, which make modest well-being possible.

However, on the basis of a study of 159 economies over the period 1980–2012 the International Monetary Fund concluded that the growing income inequality in the world negatively affects economic growth and that increasing the income share of the poor and middle class actually increases growth. The Inclusive Growth and Development Report 2015 of the World Economic Forum also states that reducing inequality can strengthen economic growth.[22] This conclusion seems to fall on deaf ears in modern capitalism, as it clashes with the system's founding principles of competition, maximising profits and continuous economic growth fostering the amassing of concentrated private wealth. These principles are driven to the extreme, and the harsh consequences are becoming increasingly visible: deteriorating environmental sustainability and public welfare, to the point of 'public squalor'.[23] Given these consequences and the fact that inequality negatively impacts economic growth, this system no longer makes sense. We have reached 'the end of rational capitalism'.[24]

'It does not have to be like this!'

A number of political economists argue that one of the major characteristics of the recent financial crisis (2008–2016) in Europe and the United States was that a huge upward redistribution of wealth took place. So, not from the well-to-do to the less privileged, but from poor to rich.[25] Poor and marginalised communities worldwide are suffering from an economic decline that is not of their own making.

21 In a review of Wolfgang Streeck's book about the end of capitalism (Welton, 2016)

22 Dabla – Norris, 2015 and Samans et al., 2015.

23 See McChesney and Bellamy Foster who refer to John Kenneth Galbraith's observations of U.S. capitalism half a century ago, in: McChesney and Bellamy Foster, 2010.

24 McChesney and Bellamy Foster, 2010.

25 Baker, 2016.

Worldwide there is growing resistance from especially social movements and civil society organisations against this unsustainable development model.[26] Economists speak out as well, including the late South African Margaret Legum who once stated that 'Old Economics has failed': 'A visitor from Mars today might assume that our planet had suffered an appalling catastrophe that has destroyed our resources, leaving us in the grip of scarcity.' She considers the distance of the wealthy elite from the rest of the population an extremely unhealthy development and is outraged by the effects of the current economic system. Her last book carries the title: 'It does not have to be like this!'[27] Other political economists from across the world join Legum in her motto and offer alternative models, transition models and solutions.[28]

More and more thought leaders in the corporate sector also start expressing concerns about the sustainability of the present development model, however without giving in on shareholder value.[29] For instance Arun Maira, former member of the Planning Commission of the Government of India, who earlier worked for one of the biggest corporate firms in India (Tata) and is now with the Boston Consulting Group, argues that there is an urgent need to transform capitalism: 'The rules of the game must be changed to create a society that is fair and good for everyone. Citizens want corporations to pay more attention to society needs, not merely to shareholders.'[30]

There is indeed a growing unease within the corporate sector about shareholder value. Maira quotes a McKinsey Global Survey of 4,000 executives in 116 countries that found that 84% of respondents embrace the idea that 'the social role of the corporation goes far beyond meeting its obligations to shareholders'.[31] He finds support in Galston, who calls the stubborn belief of many corporations that business begins and ends with maximising shareholder value, a 'misunderstanding'. And it's a costly misunderstanding, also for corporations: 'Now we can see what four decades of pursuing shareholder value at the expense of everything else has yielded. Public confidence in corporations is at the rock-bottom, and public anger is sky-high. The revolt of the voter against the corporate economic agenda ... is sweeping the country.'[32]

---

26 For instance, Oxfam and like-minded (international) civil organisations reason that it is no longer acceptable that national governments, international organisations and corporate sector entities are 'ducking their responsibility for tackling the big issues, often compromised by political weakness, political expediency or powerful vested interests'. The organisation has 'a vision that sets local communities and the voices of women, men and young people at the centre of change. Through dialogue and pressure on governments and business, and through political programs that enable human development, dignity and well-being, it is those voices that are the best hope for ending discrimination, exclusion and the injustice of poverty.' (Oxfam 2012: 5.)

27 Legum, 2002: pages 7, 13, 26 and 29.

28 See among others: North & Cato (eds.), 2017; Calvo & Morales (eds.), 2017; Utting (ed.), 2015; Kielburger, Branson & Kielburger, 2018.

29 In fora such as the World Economic Forum ('Davos'); Bilderberg. Media include The Economist and Financial Times.

30 Maira, 2011: 11. (The interesting issue here is that this argument was first published in his column in The Economic Times, the leading business newspaper in India.)

31 Maira, 2011: 6. Brian Iversen, director at Cimbria Capital, argues: 'We are ensnared by the wrong kind of capitalism – one that allocates capital towards conventional sectors creating entrenched problems rather than solving longer-term fundamental needs'. (Iversen, 2017.)

32 Galston, 2016.

The end of the golden triangle: Hybridisation and the 'plural sector'

These global trends can be seen in the context of the end of the golden triangle: state-market-civil society. In September 1970 the (later) Nobel Prize laureate Milton Friedman wrote an article in The New York Times Magazine in which he states that business men who speak about the social responsibility of businesses '... are unwitting puppets of the intellectual forces that have been undermining the basis of a free society these past decades.' Friedman writes: 'The corporate executive would be spending someone else's money for a general social interest ... reduce returns to stockholders, he is spending their money.' He concludes with the observation that '"Social responsibility" involves the acceptance of the socialist view that political mechanisms, not market mechanisms, are the appropriate way to determine the allocation of scarce resources to alternative uses'.[33]

However, perceptions of the position and responsibilities of business entities and 'business men' have changed considerably over the past 48 years, moving away from Friedman's stance. Two major interrelated changes can be observed: there is – as indicated above – a growing realisation that corporates cannot exclusively focus on shareholder value. As a matter of fact, more and more companies do pay (some) attention to corporate social responsibility (CSR)[34] and/or focus on shared value creation (see the next section of this chapter).

Diagram II.2: The Hybridisation movement[35]

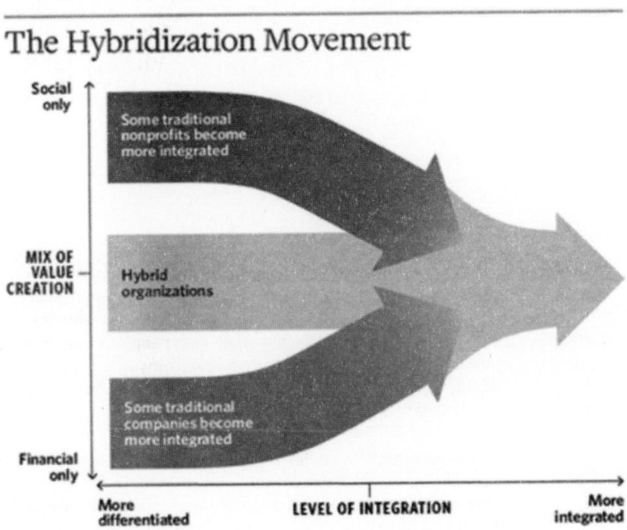

33 Friedman, 1970.
34 In some countries CSR has become mandatory, i.e. South Africa and India.
35 Battilana et al, 2012.

Secondly, the traditional division of societies into three pillars (state, market and civil society) is no longer an appropriate reflection of the somewhat chaotic and complex current reality where markets, government and civil society are converging.[36] In an article in the Stanford Social Innovation Review, Henry Mintzberg speaks about the interface between government, corporate sector and civil society as the 'plural sector' that is neither public nor privately-owned and that 'deserves greater recognition of the critical role it will have to play in restoring the balance in this troubled world'.[37] Others speak about the emergence of hybrid organisations that combine elements of non-profits and profits (see Diagram II.2).

Box II.4: Democracy under pressure

The growing inequality and the ecological crisis are intertwined with a third major challenge: the increasing erosion of political institutions. In many countries (including North Atlantic states) democracy is under pressure and the space for civil society organisations is shrinking.[38] For almost half a century, scholars have been arguing that ill-functioning economies, vast income disparities and poverty affect the social cohesion of countries and the legitimacy of public institutions and liberal democracy.[39] In many parts of the world the legitimacy and moral authority of governments and mainstream political parties is low. In a number of cases the performance of government leaves a lot to be desired and financial institutions and multinational corporations have come to rule the world.[40] Both have gained excessive influence over governments and the general public. Today's inequality, environmental problems and damaged democracy reinforce each other.

In many countries the space to manoeuvre for emancipatory civil society organisations (such as leftist trade unions, human rights organisations and environmental groups) is decreasing gradually but steadily. The 2017 State of Civil Society Report of CIVICUS highlights a global emergency on civic space as 'democracy is being undermined by right-wing populist and neo-fascist leaders', while the power of businesses continues to grow, having a greater impact on all spheres of life than ever. 'A consistent pattern is emerging of attacks on civil society organisations (CSOs) and activists engaged in defending human rights and fundamental freedoms from repressive state machinery, extremist groups and criminal forces linked to big business'.[41]

Social business and social and solidarity economy

Taking a bird's eye view of the social, economic and political developments over the past one to two centuries, one sees a broad consensus emerging that a change is needed. There is, as indicated above, much discontent about the current neo-liberal development model. Arguments are many: the assumption that individual rationality leads to collective rationality does not seem feasible any longer. Means of production

36 Ref. among others Fowler & Biekart, 2008: Chapter 10. In a thought piece for the UNDP Fowler (2011) writes: 'In practice, separation between people in the sectors makes less and less sense'. '... a growing societal response to solving wicked problems is found in blending between 'sector' logics and measures of performance'. (Fowler 2011: 17 - 18).

37 Mintzberg, 2015. He quotes the examples of the Amul Cooperative in India, Mondragon the world's largest federation of worker cooperatives.

38 See among others the writings of Colin Crouch who has been writing since 2000 about the 'poor health of democracy' and 'post-democracy'. (Crouch, not dated).

39 Ref. among others: Wharton, 1969.

40 Korten, 1995.

41 CIVICUS, 2017: 7.

are in the hands of few. Financial capital has become more important in the past half a century. Despite the free market ideology, the model is being supported by state interventions and finance capital. Accumulation takes place through acquisition of surplus of labour[42] and exploitation of nature. The vast and growing inequality and damaged democracy reinforce each other. Companies and the economy have lost their embeddedness in social relations and nature. The emphasis is on the production of exchange instead of on use value.

Box II.5: Some data about the state of democracy in the world

- 'Autocratization is now manifesting in a number of large countries including Brazil, India, Russia, Turkey and the United States. It affects one third of the world's population – some 2.5 billion people.
- Even in democracies, some groups – women, social groups, and the poor – are systematically excluded from access to political power.
- Only 15% of the world's population, or 1.1 billion people, live in a society where political power is distributed at least somewhat equally by gender or socio-economic group.
- Exclusion due to socio-economic status has become more severe since the 1970s. Intensified political exclusion now affects poorer groups in countries that are home to one-quarter of the world's population, or almost 2 billion people. Despite some advances, inclusion remains an illusion.
- The aspects of democracy that make elections truly meaningful are in decline.[43]
- It is highly improbable that development has any chance of producing equitable, sustainable, or inclusive outcomes under conditions where civic space is restricted or closing up.'[44]

Ours is also a time when just three per cent of the world's population live in countries where civil space is fully open, meaning that the exercise of their freedom of expression, association and peaceful assembly is not being unduly restricted.[45]

One of the positive outcomes of the recent financial recession is the increasing interest in social economy and social business as an alternative, more sustainable development model. It is – as emphasised by Jed Emmerson (see his quote at the beginning of this chapter) – time to revisit the concept of value addition and creation.

However, there is no consensus about which route to follow. The transition discourses can basically be divided into two broad categories: political and technocratic.[46] The technocratic approach primarily promotes technological innovations in order to foster sustainable development. The concepts related to the economic system are 'inclusive development' 'creative capitalism', 'circular economy', 'from cradle to cradle' and fostering 'green economy'. In such an approach transition is not positioned within the political and economic context of the world's contemporary challenges, and

42 Labour performed in excess of the labour necessary to produce the means of livelihood of a worker.
43 https://www.v-dem.net/en/news/democracy-all-v-dem-annual-democracy-report-2018/ and V-Dem Institute, 2018.
44 Hossain et al.2016.
45 www.civicus.org
46 Audet, not dated.

change processes are perceived as predominantly technical, value-free and neutral trajectories.[47]

The political approach acknowledges that 'transition is a broader process than mere technological improvement – it is about deep radical, and fundamental social transformation'.[48] Here, social business is – as outlined in the Introduction – conceptualised as a political and radical (read 'transformative') element in a transformation process that centers around interrelated local and global action towards a social and solidarity economy. The theory and practice of social business and social economy should be seen as attempts to contribute to the transformation of capitalism towards an SSE, by way of generating highly practical experiments and examples that provide insights into fundamental transition processes.[49] In the introductory chapter of this book, the concept of a social and solidarity economy sector is defined as a system that 'aims to replace fundamentally unjust or unequal social, economic and power relations with democratically run institutions providing sustainable livelihoods, in order to bring democratically run, economically just, socially inclusive and environmentally sustainable futures.'[50] Although different world views and understandings of change can be found under the umbrella of an SSE, there is some consensus emerging that it is primarily about '... expanding the economic space where people-centred organisations and enterprises can operate'.[51] In the last chapter of this book – a contribution by Moolla and Van der Velden – the concept of SSE will be further developed.

Re-emergence of the concepts of social business and social enterprise

The concept of social business and social enterprises is not new. Social businesses and enterprises have existed throughout the ages, even St. Francis of Assisi, founder of the Franciscan Order, could be considered to have been one.[52] Jerr Boschee's Institute for Social Entrepreneurs produced a chronology that – despite a strong bias towards

47 Such an approach is often linked with what Harry Boytes call 'a culture of rescue': an expert who identifies deficiencies, takes the lead and is in control and negates capacities and opportunities of those who are affected. The rescue approach is the opposite of an agency approach, in which competencies and capacities of people are acknowledged to take responsibility for their own development of their families, communities and society at large. (Boyte, 2008: 123 - 125). The South African intellectual Xolela Mangcu calls this 'technocratic creep'. 'Technocratic creep creates professional identities separated from civic identities. It embodies instrumental rationality which holds "why" questions as a given and focuses on efficiency of means. It holds a view of scientific knowledge as objective truth rather than as power resources which need to be in relationship to other kinds of knowledge for effective action'. (Boyte, 2013.)

48 Audet, not dated: 6.

49 Ref. also the work by Miller (not dated). Internationally, the New Economics Foundation is one of the leading knowledge institutes in this area. http://neweconomics.org/ 'Together we will build a new economy where people really take control'. See as well NEF, not dated. In the present chapter it is acknowledged that 'share holder capitalism' as part of the neo-liberal development paradigm is 'past its sell-by date' as corporate governance (even of companies that advocate CSR and SVC, and B corporations) is dominated by the urge to maximise shareholders' return. In a publication of the NEF McCann and Berry rightly argue: 'There is nothing natural or inevitable about the shareholder-owned corporation as it currently exists. Like all economic institutions, it is a product of political and economic choices which can and should be remade if they no longer serve our economy, society, or environment'. (McCann & Berry, 2017: III).

50 North & Scott Cato, 2017: 6 -7.

51 Utting, 2015: 2.

52 Bornstein & Davis, 2010: 2 - 7.

the Northern hemisphere – provides interesting insights into the overall evolution of the concept.[53] Historical antecedents may be monasteries, missionaries and hospitals worldwide. Forerunners in the United States include Andrew Carnegie in the 1890s, Julius Rosenwald in the 1910s–1920s and William Norris with his Control Data Cooperation in the 1960s–1980s. The Mondragón Corporación Cooperative (established in 1956) may still be considered the world's largest social enterprise by annual sales and size of staff. In the 1970s, The Shore Bank in Chicago applied social activism in the banking industry.[54]

On a different note, in India Mahatma Gandhi may be considered an advocate of a social business approach to change processes avant la lettre as his 'village industries movement'[55] has many characteristics of the contemporary social business movement. With the emergence of the Ashoka Foundation[56] in the 1980s, the concept received a tremendous boost globally, both at conceptual and operational level. For instance in the UK, Liam Black and Jeremy Nicholls have been frontrunners at policy and operational level.[57] David Bornstein's publications with case descriptions of social entrepreneurs from different parts of the globe have contributed tremendously to the understanding of this approach to change process.[58] In 2008 the Social Enterprise World Forum was established, holding annual conferences to discuss the major developments in this discipline.[59] From a different angle Jeff Skoll, the first president of eBay, in 1999 created the Skoll Foundation supporting social entrepreneurs.[60] Muhammad Yunus and the Grameen Bank were awarded the Nobel Peace Prize 2006 'for their efforts to create economic and social development from below'.[61] Many universities worldwide have started Master's Diploma Courses in social entrepreneurship.[62] A number of social investment funds and companies have been set up, and in a number of countries, quite often with the support of the British Council,[63] a social business ecosystem has been created.

In short: the history of the concept of social business is long and rich. It has a global reach and meaning. Over the last four decades social entrepreneurship is becoming established 'as a vocation and a mainstream area of inquiry' not only in high- but also medium- and low-income countries.[64]

---

53 http://www.socialenterprise.org/index.htm and Bornstein, 2017: 3.
54 Institute for social entrepreneurs 2008.
55 Ref. among others Gandhi, 1960.
56 https://www.ashoka.org
57 Ref. among others their book 'There is no business like social business' (2004).
58 Bornstein 2007.
59 http://sewfonline.com/
60 http://skoll.org/ 'The Skoll Foundation drives large-scale change by investing in, connecting, and celebrating social entrepreneurs and the innovators who help them solve the world's most pressing problems'.
61 https://www.nobelprize.org/nobel_prizes/peace/laureates/2006/ In a country such as the Netherlands the subject of social business is 'hot'. Some Dutch Non-Governmental Development Organisations that have acted as funding agencies for decades are transforming themselves into social enterprises (with business units) and investment bankers.
62 E.g. Goldsmith University London; Deshpande Educational Trust, Hubli, India (http://www.detedu.org).
63 See: https://www.britishcouncil.org/society/social-enterprise
64 Bornstein, 2007: 3.

The landscape is however very diverse. In everyday reality at conceptual, policy and operational level there is quite a bit of confusion about the meaning of the term 'social business'. Often the term is used too loosely and a number of – generally quite different – concepts such as 'social entrepreneurship', 'B Corporation'[65], 'Corporation 2020'[66], are being used interchangeably. The next paragraph strives to bring some clarity.

What is actually a social business?

Typology of businesses: Eight archetypes

The insights and developments of the last few decades trigger the question: 'What is actually a social business?'

At least on paper, eight different archetypes of businesses can be distinguished (see Diagram II.3).

Diagram II.3: Typology of businesses

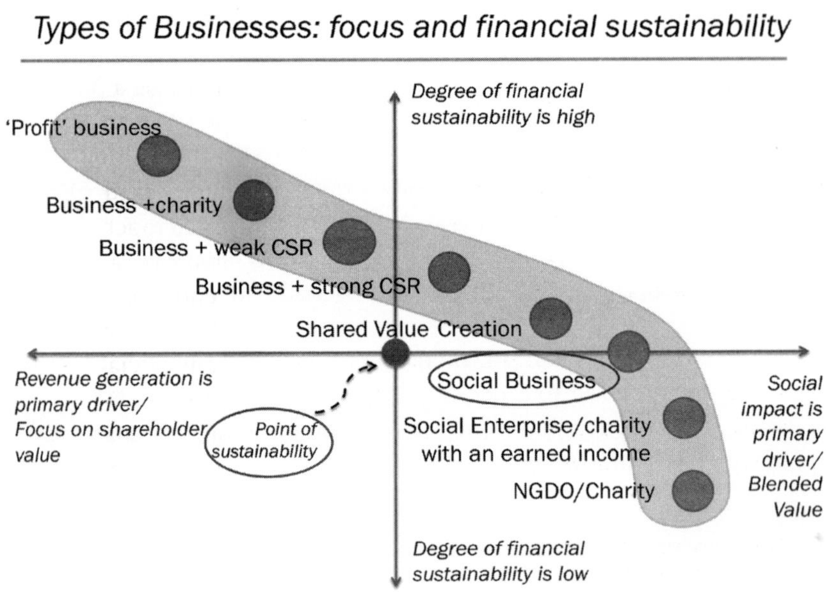

Source: Van der Velden in collaboration with De Greve and Van der Spek.

65 A term which is used in the United States of America for organisations that 'are for-profit companies certified by the nonprofit B Lab to meet rigorous standards of social and environmental performance, accountability, and transparency' (https://www.bcorporation.net/what-are-b-corps)

66 Sukhdev, 2012. Some organisations that have a history in the development sector use the concept of social business so loosely that almost every organisation that operates in the domains of 'social' and 'business' falls in the category 'social businesses', which is not helpful for conceptual, policy and operational reasons.

- Traditional 'for profit' business, mainstream market company with exclusive emphasis on shareholder satisfaction;
- Traditional business with a link to a charity foundation (e.g. Bill and Melinda Gates Foundation, Safaricom Foundation and W.K. Kellogg Foundation);
- Business with 'weak corporate social responsibility' ('do not do too much harm');
- Business with 'strong corporate social responsibility' ('do good for people, planet and profit, as long as this does not affect the financial return on investment')[67];
- Business focusing on shared value creation, which can be defined as 'policies and operating practices that enhance the competitiveness of a company while simultaneously advancing the economic and social conditions in which it operates'.[68] The case study presented in this volume by Jack van Dokkum about Pactics in Cambodia is a clear example of such an approach.
- Social businesses are organisations that use business principles to create 'blended value'[69] in a (financially) sustainable manner in order to contribute to systemic societal change. In a social business the social and financial purposes are intertwined. The case descriptions in this volume of the Apple Project by L.P. Semwal and InternetNow! by Pol De Greve fall into this category. The Inspire2Care programme presented by Betteke de Gaay Fortman also has major characteristics of a social business approach.
- Social enterprises are organisations that have as their primary purpose a social objective but are engaged in regular business activities (unlike the social businesses, where the actual operation of the business activities needs to achieve certain social objectives as well, i.e. the socio-political and financial purpose are intertwined in the business model). The surpluses of social enterprises are then reinvested to achieve a wider social or community objective. Key distinguishing characteristics of a social enterprise are the social and societal purposes combined with an entrepreneurial, private sector spirit. The Boma Hotels run by the Kenyan Red Cross are a clear example of a social enterprise. The hotels are exploited on a purely commercial basis and 'All profits fund the Kenya Red Cross Society's Humanitarian activities'.[70]
- Traditional not-for-profit organisations (different manifestations such as charities, Non-Governmental Development Organisations, community-based organisations). (See Diagram II.3)

---

67 The distinction between weak and strong corporate social responsibility originates from Yunus, 2010. CSR should be positioned with the Triple Bottom Line approach ('people, planet and profit') that has been developed in 1994 by John Elkington (Elkington 1994).

68 Porter & Kramer, HBR, January 2011. Porter and Kramer's concept of shared value creation, defined as 'policies and operating practices that enhance the competitiveness of a company while simultaneously advancing the economic and social conditions in which it operates', is basically a plea that companies should re-establish their relationship with communities and society at large. The recent cases (2017) of e.g. Unilever and AKZO Nobel in the Netherlands illustrate that, despite good intentions and attention for a win-win approach vis-à-vis community interests, shareholder value is and remains the leading guiding principle for business operations.

69 With components such as reducing inequality, contributing to global social justice, improved environment and enhanced democracy.

70 http://www.theboma.co.ke/pages/about.html

All these business models have their own characteristics and logics and they differ substantially in their contribution to societal change.

The concept of blended value and social and solidarity economy

The essence of a social business is creation of value(s) that is relevant for society as a whole and that contribute to systemic change. Social businesses function in a financially sustainable manner. The simultaneous achievement of multiple values is what Jed Emerson, one of the founding fathers of the concept, calls 'blended value'. 'B[lended] V[alue] is simply a conceptual framework for advancing a vision of value creation which is not based upon a bifurcated understanding of the nature of value (either/or), but rather a unified, holistic understanding of value as "both/and," integrated and non-divisible.'[71] In their book Impact Investing, Bugg-Levine and Emerson explain it succinctly as follows: ' ...using the best of business thinking and practices to pursue value integrative and not exclusive either socially or financially directed'.[72]

The concepts of corporate social responsibility and shared value creation have of late become popular within the corporate sector.[73] Both approaches may have their own rationale and value but have actually not much in common with social business. In the case of shared value creation 'competitiveness of a company' and shareholder satisfaction remain the primary purpose of the business. This is also the case with CSR. David Sogge quotes a study that was commissioned by the European Commission which had as its key research question: 'What benefits and impacts does CSR actually bring beyond company borders to the economy and society at large?'. The headline conclusion was:

> There is little empirical evidence which explains the concrete impacts of CSR activities and programmes on the organizational performance of companies, the wider economy, or the social and environmental fabric of Europe, its nations and regions. By implication, the aggregate CSR activities of European companies in the past decade have not made a significant contribution to the achievement of the broader policy goals of the European Union.[74]

Such models, though significant in re-evaluating the way business is being done, are not enough to bring about systemic change and to ensure a focus on new, social value creation.

---

71 http://www.blendedvalue.org/framework/

72 Budd-Levine and Emerson, 2011: 62 – 63. 'In fact, all organizations have the potential to generate a blend of economic, social and environmental value. Most for-profit corporations, however, have historically under-performed on a social and environmental basis and most nonprofit organizations have under-performed on an economic basis. Pursuing blended value enables them to capture efficiencies not possible through pursuing purely commercial or purely social strategies. This strategy not only appeals to many on an intuitive level—it provides a framework to assist us in better understanding the growing wave of practice across the for-profit and nonprofit sectors, and the concurrent interest by academics, business writers and the press'. Sheila Bonini & Jed Emerson, 2005.

73 Ref. also Chapter V in this volume, the contribution by Jack van Dokkum about Pactics in Cambodia.

74 Sogge, 2016. (Ref. also: CSR Impact, 2013).

Ten characteristics of a social business

Based on our collaborative action research, it can be asserted that the 'ideal type' of a social business has the following ten interrelated characteristics. [75]

1. Primary purpose: Contribution to systemic change

The primary purpose of a social business is twofold: bringing about changes in the lives of people, as well as a shift in power equations in order to contribute to systemic change. This is about promoting global social justice, an improved environment and enhancing the functioning of democratic institutions. A social business is 'a business that generates revenue through the sales of products and services with the fundamental purpose to make the world better'.[76] The primary focus is not on shareholder value or on maximising profit, but on maximising impact, which may be social, environmental, political, or cultural. This is an essential element. Many definitions of social entrepreneurship do not capture this. They remain blind to the structural difficulties that societies face and come up with solutions within parameters of the neo-liberal development paradigm.[77] The term 'social business' is under threat of being high-jacked by the neo-liberal paradigm (thus proving its popularity and the need for change in the neo-liberal realm) which may cause it to lose its transformative meaning, its 'sting'.

Box II.6: Definitions of social entrepreneurship and business[78]

- 'A social enterprise is an organisation that is run like a business but that has a social purpose.' (ILO)
- 'Social business = (social improvement and verification) + competition and innovation.' (Black and Nicholls)
- 'A non-loss non-dividend company devoted to solving a social problem and owned by investors (or people) who reinvest all profits.' (Yunus)
- 'Businesses with primarily social objectives whose surpluses are principally reinvested for that purpose in the business or in the community, rather than being driven by the need to maximise profit for shareholders and owners'. (UK Government)
- 'A business that seeks, above all, to make a better world – a business for a common good.' (Lynch & Walls)
- 'A social entrepreneur identifies practical solutions to social problems by combining innovation, resourcefulness and opportunity.' (Hartigan and Billimoria).
- 'A social enterprise [is] a private and autonomous organization, providing goods and services, with an explicit aim of benefitting the community, that is owned and managed by a group of citizens, and in which the material interest of investors is subject to limits.' (UNDP).

75 An earlier version of this overview was published in Van der Velden, 2011. These characteristics have emerged from interactions (collaborative action research, Business Development Support, trainings, et cetera) with client organisations of Context, international cooperation.

76 Kielburger, Branson & Kielburger, 2018: 54.

77 Moseley, 2014. (They pursue what Audet (not dated) calls the technocratic approach.)

78 ILO, 2011; Black & Nicholls, 2004: 33; Yunus, 2010; Lynch & Walls, 2009: 33; Borzaga, Galera & Nogales, 2006 in a UNDP publication; Hartigan & Billimoria, 2005: 19. The definition of the UK Government can be found at: https://www.socialenterprisemark.org.uk/what-is-social-enterprise/

Unlike what Muhammad Yunus may seem to suggest, the defining feature of a social business is not its form but its function.[79] Form should follow function and the quality and verifiability of the service and product are more important than the legal structure of the delivery organisation.[80]

2. Social businesses operate through the market

Social businesses use market-based business models: trading of goods and services within a market. Unlike Non-Governmental Development Organisations, social businesses do not work on the basis of grants[81] and do not operate in a parallel economy, but are part of the regular market and competition (in order to achieve financial sustainability, among other things). Real trade with real paying customers, generating services aimed at reducing inequality and including people who are usually left out. [82]

3. A social business is financially sustainable

For a real social business, the bottom line is financial sustainability. Among entrepreneurs and in literature, there is much debate about the percentage of income that should be generated through the market. The Social Enterprise Mark (UK) sets the percentage at 50.[83] This may be too low. For many organisations the journey from a grant-funded organisation to sales-led social business requires a massive change in leadership and organisational culture. Quite often this is no easy feat, as mindset, strategy, systems, procedures, staff competencies, leadership, et cetera all need to be changed accordingly. Against this background it may be advisable to earn a higher percentage of income through the market in order to promote and maintain an entrepreneurial spirit within the organisation.

Although social businesses strive for financial sustainability independent of grants, most of them cannot always fully rely on the market for their income due to the fact that they have often higher transaction costs. Social businesses often provide services and products in markets and areas where private business, public sector and civil society organisations have not been able to act adequately and where competencies, collective capabilities and capacities are generally low.[84] That brings extra (transaction) costs which may have to be compensated by grants or subsidies. Black and Nicholls suggest, in this context, replacing the word 'subsidy' with 'compensation'.[85] Social entrepreneurs, especially those who work in low- and medium-income countries,

---

79 Lynch & Wall, 2009: 40.

80 Black & Nicholls, 2004: 33.

81 'You want to be freed from the tyranny of grant money', Ibid, page 29.

82 Black and Nicholls state: 'Social enterprises are making money while at the same time addressing social issues'. 'Real trade with real paying customers is at the heart of things.' 'Thriving business, part of the enterprising economy, generating services and products which reduce inequality and create new opportunities for people who are usually left out'. (Black & Nicholls, 2004: 9.)

83 www.socialenterprisemark.org.uk

84 Black & Nicholls, 2004: 25.

85 Ibid, page 27.

tend to (certainly initially) have extra management burdens and costs that need to be compensated.[86]

4. *Multi-actor environments: Value chain development*

Social businesses operate in a wide variety of contexts but often in complex environments with diverse client groups and stakeholders. This is because such businesses operate ideally as part of a value chain (instead of a supply chain) which may be described as interlinked value-adding activities that convert inputs into outputs, which, in turn, add to the bottom line and help create competitive advantage.[87] The nature and character of a value chain differs from case to case and depends to a large extent on the nature of the product and on the context, actors and factors involved. Stakeholders in a value chain may include producers, traders, those involved in processing the product, wholesalers and retailers. The level of influence and importance may differ from actor to actor.[88]

It is important for a social business to ascertain where major value addition takes place, to position itself strategically within a value chain, and to manage relationships with stakeholders proactively.[89] Experience shows that appropriate and effective embedding in the institutional context and support services are critical factors for the well-being of a social business.[90]

5. *Social entrepreneur*

One of the early and longstanding authorities on (social) entrepreneurship, J. Gregory Dees of the Duke Innovation and Entrepreneurship Initiative, developed a somewhat idealised concept of the social entrepreneur as a 'bold and opportunistic change agent working to create and sustain social value, and working innovatively and adeptly to overcome resource constraints.'[91] A social entrepreneur has a clear political vision, awareness about the destructive nature of the current economic system, a passion and determination to do things differently and combines this with risk-taking, a business approach and innovation. The complexity of running a social business implies that a social entrepreneur needs to draw heavily on existing social capital (in terms of relationships and networks) or the development of it, which is a prerequisite for the participation of people, regions, groups and individuals (networking). Business has always been as much about who you know as what you know. 'Your ability to create robust networks across systems which enable you to build, sell, fundraise, access supply chains, recruit, influence, will determine how effective you will be.'[92]

---

86 See also in this chapter: Characteristic 6: Slow capital – 'the missing middle' and Challenge 4: Access to capital for social business start-ups.

87 http://www.businessdictionary.com/definition/value-chain.html See e.g. Steenhuis Pieters et al., 2006.

88 Brouwers et al, 2010: 20.

89 Yunus, 2006: 86.

90 Yunus writes with regard to this subject: 'The ability to forge and maintain positive, creative relationships with partner organizations is likely to be one of the hallmarks of the most successful social businesses'.

91 Dees, 2001.

92 Black, 2014: 71.

Box II.7: Qualities of social entrepreneurs

'A social entrepreneur has many qualities:
- A pragmatic visionary who achieves large scale, systemic and sustainable social change through a new invention, a different approach, a more rigorous application of known technologies or strategies, or a combination of these.
- Is able to unlock, stimulate and lead the innate capacity of people to contribute meaningfully to economic and social development.
- A driving passion to make that happen.
- A practical but innovative stance to a social problem, often using market principles and forces, coupled with dogged determination that allows them to break away from constraints imposed by ideology or field of discipline, and pushes them to take risks that others wouldn't dare.
- A zeal to measure and monitor their impact. Entrepreneurs have high standards, particularly in relation to their own organisation's efforts and in response to the communities with which they engage. Data, both quantitative and qualitative, are their key tools, guiding continuous feedback and improvement.
- A healthy impatience. Social entrepreneurs don't do well in bureaucracies. They cannot sit back and wait for change to happen – they are the change drivers.' [93]

Action research by Context, international cooperation and the Leadership Development and Support Programme (LEAP+) in collaboration with client organisations such as SNV, Netherlands Development Organisation, showed that personal leadership, business management competencies and the ability to embed a social business in a community and society ('societal leadership') are of crucial importance.[94]

Business leaders are often 'doers' and Peattie and Morley argue rightly that 'such personality types may be inclined towards benign autocracy rather than participation and particularly democratic approaches'.[95] Benign autocracy seems out of place in social business. But, although much of the literature and practice of social business relates business leadership to an individual person, this should not be the case. Leadership in social business is an organisational function that can be carried out by more people (even teams) with complementary competencies.[96] This also safeguards the social business against mission drift (see Challenge 1, later in this chapter).

The emerging social trend of 'downshifting, the adoption of a less pressurised and materially intensive lifestyle in search of an improved quality of life'[97] has the potential to generate more social entrepreneurs. It will be interesting to see if that occurs.

---

93 Reference is made to the website of Nyenrode Business University. See http://www.nyenrode.nl/FacultyResearch/BMI/CE/SVE/Pages/Social-Entrepreneurs.aspx

94 Van der Spek, Schreven & Van der Velden, 2013. More on the LEAP+ programme and its outcomes can be found in Chapter IV.

95 Black, 2014: 8.

96 Ref. as well Chapter IV by Behonegne & Van der Velden about leadership in social business.

97 Peattie & Morley, n.d.: 16.

6. Slow capital: 'The missing middle'[98]

All businesses need capital, social businesses as well. Access to secure and sustainable funding remains the key determinant of the success of social businesses. [99] Access to such capital is often a constraint for a number of reasons:

- Investors are normally risk adverse, i.e. they seek certainties about financial return that require proof of commercial viability of the start-up which cannot be provided at an early stage, especially if the venture enters a 'complex territory' (often the case for start-ups aimed at positive social impact);
- Social entrepreneurs often lack collateral, credit history and/or perceived financial competency or stability sufficient to attract regular loans (debt);
- Capital markets for this type of non-conventional business are still immature and there is little availability of financial instruments appropriate for capitalising social business, especially in the early start-up phase (too late for innovation, too soon for investors);
- Ownership and regulatory issues can pose hindrances in access to capital in some countries.

Social entrepreneurs, who work in situations where market, civil society and state fail[100], are in investment terms a difficult category: too small and risky for big finance institutions; too big for microfinance. In a report by the Shell Foundation[101] it is testified: 'We have been struck by the paucity of foundations and donors willing to provide all-important flexible and long-term subsidy support to start-up and growing for profit social enterprises.' Especially where the potential social return and the risks are high, capital is a scarce commodity. The cover of J.P. Morgan's publication about 'Impact Investments' shows a big gap in the middle of an enormous bridge: 'the missing middle' in terms of finance.[102]

Microfinance is not an option for social businesses, not just because the amounts provided by microfinance are normally too small for a social business, which makes them too big to qualify. There are many downsides to microfinance, which make it less suitable to social businesses – see Box II.8.

98 In this section the term social capital is used, not in the sociological meaning of network (Bourdieu and Putnam) but as capital that is being provided to entrepreneurs against concessional conditions. See also further on in this section.

99 Peattie & Morley, n.d. 29

100 Or made to fail by off-loading of tasks from the public to the private sector, 'Big Society' (Cameron in UK), 'Participatiemaatschappij' (Prime Minister M. Rutte and his colleagues in the Netherlands).

101 West & Woodcraft, 2010.

102 O'Donohoe et al, 2010.

Box II.8: The myth of microfinance[103]

Over the past two decades, microfinance, the provision of financial services to micro-entrepreneurs and small businesses, has become a popular approach for poverty alleviation.

A body of research literature has emerged over the last few years that questions the reliability and validity of this approach. Empirical evidence shows that quite often:

- The effect of microfinance on 'consumption is insignificant or negative, no huge improvement in welfare, no effect on starting new economic activities ... no impact on education, no impact on women empowerment' (Banerjee, 2013);
- Microcredit is only 'half right'; loans are often too small to start a feasible and viable business (Bauchet & Morduch, 2011);
- Borrowers above the poverty line benefit more from microfinance than those below the poverty line (largely due to the risk-income ratio; clients with more money are in a better position to take risks) (Karnani, 2007);
- Interest rates are normally far too high and quite often reduce cash flow of the poor and therefore do more harm than good (Karnani, 2007);
- The repayment period is usually too short for any enterprise to have generated enough cash flow to support the repayment of the loan and operations of the enterprise;
- Microfinance has often been commercialised to such a degree that targets for staff of microfinance institutions were set too high, which led to an oversupply of loans, as well as multiple indebtedness which a large number of the poor did not know how to repay - and the credit bubble burst (this is what happened in the state of Andhra Pradesh, India) (Hulme & Arun, 2011);
- Vital management and leadership inputs are often not provided alongside microcredit (Saxena, 2011);
- Poverty alleviation cannot be defined solely in economic terms, which is the focus of microfinance institutions; 'It is also about addressing a much broader set of needs' (Yunus, 2010).

Saxena's (2011) conclusion about microfinance is that it is: 'an activity that provides an avenue of generating high returns on urban capital through entrepreneurial efforts of members of the underprivileged section of the society in creation and expansion of rural market for consumerism'.[104]

Analysis of macroeconomic data by Karnani (2007) suggests that microfinance may yield some non-economic benefits, but it does not significantly alleviate poverty. In actual fact, instances exist where microfinance has worsened conditions at the bottom of the pyramid. Karnani argues that 'Contrary to the hype about microcredit, the best way to eradicate poverty is to create jobs and to increase worker productivity'.[105]

Despite the above-mentioned constraints, impact investment is a new, some say fast-growing, market. Balandina Jaquier quotes the Monitor Institute that has 'projected the market to grow from $50 bn in 2009 to $500 bn by 2019'.[106] (This is however still less than 1% of all global financial assets.)

---

103 Titus van der Spek provided valuable research assistance with regard to this subject of microfinance.

104 For a more comprehensive assessment of the microfinance phenomenon and the way it has betrayed 'the poor', reference is made to Sinclair's book Confessions of a microfinance heretic (2012) and the documentary by Tom Heinemann, The Micro Debt - a critical investigation into the dark side of Microcredit (2010).

105 Karani, 2007.

106 Balandina Jaquier, 2011.

In view of the fast-growing demand for capital for social businesses, the Shell Foundation emphasises 'that more foundations need to be willing to give flexible subsidy support to for-profit organisations to enable them to achieve social change rather than just restrict their giving to not-for-profits'. In the journey to facilitate the further development of impact investment as a so-called 'asset class' (a group of securities that exhibit similar characteristics) governments can play an important role, for instance by acting as a risk guarantee, starting or promoting social investments funds and/or by contributing to a conducive environment, including encouragements through tax-incentives.

The social investment market is indeed growing. Over the past two decades an increasing array of specialised funding sources for social businesses has emerged, 'from angels to venture capitalist to foundations.'[107] For generations, most of this capital has been publicly funded through tax breaks and tax spending (subsidies) to the corporate sector in OECD countries.

Impact investing may be defined as 'investing with a specific objective of achieving positive social and/or environmental impact as well as financial return'.[108] 'Finance first' investors concentrate on shareholder value and financial returns; philanthropists focus on charitable models; 'impact first' investors (who provide what is called 'patient' as well as 'social' capital) seek to balance the two, thereby optimising the mix between social impact and some financial return (see Diagram II.4).

Some of these investors look for mission-driven businesses that do not sacrifice return at all, while others provide capital for ventures that may trade for some non-financial returns. Grace periods are often extended and financial returns on investment are lower than the prevailing market rate: this is 'slow', 'social' or 'patient' capital.[109]

The social investment capital market can be divided into two categories: the first being direct investors (such as wealthy individuals who typically invest in early-stage businesses, so-called 'angel investors'; philanthropic foundations; endowed non-profits; international development agencies and pension funds) and the second being intermediaries that invest other people's money in social enterprises (social venture capital funds; venture philanthropists; social enterprise and non-profit loan funds).

107 Tozzi, 2009. Many of them are owned by so-called High Net Worth Individuals'.

108 Balandina Jaquier, 2011.

109 Social investors are driven by a clear vision on solving societal issues and a dedicated world view. They invest in society via products and services to stimulate people towards independent action and self-sustainability to enable the achievement of equal (economic) positions in an entrepreneurial and lasting way.

Diagram II.4: Investment spectrum[110]

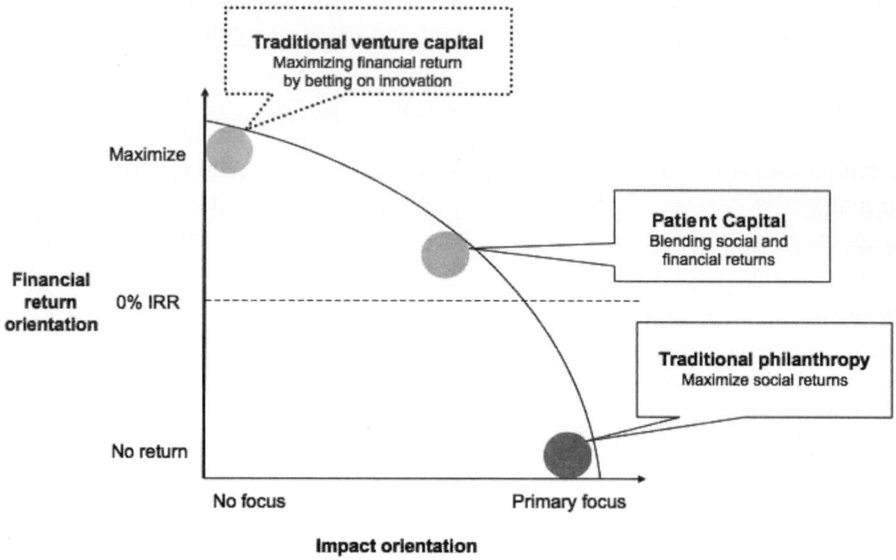

Impact investment can be provided in many different ways. The majority currently represents private equity (shares not quoted on a stock market) and debt. [111] It should be noted that social investors quite often not only provide capital but also their creativity, networking skills, technological competency, life experience and other resources.[112]

7. Social accountability

Recent debates about sustainable development have led to some positive developments, i.e. there is now a growing realisation that negative non-financial effects, such as environmental degradation or social decline, can no longer be labelled 'externalities'. Business performance measurement needs to be improved for operational and for strategic reasons. In 2010 Nobel Prize laureates Joseph Stiglitz and Amartya Sen published the report Mis-measuring our lives; Why GDP doesn't add up. The report was written at the request of the then President of France, Mr Nicholas Sarkozy, who states in its foreword 'We will not change our behavior unless we change the ways we measure our economic performance'. In the book the authors argue in favour of multiple metrics that encompass social progress and societal well-being, in addition to the standard metric of market activity.[113]

110 https://www.slideshare.net/adhersdomain/a-2-aumen-fund-measuring-social-impactmolly-alexander

111 Mohammad Yunus states: 'In a social business an investor aims to help others without making any financial gain himself'. He speaks about a 'non-dividend company'. With all due respect to the Nobel laureate, this view may be and is contested. Social investors do obtain a financial return, but accept a lower return and/or a longer grace period ('slow', 'patient' capital) which is compensated by demonstrating non-financial returns as well.
Yunus, 2010: xvii.

112 Yunus, 2006: xviii.

113 Stiglitz, Sen and Fitoussi, 2010: xxv.

This is certainly true for social businesses. Black and Nicholls make a case in point: 'Without verification the label "social" in "social enterprise" is meaningless.' They call social accountability a moral imperative, and the willingness to be independently scrutinised and held accountable 'the acid test of the social business'.[114]

The importance of social reporting reflects the continuous balancing act between the economic and social purposes of a social business. Performance measurement, benchmarking and reporting are crucial for three reasons: social reporting enhances the quality of results of a social enterprise and business; to prove its worth to people who matter to the business; there is a moral responsibility towards those who have invested in the company.[115] Lynch and Walls state: 'Your business isn't a social enterprise until you can prove it with blended social and financial returns.'[116]

Verifying the financial bottom line (Return on Investment) is relatively easy; establishing social impact requires more effort. Over the years several social impact assessment approaches and tools have been developed to assess the financial, social, political and environmental returns on investment.[117] The various methodologies can be grouped into three to four types according to the function they fulfil: rating system (this is particularly useful for generating PR, for communication purposes and for screening of investment opportunities); assessment system (particularly useful for summarising results); management system (useful as an ongoing management tool); and learning system (particularly useful as an approach for organisational learning). Some methodologies can be used across functions.[118]

In a Social Return on Investment approach, which is being practised among others by Context, international cooperation, attention is paid to all visible and invisible, official and unofficial externalities and inputs and outputs of a social business. Such an assessment is done in an interactive, participatory manner whereby – in order to avoid technocratic creep – valuation is done by the end-users themselves.[119] In such a manner organisational learning, and application of the learning, is being fostered.

8. Citizen involvement

The notion of Peattie and Morley of a social entrepreneur as a somewhat 'benign autocrat' may actually fit the functions that need to be performed. At the same time, a social entrepreneur is, in the terminology of Easterly, a searcher who believes that only

114 Black & Nicholls, 2004: 20.

115 Black & Nicholls, 2004: 142 – 143.

116 Lynch & Walls, 130.

117 Ibid: 132–134. In her PhD, Maas provided an overview of different social impact assessment methodologies and an appraisal thereof. (Maas, 2009: Chapter 3; a succinct version is being presented in Maas, 2014). A summary of different impact measurement methodologies is also provided by Balandina Jaquier, 2011: 109–111.

118 Inspired by Balandina Jaquier, 2011: 109–111.

119 De Greve. Lont & Van der Velden, 2013.

insiders have enough knowledge to find solutions. These can therefore not come from consultants, experts or other outsiders; most solutions must be home-grown.[120]

Moreover, there is a whole body of literature indicating that change processes can only be successful if there is active involvement of citizens in different stages of the business process.[121] People may be involved as producers, consumers, as managers of natural resources or for instance as users of a public space.[122] The adage: 'do not give them [help]; give them respect' means people need to be engaged.[123] This implies a democratic, participatory culture in social businesses. 'Social business gives everybody the opportunity to participate in creating the kind of world we want to see ... citizens don't have to leave all problems in the hands of the government.'[124] Such a social business approach combines the best of both worlds, the corporate sector and the development sector.[125]

9. The need for innovation

Social businesses often arise as a response to market failures or problems with funding or management of traditional public service provision.[126] Social business generally provides services in markets where private businesses, civil society organisations and the public sector have been unable to deal adequately with injustices, environmental issues and issues of governance. 'Business as usual' has not worked, hence the need to redesign models and change mindsets. Black and Nicholls put it very succinctly: 'Finding answers to problems where others have failed demands innovation. No innovation – no social business'.[127] Innovation in the realm of social business should therefore not be treated as an add-on, or made the sole responsibility of an innovation officer, but as an integral part of social business.

10. Contribution to systemic change: Policy advocacy

In the first section of this chapter the major global challenges currently facing mankind were summarised: inequality, environmental degradation, crisis in democracy manifested among other things by a shrinking space for participation of citizens in political decision-making processes. Yunus states that 'Poverty is not created by poor people. It is created by the system that we have built, the institutions that we have designed, and the concepts that we have formulated'.[128] When the social business discourse is positioned in an a-political technocratic perspective, the focus gets distracted from these systemic, political realities. It may then look like

120 Easterly, 2006: 6.

121 Ref. for an overview of the literature about this subject Chambers, 2005.

122 Bhardan, 2006.

123 Prof Dr Gert van Dijk, personal communication during Blooming Events Network meeting, 19 November 2009.

124 Yunus, 2006: xxiv.

125 In this context it needs to be mentioned that the civic driven change discourse, provides an important conceptual and operational framework for citizen involvement. See: Fowler & Biekart, 2008; Fowler & Biekart, 2013.

126 Peattie & Morley, not dated, page 5

127 Black & Nicholls, 2004: 25.

128 Yunus, 2010: xii.

social businesses are the answer to many deeply rooted problems. But the solutions for problems related to poverty and marginalisation, environmental issues and the crisis in democracy require more than efforts by social businesses, they demand far reaching structural, systemic changes in the way economies and states work. And those are ultimately political choices. Black and Nicholls make the following point: 'A million social business entrepreneurs can show how things can be done in radically different ways but they cannot redistribute wealth or compel large businesses to take responsibility for the mess they make. Systemic changes require government action.'[129]

Such radical changes – in terms of a change in the dominant mode of production[130] – do not seem likely to happen soon or easily. In fact, in many countries 'It seems less and less likely that radical change in economic conditions will emerge from the usual political processes that are the domain of a few government departments, powerful interest groups, and consultants'.[131] Therefore, a social entrepreneur should position a social business within this broader perspective: social business as a transformative approach to change processes needs to contribute to systemic change. This can be done through activities in policy advocacy, aiming to contribute to three objectives:

- Promotion of a social business and SSE approach: to engage in advocacy in order to raise awareness about social business and SSE as an alternative approach to pro-poor systemic change processes.
- Conducive environment: contributing to the emergence of a conducive environment for social businesses and SSE. There is a need to build an institutional architecture (finance, resources, advice, legal framework, educational institutes, and support structures).[132]
- Support systemic changes: bring a social business and SSE approach to the political domain in order to contribute to systemic changes.

The value of social businesses lies therefore not only in mitigating or ameliorating desperate circumstances (where expectations of results may not be grandiose, as such experiments are generally constrained by structural contexts), but also in demonstrating that things can be done differently and generating practical experiences that 'a better world is possible'.

Main challenges for social businesses

In a recent publication, Liam Black (one of the thought leaders and practitioners in the field of social business) shares the following anecdote:

129 Black & Nicholls, 2004, p. 49.

130 Ref. the last chapter of this book by Moolla & Van der Velden.

131 Moolla, 2014: 145.

132 This implies '... legislation that provides legal recognition to social business and creates regulatory bodies to ensure transparency, integrity, and honesty in this sector. They can also provide tax incentives for investing in social businesses as well as for social business themselves'. (Yunus, 2010: xxv).

> At the height of my messianic fervour about social enterprise in the late 1990s, I opened the Liverpool Echo newspaper and basked in the glory of an interview I gave in which my brilliant insights about enterprise and regeneration were laid out for all of the Merseyside to see. ... My wife said that she was very impressed and handed me a glass of red wine. And I think that was being sincere. On returning to my office in the morning there was a piece of paper stuck to the door. It was from Stan Riley, one of the upholsterers and our trade union convenor. 'Liam, I read in the Echo you will be transforming the city. You can't even get our wages right. Good luck with Liverpool'. ... By all means aspire to change the world but make sure the vehicle you are using to drive that change has an engine that works.[133]

A decade ago, the social business agenda was absorbed mainly with answering and advocating the question: what is a social business? Today practitioners, policy-makers and academic researchers are asking the question: 'how' do social businesses function optimally? Yes, social businesses face many challenges at operational level. Some of the main ones can be summarised as follows. [134]

Challenge 1: Mission drift: Retaining a social purpose while driving a profit

The task of reiterating and steering a business towards a social vision is difficult. Especially when strategic choices must also ensure that the business model remains feasible and sustainable.

The challenge of mission drift refers to this need to continuously reassess the value orientation of a social business: making sure the venture does not 'drift' away from its core purpose, to create positive social change. Social businesses that straddle both social value creation and revenue generating strategies can benefit from strong leadership at management level with a focus on strategies that aim to integrate social and financial objectives.[135]

Challenge 2: Improving social impact through community participation

The core function of a social business is to instil positive social change. In order to optimally understand the needs and desires of people, social entrepreneurs can benefit from a model that strives to actively include communities within the decision-making and functioning of their business.

The challenge lies in finding the most appropriate level of community participation that will improve, rather than hinder, an entrepreneurial approach (which tends to be

---

133 Black, 2014: 23 – 24.

134 This section has emerged from a collaborative action research process about the potential role of Non-Governmental Development Organisations vis-à-vis social businesses that was supported by ICS (Investing in Children and their Societies) (www.ics.nl). The section is co-authored by Titus van der Spek and Fons van der Velden and was published earlier as 'Trending challenges to running a social business' in The Broker online, 15 July 2014. See on this subject also: Battilana et al, 2012.

135 Ref. among others: Ebrahim, Battilana & Mair, 2014.

a bit top-down, capital intensive and task-oriented rather than process-oriented) and support both the social and commercial success of the social business.

Challenge 3: Social, financial performance measurement, or both?

As social businesses are tasked with the creation of social value, it is important that they remain accountable to themselves and their stakeholders. Transparency in accountability and solid performance measurement, in terms of social and financial performance, are aspects to running a social business that cannot and should not be ignored.

However, the process of measuring one's impact remains complex and extremely bespoke. The question is not only how to measure the impact of a social business, but also when to start measuring. Measures are often adopted late in the organisational life cycle or on a demand-driven basis. Hence, social entrepreneurs are challenged, not only with finding the right tools for the job, but they must also decide when they should (and are able to) implement impact measurement tools.

Challenge 4: Access to social capital for social business start-ups

A quick search for financing opportunities yields a plethora of impact investors, funds and grants made available to social businesses around the globe. Although various funding options exist, very few impact investors cater to social entrepreneurs pre-start-up. This may be partly due to the fact that unlike non-profit organisations, social businesses are not only assessed on their ability to create social change, but also on their potential for financial return on investment. To invest in a social venture pre-start-up is often high-risk.

In the past years, the social business agenda placed a strong focus on understanding the scalability and sustainability of social businesses. Such focus areas tend to place more attention on enterprises that proved successful rather than those which are yet to lift off. However, risk-taking and innovativeness are defining the sector. It is thus vital that efforts are made to readdress the case for social businesses and social entrepreneurs that need support to take their businesses from raw idea to start-up.

Challenge 5: Organisational form

The famous motto from functionalism 'form follows function' is a complicated issue for social businesses. More often than not there are no legally recognised forms that cater to their specific needs. Even though some countries have developed legal forms that give social businesses more leeway, in many cases the environment, institutional architecture and existing legalities are not very conducive to social businesses.[136]

136 It is, for instance, in only a limited number of countries possible to register as a hybrid organisation, i.e. an organisation that tries to find the balance between profit maximising and creating blended value for society.

In the early stages of start-up, a social business may, for example, still be partially grant-funded. It may then be beneficial to register the organisation as a charity rather than a company. As the enterprise transitions into a wholly self-sustainable model, it may be time to change legal forms and become a company limited by shares, so as to function more like a business. In such instances, it would be wise to ensure that the social mission is written into the company's memorandum and articles of association to make it clear that profits should be reinvested into the social business.

Critique of social business approach to change processes[137]

'After six decades of development initiatives, social entrepreneurs are now the child star in an otherwise much-maligned space. Governments sing their praises, business schools teach their methods and award schemes elevate them to iconic status. But can social enterprises fill the gaps left by traditional state and NGO-led development?'[138] The concept of social enterprises and businesses is indeed not uncontested. The critique can be clustered into five main categories.

Social business is not a panacea for every problem

Doane argues that there are areas in which social enterprises clearly outplay traditional development – fair trade businesses, employment training, green energy providers – but there are also areas, such as health care and non-vocational education, where a social business approach to change processes is not a solution to the problem.[139] Further and more in-depth research is necessary to explore which products and services can be best provided in a financially sustainable manner. But it is safe to acknowledge that a social business approach will not be the panacea for addressing all problems in the area of justice and mercy. Many government institutions and grant-funded organisations are doing great work. 'As long as they can verify the value and impact then good luck to them.'[140] Social business is not – and should not be – for everyone.[141]

Role of the state

Moreover, it is thought by many critical observers that it is incorrect to put a market price on what should arguably be provided by the state through public services. In a number of cases, social entrepreneurs let governments off the hook. Anthony Bugg-Levine, a pioneer in impact investing, argues that social enterprises are 'second-best solutions'. Social enterprises that provide access to clean drinking water, for example, only exist when government or the private sector fail to provide such access. Ravi Venkatesan, the former head of Microsoft India who has become a strong proponent

137 Laila Bouallouch and Caroline de Vogel (then research assistants at Context, international cooperation) provided valuable research assistance with regard to this paragraph. See as well the last chapter of this volume in which especially neo-Marxist critiques of the concept of social entrepreneurship and social business are being summarised.

138 Doane, 2014.

139 Ibid.

140 Black & Nicholls, 2004: 26. 'There is nothing wrong with tax payers' or donors' money being used to keep open services to excluded people who otherwise would go without or to subsidize recycling in low income countries' (page 26).

141 Ibid, 65.

of social business, admits that they cannot and should not replace the public sector; the state has to provide public goods. Such public goods should include health care, education and water and sanitation.[142]

Too high return on investment demanded

The DFID India Impact Fund expects a 12% return on its investment.[143] Such a return may be reasonable for regular mainstream business and private investors but is not likely to be desirable or realistic for social entrepreneurs (at the risk of becoming heavily indebted)[144] who are creating blended, and not only financial, value.

Need for systemic changes

A crucial objective for social businesses is the need to contribute to systemic changes. It is also the most difficult to achieve and the easiest to lose focus of. As Mehr states: 'Yet, a social entrepreneur can run the most transparent, well-managed, profitable social enterprise in the world, and still not be solving the social problem their business is founded upon.'[145] Yunus is absolutely right when he argues that inequality and poverty are not created by poor people; they are produced by a system.[146] Black and Nicholls have – as stated earlier – rightly argued that 'A million Social Business entrepreneurs are not going to change the world'.[147]

The Indian activist and writer Rajni Bakshi, who has a lot of respect and appreciation for practical social business initiatives, states: ´However, experience of the last half century shows that merely multiplying successful micro-efforts of this kind is not enough. It is far more important to work for change at the level of ideas and in macro, national policy'.[148]

Michael Edwards argues the structural problems of poverty, marginalisation and violation of human rights require a 'structural solution' and 'solutions have to be fought for and negotiated – not produced, packaged and sold'.[149] He states that it is of crucial importance that social investors '... payout on "social justice philanthropy"-investments that tackle causes and not just symptoms; build institutions and relationships; increase the power and the voice of those left outside the mainstream; protect public sphere; strengthen social movements; and change the systems and structures that keep certain

142 Although there are many organisations that promote a social entrepreneurial approach in this area as well. Ref. among others 'Teach a man to fish': 'Our organisation works with schools to set up school businesses. These businesses are both educational and profitable – teaching students business and entrepreneurial skills, and generating much-needed income for schools'. http://www.teachamantofish.org.uk/

143 Doane, 2014. See also: http://www.theimpactprogramme.org.uk/investments-dfid-impact-fund/

144 Ref. Box II.8 about the myth of microfinance.

145 Mehr, 2014.

146 Yunus, 2010: xii.

147 Black & Nicholls, 2004, p. 49.

148 Bakshi, 2016.

149 Edwards, 2010: 8.

poor people poor.'[150] In his book Small change; Why business won't save the world, he adds succinctly: 'Social transformation is not a job to be left to market forces or to the whims of billionaires.'[151]

Shore and Hammond write in a Stanford Social Innovation Review article:

> The foundation on which many non-profits are built is flawed and simplistic, focused on a symptom rather than the underlying set of problems, developed in isolation rather than as part of an integrated system, and organized to administer a narrowly tailored program or benefit rather than generate sustained, significant change for a person or community. As a result, change is incremental, not big or bold enough to make a lasting and transformative impact. To be truly impactful, social enterprises need to think about their cause and community holistically and incorporate that understanding into their theory of change. This is where the tools and ethos of human-centred design can be powerful.[152]

What social business can and cannot do

One of the greatest aspects of social businesses is that they offer proof of a concept for new business models and for solving problems from different angles, which governments and businesses can (and actually should) later adopt. Zunaid Moolla, a South African political economist, formulates this as follows: 'There is a case then to make for community-based organisations to undertake alternative economic growth and development initiatives'. ... 'We must acknowledge that decisions regarding major macro-economic policy levers could never devolve to communities'.[153]

Inequality, environmental degradation and shrinking space for political participation are – indeed – political conditions. Therefore, they require political solutions with attention to change in power relations and ownership of assets; and with poor people and other marginalised communities in 'the driver seat'.[154] If advocates of a social business approach to change forget to advocate for those changes at the policy and strategic level or neglect to encourage or pressurise businesses to change radically, they are failing to create long-term, holistic impact. In the introductory and last chapters of this book it is therefore argued that a social business approach to changes processes should be positioned at conceptual and operational level in an attempt to promote a new mode of production that leads to systemic changes.[155]

---

150 Edwards, 2008: 89–90.

151 Edwards, 2010: xiii.

152 Shore, Hammond & Celep, 2013: 42.

153 Moolla, 2014. At the same time, it should be acknowledged 'that decisions regarding major macro-economic policy levers could never devolve to communities'. (Ibid.) For an elaboration of this argument, reference is made to the last chapter of this book.

154 Edwards, 2010: 12.

155 Ref. Chapter X by Moolla & Van der Velden.

Epilogue

Over the past three decades the approaches to pro-poor change processes have undergone several changes themselves. Many approaches, methods and tools have become fairly standardised if not 'instrumentalised'. The ten characteristics of a social business mentioned earlier in this chapter should not face the same fate. There are sufficient proxy indicators that social business in combination with SSE is an emerging strategy to facilitate systemic socio-political change.[156] There is still a lot of 'work in progress' and hence the framework should primarily be used as a thought discipline and not as a 'lock frame'. It is a state of mind and not a technical approach.[157]

Conceptually, social business may be seen as a rejection of the bifurcated world of capitalism and charity. It is a shift from the 'either/or' world, where capitalism exists on the one extreme and charity on the other, to an integrated system of both, where it is possible to generate blended value within one system. Social business is a phenomenon where markets, government and civil society are converging. Kievit et al. state that practical examples of social businesses are: 'proof that a silent revolution is taking place which offers solutions to problems in areas where both the government and markets are falling short'.[158]

References

Audet, R. (2016), Transition as discourse, in: International Journal of Sustainable Development, Vol. 19, No. 4, pp. 65 – 82.

Audet, R. (not dated), Transition as a discourse and the issues of interventionism, justice and innovation. (http://www.isecoeco.org/conferences/isee2012-versa03/pdf/716.pdf)

Baker, D. (2016), How globalization and the ruled of the modern economy where structured to make the rich richer, Washington, Centre for Economic and Policy Research.

Bakshi, R., (2016) Learning from Mahatma Gandhi's insights on economic democracy, Village Square, October 2. (https://www.villagesquare.in/2016/10/02/learning-from-mahatma-gandhis-insights-on-economic-democracy/)

Balandina Jaquier, J. (2011), Guide to impact investing for family offices and high net worth individuals – managing wealth for impact and profit, Zürich, Winkel. (www.guidetoimpactinvesting.org)

Barrez, D. (2016), Transitie; Onze welvaart van morgen, Kaltmthout, Pala vzw/Pelckmans Pro.

Bardhan, P. (2006), Globalization and rural poverty, World Development, volume 43, pp. 1393 - 1404

Banerjee, A. et al. (2013) The miracle of microfinance? Evidence from a randomized evaluation, Boston, MIT. https://economics.mit.edu/files/8818

Battilana J. et al, (2012), In Search of the Hybrid Ideal, Stanford Social Innovation Review, Summer, pp. 51-55.

156 Much writing on social business and SSE is very unfortunately promotional. There are basically three main studies that provide proxy indicators for the potential of social business and SSE: Utting, 2015; North and Cato (eds.), 2017; Calvo & Morales (eds.), 2017.

157 Black & Nicholls, 2004: 40.

158 Kievit et al., 2008.

Bauchet, J. & Morduch, J. (2011) Is Micro too Small? Microcredit vs. SME Finance, New York: New York University.

Black, L. & Nicholls, J. (2004), There is no business like social business – how to be socially enterprising, London, the Cat's Pyjamas.

Black, L. (2014), The social entrepreneur's A to Z; On anxiety, leadership and getting enough sleep, London, London Fields Publishing Ltd.

Bonini, S. & Emerson, J. (2005), Maximizing Blended Value – Building beyond the blended value map to sustainable investing, philanthropy and organisations, 2005. (www.blendedvalue.org)

Bornstein, D. (2007), How to change the world; Social entrepreneurs and the power of new ideas, Oxford, University Press.

Bornstein,D. & Davis, S. (2010), Social entrepreneurship; What everyone needs to know, Oxford, Oxford University Press.

Borzaga, C., Galera, G. & Nogales, R. (2006), Social enterprise: A new model for poverty reduction and employment generation; An examination of the concept and the practice in Europe and the Commonwealth of Independent States, Bratislava, UNDP Regional Bureau for Europe and the Commonwealth of Independent States.

Borzaga, Galera & Nogales, (2008) The Concept and Practice of Social Enterprise. Lessons from the Italian Experience, International Review of Social Research, Volume 2, Issue 2, June 2012, pp. 85 - 102.

Boyte, H. (2008), The Citizen Solution; How You can Make a Difference, Minnesota, Minnesota Historical Press.

Boyte, H. (2013), Reclaiming Our Democracy – Lessons From the Trenches of Citizen Advocacy, Huffington Post October 15 (https://www.huffingtonpost.com/harry-boyte/reclaiming-our-democracy_b_4089895.html)

Brouwers, J. et al. (2010), Social Return on Investment. A practical guide for the development cooperation sector, Utrecht, Context, international cooperation.

Bugg-Levine, A. & Emerson, J. (2011), Impact investing; Transforming how we make money while making a difference, San Francisco, John Wiley & Sons.

Calvo S. & Morales A. (eds.) (2017), Social and solidarity economy; The world's economy with a social face, New York, Routledge.

Chambers, R. (2005), Ideas for development, London, Earthscan.

CIVICUS (2017), State of civil society report 2017 (executive summary), Johannesburg, CIVICUS (http://www.civicus.org/documents/reports-and-publications/SOCS/2017/state-of-civil-society-report-2017-executive-summary-en.pdf)

Crouch C. (n.d.), Coping with Post-Democracy, Fabian Society. (https://www.fabians.org.uk/wp-content/uploads/2012/07/Post-Democracy.pdf)

CSR Impact (2013), Impact Project; Executive Summary. Headline findings, insights & recommendations for policy makers, business & stakeholders, Brussels, 7th Framework Programme European Commission.

Dabla – Norris, E. (2015), Causes and consequences of income inequality: A global perspective, IMF (International Monetary Fund).

Dees, J. G. (2001), The meaning of social enterprise. Stanford University, Palo Alto, CA.

De Greve, P., Lont, H. & Van der Velden, F. van der (2013), Narrative numeracy: social impact assessment – a brief guide to Social Return on Investment, Utrecht, Context, international cooperation

(Contextual 10).

Doane, D. (2014), Social enterprise: can it succeed where traditional development has failed, The Guardian on line, February 24. (https://www.theguardian.com/global-development/poverty-matters/2014/feb/25/social-enterprise-succeed-traditional-development-failed)

Easterly, W. (2006), The white man's burden; Why the west's efforts to aid the rest have done so much ill and so little good, New York, Penguin Books.

Ebrahim, A., Battilana, J. & Mair, J. (2014), The governance of social enterprises: Mission drift and accountability in hybrid organizations, in: Research in Organizational Behavior, vol. 34, pp. 81 – 100.

Edwards, M. (2008), Just another emperor? The myths and realities of philanthrocapitalism, New York, Demos.

Edwards, M. (2010), Small change; Why business won't save the world, San Francisco, Berrett-Koehler Publishers.

Elkington, J. (2004), Enter the Triple Bottom Line. (http://www.johnelkington.com/archive/TBL-elkington-chapter.pdf)

Emerson, J. (2003), The Blended Value Proposition: Integrating Social and Financial Returns, in: California Management Review, Summer 2003, Vol. 45, No.4, pp. 33 – 51

EMES European research network and UNDP (2008), Social Enterprise: a new model for poverty reduction and employment generation. UNDP regional bureau.

Fowler, A. & Biekart, K. eds. (2008), Civic Driven Change; Citizen's Imagination in Action, The Hague, Institute of Social Studies.

Fowler, A. & Biekart, K. (2013), Relocating Civil Society in a Politics of Civic-Driven Change, Development Policy Review, 2013, 31 (4), pp. 463 – 483.

Fowler, A. (2011), From sectors to process: understanding civil society in action, in: Anheier, H. et al. (2011), The future of participatory civil society assessments: a conceptual analysis, New York, UNDP pp. 10 – 22.

Friedman, M. (1970), The social responsibility of business is to increase its profits, in: New York Times Magazine, September.

Futurearth (2017), The 10 Science 'Must Knows' on Climate Change, Prepare b the Earth League and Future Earth for the UNFCCC 23rd Conference of the Parties,2017 (http://futureearth.org/sites/default/files/the_10_science_must_knows_on_climate_change_november_2017.pdf)

Galston, W.A. (2016), A voter revolt against 'shareholder value', The Wall Street Journal, October 4.

Gandhi, M.K. (1960), Village Industries, Ahmedabad, Navajivan Publishing House.

Hardoon, D. (2017), An economy for the 99%; It's time to build a human economy that benefits everyone, not just the privileged few, Oxfam Briefing Paper, Oxford, Oxfam, January.

Hartigan, P. & Billimora, J. (2005), Social entrepreneurship: an overview, Alliance (http://www.allavide.org/alliance/mar05f.html)

Harper, M. (2010), Book review of Bateman, M. (2010) Why microfinance doesn't work. London: Zed Books Limited.

(http://www.microfinancefocus.com/news/2010/06/07/book-review-why-microfinance-doesn%E2%80%99t-work%E2%80%9D/)

Hulme, D. & Arun, T (2011), What's Wrong and Right with Microfinance – Missing an Angle on Responsible Finance? BWPI Working Paper 155, Manchester, Brooks World Poverty Institute.

Hossain, N. et al. (2018), What Does Closing Civic Space Mean for Development? A Literature Review and Proposed Conceptual Framework, Sussex, IDS Working Paper, Volume 2018 No 515.

Institute of Social Entrepreneurs (2008), Evolution of the social enterprise industry: A chronology of events, Revised August 1. (http://socialent.org/documents/EVOLUTIONOFTHESOCIALENTERPRISEINDUSTRY--ACHRONOLOGYOFKEYEVENTS.pdf)

Iverson, B. (2017), The wrong kind of capitalism, https://www.linkedin.com/company/cimbria-capital/

O'Donohoe, N. et al. (2010), Impact investments; an emerging asset class, J.P. Morgan Global Research/The Rockefeller Foundation/Global Impact Investing Network, Inc. (www.morganmarkets.com)

Karnani, A. (2007), Microfinance misses its mark, Stanford Social Innovation Review, 5 (3).

Kielburger, C., Branson, H. & Kielburger, M. (2018), WEconomy; You can find meaning, make a living, and change the world, Hoboken. John Wiley & Sons.

Kievit, H., Van Dijk, G. & Spruyt, B.J. (2008), De stille revolutie van social venturing entrepreneurs [The silent revolution of social venturing entrepreneurs], in: Holland Management review, Number 120, 2008 pp. 20-25.

Kinsley, M. et al. (2009), Creative capitalism; A conversation with Bill Gates, Warren Buffet, and other economic leaders, London, Simon & Schuster.

Korten, D. (1995), When corporations rule the world, West Hartford, Kumarian Press.

Legum, M. (2003), 'It doesn't have to be like this': global economics – a new way forward, Glasgow, Wild Goose Publications.

Lynch, K. & Walls, J. (2009), Mission, Inc. The practitioners guide to social enterprise, San Francisco, Berret Koehler Publishers.

Maas, K. (2009), Corporate Social Performance, From Output Measurement to Impact Measurement, Rotterdam, Erasmus University (ERIM PhD Series in Research in Management, 182).

Maas, K. (2014), Classifying social impact measurement frameworks, paper for Giving Thoughts The conference board initiative on corporate philanthropy, March http://citeseerx.ist.psu.edu/viewdoc/download?doi=10.1.1.679.4208&rep=rep1&type=pdf

Maira, A. (2011), Transforming capitalism; Improving the world for everyone, New Delhi, NIMBY books.

Mangcu, X. (2014), Biko a life, London, I.B. Tauris.

McCann, D. & Berry, C. (2017), Shareholder capitalism; A system in crisis, London, New Economics Foundation.

McChesney, R.W. & Bellamy Foster, J. (2010), Capitalism the absurd system, Monthly Review Vol 62.No 2, June, pp. 1 – 16.

McDonough, W. & Braungart, M. (2002), Cradle to cradle; Remaking the way we make things, New York, North Point Press.

Mehr H. (2014), Social Entrepreneurs Need to Think Beyond the Business, The Blog Huffington Post, 8 April (https://www.huffingtonpost.com/hila-mehr/social-entrepreneurs-reme_b_5646428.html)

Miller, E. (not dated), Solidarity Economics; strategies for building new economies from the bottom-up and inside out. (http://www.geo.coop/search/node/Miller)

Mintzberg, H. (2015), Time for the plural sector, Stanford Social Innovation Review, Summer 2015, Volume 13, number 3, pp.29-33.

Moolla, Z. (2014), Doing popular economics in South Africa, in: Hope, A. & Timmel, s. (ed.), Training for transformation in practice, Warwickshire, Practical Action Publishing Ltd, pp. 142 – 145.

Moseley, W. (2014), The limits of new social entrepreneurship, Aljazeera on line, December 22. (http://www.aljazeera.com/indepth/opinion/2014/12/limits-new-social-entrepre-neu-20141221113250395741.html)

North, P. & Scott Cato, M. (eds) (2017), Towards just and sustainable economies; The Social and Solidarity Economy North and South, Bristol, Poly Press.

Oxfam, (2017) An economy for the 99%; It's time to build a human economy that benefits everyone, not just the privileged few. (https://www.oxfam.org/sites/www.oxfam.org/files/file_attachments/bp-economy-for-99-percent-160117-en.pdf)

Peattie, K. & Morley A. (n.d.), Social Enterprises: Diversity and dynamics, contexts and contributions, Cardiff, Economic & Social Research Council.

Porter, M.E. & Kramer, M.R., 2011, Creating shared value. How to reinvent capitalism – and unleash a wave of innovation and growth, in: Harvard Business Review, January – February 2011.

Rostow, W. (1960), Stages of economic growth, a non-communist manifesto, Cambridge, Cambridge University Press.

Samans R. et al, (2015), The inclusive growth and development report 2015, Geneva, World Economic Forum.

Saxena, M. (2011), New Dimensions of Sustainability through Social Entrepreneurship. http://ssrn.com/abstract=1780848

Shore, B., Hammond, D. & Celep, A. (2013), When good is not good enough, Stanford Social Innovation Review, Fall, pp. 40 – 47. (https://ssir.org/pdf/Fall_2013_When_Good_Is_Not_Good_Enough.pdf)

Sinclair, H. (2012), Confessions of a microfinance heretic; How Microlending Lost Its Way and betrayed the poor, San Francisco, Brett-Koehler Publishers.

Sivaraksa, A. (2009), The wisdom of sustainability; Buddhist economics for the 21st Century, London, Souvernir Press.

Sivaraksa, 1992, Seeds of peace; A Buddhist vision of renewing society, Berkley, Parallax Press.

Sogge, D. (2016), The corporate wax nose, Open Democracy, 17 November. (https://www.opendemocracy.net/transformation/david-sogge/corporate-wax-nose)

Steenhuis Piters, B. (eds.) (2006), Chain empowerment; Supporting African farmers to develop markets, Amsterdam. Royal tropical Institute.

Stiglitz, J., Sen, A. & Fitoussi, JP, (2010), Mis-measurement our lives; Why GDP doesn't add up; Report by the commission on the measurement of economic performance and social progress, New York, The New Press.

Straus, T. (2010) A Sobering Assessment of Microfinance's Impact, Stanford Social Innovation Review, October 27. http://www.ssireview.org/blog/entry/a_sobering_assessment_of_microfinances_impact

Sukhdev, P. (2012), Corporation 2020; Transforming business for tomorrow's world, Washington, Island Press.

Tozzi, J. (2009). Social Entrepreneurship: resources for 'patient' capital, in: Bloomberg Businessweek, April 4 (https://www.bloomberg.com/news/articles/2009-04-03/social-entrepreneurship-resources-for-patient-capitalbusinessweek-business-news-stock-market-and-financial-advice)

Utting, P. (ed.) (2015), Social and Solidarity Economy; Beyond the Fringe, London, Zed Books/UNRISD.

Van Dijk, G. & Van der Velden, F. (2012), Sociaal ondernemerschap helpt armste snelst vooruit, in: Trouw, 16 oktober. (http://www.trouw.nl/tr/nl/4324/Nieuws/article/detail/3332432/2012/10/16/Sociaal-ondernemerschap-helpt-armste-snelst-vooruit.dhtmlrouw

Van der Spek, T., Schreven, A. & Van der Velden, F. (2013), Leading in Social Business, Utrecht, Context, international cooperation (Contextual 11).

Van der Spek, T & Van der Velden, F. (2014), Trending challenges to running a social business' in: The Broker online, 15 July.

Van der Spek, T., Schreven, A. & Van der Velden, F. (2014), The three roles of Social Business leadership, in: The Broker online 23 October.

Van der Velden, F. (2011), Social business, a novel approach to socio-political change, in: Velden, F. van der (red.), New approaches to international development cooperation – a tribute to Meindert Witvliet, Utrecht, Context, international cooperation: 69-87.

Van der Velden, F. (ed.) (2011), New approaches to international development cooperation – a tribute to Meindert Witvliet, Utrecht, Context, international cooperation.

Van der Velden, F., 2014, Sociaal ondernemerschap als nieuwe benadering voor internationale solidariteit? In: Stefan Verwer et al., Hoe nu verder? 65 jaar Nederlandse ontwikkelingssamenwerking, Arnhem: LM Publishers, 2014 (p. 312 – 325).

V-Dem Institute (2018), Democracy foe all? V-Dem Annual Democracy Report, Gothenburg, V-Dem Institute.

Welton, M. (2016), World out of joint: Wolfgang Streeck's vision of the end of capitalism, www.counterpunch.org January 29.

West, C. & Woodcraft, C. (2010), Enterprise solutions to scale – lessons learned in catalyzing sustainable solutions to global development challenges, London: Shell Foundation.

Wharton, C. (1969), The Green Revolution: Cornucopia or Pandora's Box, Foreign Affairs, vol. 47, No. 3, April 1969, pp. 464 – 476.

Yunus, M. (2007), Creating a world without poverty; Social Business and the future of capitalism, New York, Public Affairs.

Yunus, M. (2010), Building Social Business; The new Kind of Capitalism that Serves Humanity's Most Pressing Needs, New York, Public Affairs.

Websites

https://www.ashoka.org
www.blendedvalue.org
https://www.britishcouncil.org/society/social-enterprise
https://cop23.unfccc.int
www.counterpunch.org
http://www.footprintnetwork.org
http://neweconomics.org/
http://www.geo.coop/
www.oneplanetthinking.org
www.oxfam.org
http://www.socialenterprise.org
https://www.socialenterprisemark.org.uk
http://skoll.org/
http://unfccc.int
https://www.v-dem.net/en

CHAPTER III

Inspire2Care

Application of the principles of social business in Nepal's health and disability sector

Betteke de Gaay Fortman[1]

Introduction: The challenge

Poverty and disabilities are strongly related. Eighty per cent of all people with a disability live in a low- or middle-income country. Living with a disability in a developing country has a profound effect. The vast majority of children with a disability have no access to healthcare and education and often do not participate in society. In Nepal, the census shows that approximately 2% of the population have a disability. They belong to the most marginalised groups among the poor. Their potential is largely unrecognised and unused, and they are often perceived as a burden for parents and society. Equal rights for people with a disability are not on the government's radar, and making public services like education and healthcare accessible to them, is not considered a priority.

The gap that is left by the government can be filled – at least for the time being, as poor people cannot wait for Godot - if communities themselves take matters into their own hands. With initial outside help in strengthening the existing structure and system, communities can themselves organise healthcare, education and the inclusion of children and adults with a disability and their families. They can 'take back' the development of their own communities, rather than either waiting for the government or being (fully) dependent on a Non-Governmental Development Organisation (NGDO). Based on this starting point, Karuna Foundation[2] developed the Inspire2Care

1 The author would like to express her deep gratitude to René aan de Stegge, Deepak Sapkota and Yogendra Giri for their visionary and action-oriented ideas and ways of working which form the foundation of this chapter. She also is grateful to Caroline van Slobbe for her revision and editing work.

2 Karuna Foundation Netherlands (www.karunafoundation.com) was founded in 2007 by a Dutch entrepreneur (René aan de Stegge). The ambition and role of Karuna Foundation Netherlands is to set up innovative pilot projects in developing countries with venture capital which, once established, can be scaled up by other organisations and governments. In 2007 Karuna Foundation Nepal was founded by a social entrepreneur (Deepak Raj Sapkota) from Nepal with the financial, organisational and strategic support of Karuna Foundation Netherlands. Since 2016, Karuna Foundation Nepal is an independent local organisation. Karuna Foundation Nepal is the implementing organisation of Inspire2Care and bears responsibility for the operation and partnership with the local, provincial and central governments. Karuna Foundation Netherlands invests in quality, innovation, capacity strengthening and tries to safeguard the entrepreneurial principles that form the basis of the programme approach.

(I2C) model and piloted it in 10 villages in remote areas of Nepal. The model inspires and helps local governments and remote communities to organise healthcare and education for children and adults with disabilities, as well as the societal inclusion of people with disabilities and their families. At the same time, it aims to prevent birth defects and (childhood) disabilities. The programme is executed by communities themselves: Karuna's role is facilitating the process and strengthening the capacity of participants. How does the model work and what are its results?

Inspire2Care: Background and ambition

Karuna Foundation Netherlands was founded in 2007 by a Dutch entrepreneur with the dual goal of improving the lives of children with a disability in low- and medium-income countries and preventing disabilities among children. 'Saving children from disabilities, one by one' is its slogan. In the same year, Karuna Foundation Nepal was founded on the same principles by two social entrepreneurs from Nepal, who still lead the organisation.[3] Since 2016, Karuna Foundation Nepal has been an independent local organisation.

Originating from the mission and goals, three models were developed: Share&Care,[4] Inspire2Care and Training of Professionals.[5] In the pioneer phase, from 2007 to 2014, experiences were gained and improvements made. Through trial and error, it became clear that Inspire2Care had the highest chances of successful upscaling. The Inspire2Care model has since been adapted a number of times: day-care centres were established to support children with a severe disability; adults with a disability are now more easily reached and play an exemplary role for children with a disability; and there is a mobile data system to reach and register all pregnant women. The programme period has since been shortened by one year.

After a successful pioneer phase in 10 villages in two districts of Nepal, Inspire2Care is now being scaled up to one full district (Ilam district in the eastern part of Nepal), with a scope of 120,000 young women and children and 1,000 children with disabilities. The joint ambition of Karuna Foundation Nepal and Karuna Foundation Netherlands is to replicate the model to one-sixth of the country (in two provinces) in the coming years (2018-2024), in partnership with the local governments in Nepal and several like-minded social investors. Eventually, these provinces will serve as an example to the rest of the country, which will enable the Nepalese government to organise for the care and inclusion of children with a disability based on the principles and operational guidelines of Inspire2Care. In this manner, it is the ambition of both the Netherlands and Nepal Karuna Foundations to contribute to systemic change of the health and disability sector in Nepal.

---

3 Deepak Raj Sapkota and Yogendra Giri.

4 Share&Care is similar to Inspire2Care, but has an extra component: a community-based health insurance (https://www.karunafoundation.nl/en/community-models/sharecare/).

5 Training of Professionals was developed to strengthen the existing local healthcare by building the capacity of health professionals in preventing disabilities and addressing the needs and rights of people with disabilities.

Working together for sustainability

Karuna Foundation works together with two main stakeholder groups: local and central government and local communities. As an organisation, Karuna influences and works together with local, provincial and national authorities and with (inter)national governments to make healthcare policies inclusive and support communities to build inclusive communities. Karuna brings to the attention of governments their obligation to fulfil the rights incorporated in the UN Convention on the Rights of People with Disabilities. Lobby and advocacy lie at the heart of the programme at every level: ward, municipality, district, province and central government.

The Inspire2Care model aims to motivate local governments to respect the rights and address the needs of persons with a disability. It encourages leaders to take responsibility for creating inclusive communities from the start. In fact it is an essential characteristic of the strategy that Inspire2Care is only implemented in villages where leaders have proven their commitment and political willingness to take responsibility for bringing about improved healthcare and integration. It is believed that other villages will then follow the example of these pioneers.

Local government's willingness and ability to take responsibility is crucial, as it enhances local ownership and the financial sustainability of the Inspire2Care programme. This responsibility is reflected in the distribution of costs between Karuna Foundation and the community, in which the share of the community increases gradually. From the start, the necessary resources are mobilised locally by the municipality (by allocating resources from the municipal budget) and by the inhabitants of the villages. Karuna contributes financially in the first two years and provides training and coaching for three years. After the three years the Inspire2Care communities are aware, knowledgeable and experienced enough to continue Inspire2Care on their own, with their own (public) resources (more on financial sustainability later in this chapter).

In order to achieve a better quality of life for people with disabilities and prevent childhood disability, it is not only individual lives that need to change, but also the community. Awareness, acceptance and willingness to act should be anchored in the community. One of the major lessons learned is that a change of attitude is possible in a relatively short period of time by achieving visible changes in the lives of persons with a disability and in the access to and quality of healthcare. The end result is communities in which children and adults with a disability are equally included in the mainstream development of the community. No one is left behind. And the prevalence of birth defects and (childhood) disabilities is reduced as much as possible.

The process of engagement with local communities

The engagement with a community develops in four phases:

The first phase: Establishing readiness

Only communities which, in writing, show an interest in participating in the Inspire2Care programme are assessed for readiness through a Readiness Protocol. Karuna Foundation Nepal appraises this readiness and reviews the political willingness of the mayors and their team, as well as their ability to assume responsibility. In this case, responsibility is the ability to respond to the needs and rights of the most vulnerable groups within the community. The community leaders must prove that they are willing and able to mobilise the necessary resources for Inspire2Care.[6]

In addition it has to be clear that a (potentially) qualified and committed team can be formed in the village. This team consists of a responsible mayor and village leaders along with an appointed Community Based Rehabilitation (CBR) facilitator and available health workers and midwives. The CBR facilitator is selected and appointed by the mayor and the governors and is accountable to the community through the mayor.

The second phase: Building the foundation together

The community has to mobilise local financial resources before the start of implementation. An equal partnership between the municipality and Karuna Foundation Nepal is established based on a clear plan and budget, adapted to the needs in the village (sanitation, care, a birth centre or other health-related issues). Consequently, staff members of Karuna Foundation Nepal provide support to the local governments in order to enhance the competencies and the collective capabilities of the mayor and local municipal council members.

Furthermore, Karuna strengthens the competencies of the council members of the municipality, the health workers and other key leaders. The council ensures that people with a disability are represented in key positions and selects and pays a CBR facilitator. Karuna provides intensive training to all these different groups on different issues (leadership, rights, social change, disability, prevention, finance and administration).

The third phase: Implementation by the community, coaching by Karuna

In the third phase of the programme, all individuals with a disability in the community are identified. One of the first actions is to link them with the system through their identity card, which gives them the right to receive a social security allowance. Subsequently, for each child with a disability the CBR Facilitator, together with the

6 Hence both the ability and willingness to pay is being reviewed through a Readiness Protocol.

family, sets up an individual development and rehabilitation plan for healthcare, education, participation, empowerment and family income. Adults with a disability develop a personal plan, focused on their most urgent needs. The plan is implemented by means of collaborations with hospitals, provision of assistive devices, inclusive education, and access to vocational training and microcredit. Staff members of Karuna Foundation provide training to parents of children with a disability. In the area of prevention, mother and child care is improved by training health workers and midwives. All pregnant women are registered via an M-Health system that guarantees that they attend prenatal check-ups and that the delivery is guided professionally. Knowledge and awareness are provided on how mother and child mortality and birth defects can be prevented: healthy drinking water, hygiene, timely check-ups, healthy food and safe deliveries in a clinic.

The fourth phase: Exit and continuation

After 3½ years, Karuna Foundation Nepal exits the programme and the community continues Inspire2Care entirely with its own resources (approximately €15,000 per year per community with a population of around 10,000 households), but they can still make use of the Resource and Education Centre of Karuna Nepal. Exiting does not mean that Karuna Foundation has no further role to play. It means a role transformation for Karuna Foundation: from an implementing organisation to a resource centre and helpdesk where communities can ask for support, knowledge and network linking. This way, the relationship that is built with the community will endure.

The sustainability of the Inspire2Care programme and the self-reliance of the whole community is indeed crucial. There is a strong emphasis on the 'exit strategy' or 'role transformation' of Karuna Foundation right from the beginning of all the support that is being provided to communities. This approach makes the programme innovative and entrepreneurial. It requires a results-oriented process, characterised by thinking 'out of the box' and a drive and zeal familiar to many social entrepreneurs. Willingness to accept the risks regarding the social investment, as well as willingness to decide not to start or to stop when ownership is not taken up by partner organisations (including mayors, village level committees and communities) is essential. This entrepreneurial approach is relatively new in the context of healthcare provision in Nepal and international development cooperation in general.

Diagram III.1: Overview of an Inspire2Care community

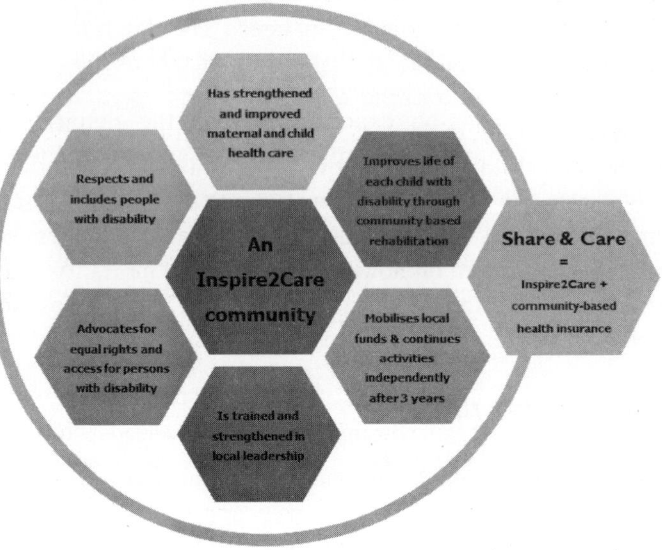

Source: Inspire2Care.

The principles

Karuna has four guiding principles in supporting the communities to implement Inspire2Care:

1 Leave no one behind – each child and every pregnant woman in the community is being reached. When Karuna Nepal goes into the villages, they enable the local leaders to go to every household to find all individuals with disabilities. For that, local committees are trained and coached for three years. Karuna Nepal supports the health workers and female community health volunteers to use the M-Health system. With this technology, all pregnant women can be identified and linked to the required health services during pregnancy, delivery and after delivery.

2 People develop themselves – Karuna Foundation assumes that people have the power to help themselves and supports them to develop their potential. The role of the Karuna Foundation Nepal is to inspire, train and enhance the capacity of the local partners and to assist communities to advocate and lobby for their rights.

3 Learning by doing and continuous improvement – this applies to the community leaders and professionals in the villages, the staff of Karuna Nepal and social investors. The principle of Kaizen[7] is applied: change for better. At all levels,

7 The Japanese word kaizen means 'change for better', with inherent meaning of either 'continuous' or 'philosophy' in Japanese dictionaries and in everyday use. The word refers to any improvement, one-time or continuous, large or small, in the same sense as the English word 'improvement'.

participants are constantly looking for the best strategy on the basis of practical experiences and insights and recommendations from adequate research.

4 Replicable and scalable – Inspire2Care is practical, cost-effective and adapted to the local needs and capacities. The replicability of the project is important, not only because it generates the most impact, but also because it is fairer. If Karuna Foundation were to implement good but expensive projects, these projects would not be adopted by other communities and this would bring further inequality. Inspire2Care is implemented as simply and cost-effectively as possible, so that people in other places can be inspired by it to take action themselves. In this manner, the Inspire2Care programme that is carried out by the community with the support of Karuna Foundation Nepal and the social investors, aims to contribute to a systemic change in the health sector in Nepal.

Replicability through financial and structural sustainability

As indicated, Inspire2Care can only start in communities where the leaders have shown responsibility (the ability to respond); where they have a capable team and where they are willing to bear the costs of this model themselves. Communities that are eligible for support must express this in writing in a letter from the mayor and his team. Thanks to this strict selection before the start, the chances for continuity are high.

As mentioned above the Inspire2Care programme runs for 3½ years in a community with the support of Karuna Nepal, of which the first six months are preparation time. In the first two years, Karuna Nepal contributes 50% of the costs of the programme and in the third year only technical support is provided to communities. Right from the start, the community contributes to the costs for the programme from the municipal budget. After three years, the communities have the capacity to continue the activities on their own, so that year after year, children with a disability, young children and pregnant women are being reached. Once this point is reached, the municipalities contribute 80% of the funds needed to run the programme from the budget they receive for the development of their community. The remaining 20% is generated through parents of children with a disability, the wealthier people of the community, and profit from cooperatives.

Through these good examples at municipal level, eventually systemic change will take place at the provincial and central government. The intention is that the Inspire2Care approach will be integrated into the regular policy/approach, plan and budget. Karuna Nepal works towards creating a tipping point for the government to be influenced by the modes and results reaped by the programme, so that it readily takes up the programme in other parts of the country on its own account. In this process, Karuna Nepal transforms into a Training and Leadership Academy and Resource Centre for government officials, health workers, CBR facilitators, health volunteers, community leaders, parents of children with a disability, and children and adults with a disability.

More on financial matters

Since the political reformation after the elections of 2017, the Nepal Central Government has allocated a yearly budget to every municipality for its development. In practice, this budget tends to go to infrastructure and economic development rather than to health and disability. Through the Inspire2Care programme, municipalities are encouraged to spend at least 10% of the local budget on people with disability and on the prevention of birth defects and childhood disabilities; that is €15,000 per year per municipality. However, the external costs for the programme are relatively high in the first 3½ years (€75,000 per municipality for the entire 3½-year project period). This is applicable to a municipality with an average of 38,000 inhabitants, and is equivalent to an investment of €2 per inhabitant and €580 per child with a disability.

The multiplier effect is enormous. On the basis of the results of the pilots and the preliminary results of the replication in Ilam district, the expectation is that a minimum of 75% of the communities (98 out of 130 villages) will continue the activities after the 3½-year period, with €15,000 per year per village as a regular part of the annual budget and plans. This means that in 2024 a structural extra €1.47-million per year will be allocated to children with a disability and mother and child care from tax revenue and from individual contributions from within the country itself. Once the government implements the programme in the rest of the country this amount will be much higher.

The Business Model Canvas

The value of Inspire2Care programme is presented in this Business Model Canvas.

Diagram III.2: Business Model Canvas Inspire2Care programme

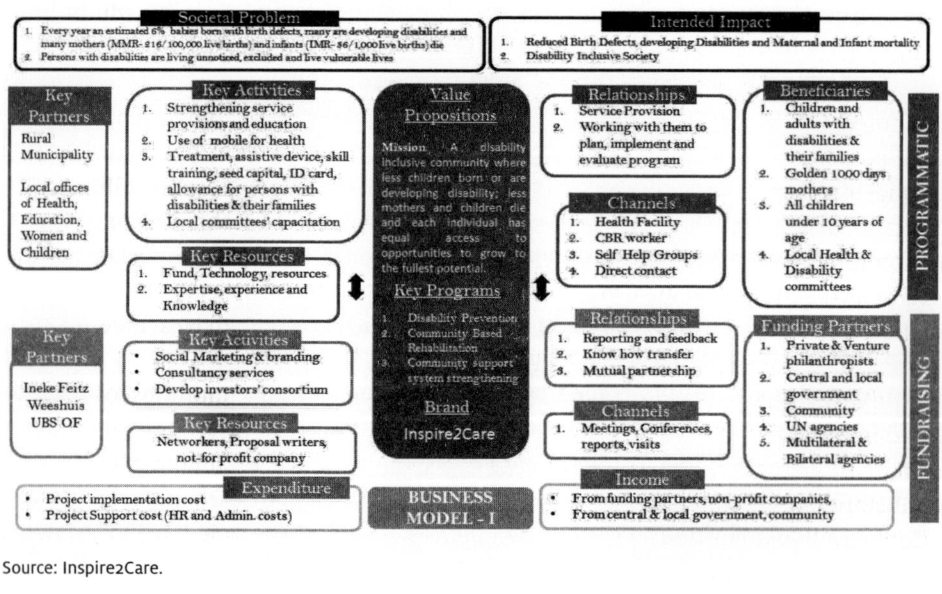

Source: Inspire2Care.

Learnings about success factors of Inspire2Care

The key success factors of this community-based model are more or less equivalent to the characteristics of a social business as described in Chapter II of this volume. It started with a social investor who entrusted his money to a local social entrepreneur. They had a joint dream to facilitate social and political changes in local communities in need. From the beginning both the social investor and the social entrepreneur realised that long-lasting change would only happen through financial and structural sustainability; a clear and relatively fast exit (role transformation) of the foreign partner, i.e. Karuna Foundation; integration of such an enterpreneurial approach to health issues within Nepalse government policies, structures and procedures, as provision of basic social services is actually a government responsibility.

For structural sustainability, active citizen involvement in the design, implementation, performance measurement and evaluation of the programme turned out to be crucial. Community leaders took responsibility for the programme and were open to learn in order to address the needs of their citizens and promote positive changes in the lives of the most vulnerable people in their community. Initially, it was an uphill battle to facilitate a situation in which local leaders were prepared to take their responsibilty. Dependency and top-down approaches have been common in many development practices in the past 70 years, especially in Nepal, and this was embedded in communities' regular ways of relating to new development initiatives. Because of the influence of many foreign organisations, the expectations of the target group in terms of money, buildings and equipment were often high. Besides, after decades of neglect and exclusion by their political leaders, the communities were not in the habit of thinking independently about their problems and needs, or about taking action. A common attitude is for communities to wait until another foreign organisation comes along, which might build a school or a hospital, or provide 'soft' loans, or give education and raise awareness.

Confronted with this situation, Karuna Foundation decided to handle each request for support from a business point of view and to view the requesting community as an equal partner. This encourages the communities to assume responsibility and simultaneously claim their rights. Once a community takes on this responsibility and accountability and sees the positive changes, it increases their enthusiasm and stengthens their perserverance to achieve more for their people, especially for the most vulnerable ones. With this bottom-up approach, systemic change can be achieved.

Over the years, Karuna Foundation has come to realise that, for communities to be able to take responsibility and work for themselves, there has to be a system and proper mechanism in place in which people living in geographically and economically harsh circumstances can express their needs and desires and also be heard and responded to. Contextual and cultural values have to be recognised and people have to believe that the envisaged development is beneficial to them. It should not be imported or transported from elsewhere. Whatever happens has to come from the local people and work for them. Communities develop themselves, and with a push from outside and some experience and technologies, the desired result will be achieved faster and more sustainably.

However, it has not always worked out as planned, which has made for valuable learnings. In some villages, leaders were not committed, or not capable of mobilising their community or not willing to allocate local resources. The programme did not get off the ground well and therefore, after careful consideration, the decision was taken to stop the programme in those particular villages. If there is no commitment from the community, the project cannot be sustained and will probably cause more harm than good. After learning this lesson, a Readiness Protocol was developed in order to assess the commitment and political willingness of the local leaders before the start of the programme.

The major innovation of Inspire2Care lies in its readiness assessment, its coordination and linkages with multiple actors throughout the country, its equal partnerships, and in the creation of frontrunner communities, which at a later stage are followed by surrounding villages. The organisation's consistant thematic and geographical focus has turned out to be one of the main factors for achieving long-lasting positive results at all levels.

Overall results: Creation of blended value

Finally, the Inspire2Care approach has proved to be successful beyond the issues of disability and prevention. It makes people confident and proud of their own competencies and collective capabilities and achievements, and optimistic about their communities' future development. Eventually, the community leaders take matters, also beyond disability, into their own hands because they now have the confidence that they can achieve this themselves, independently from external organisations or donors. This positive effect is mainly seen in the money allocated from government and local community people to the programme.

From Karuna's perspective, the value of the intervention is ultimately manifested in the allocation of resources by the local government and the people themselves. This is the evidence of the blended value created by the partnership between communities and Karuna Foundation. The allocation of resources indicates that the community has given priority to the objectives of the progamme.

External validation of the succes of Inspire2Care

To assess the cost-effectiveness and overall performance of the programme, external independent studies were carried out. They underscore that the approach creates sustainable positive change and that the targets have been reached.

Evidence and cost-effectiveness

In 2014, the Liliane Foundation and the Dutch Leprosy Relief commissioned an assessment of the cost-effectiveness, efficiency and sustainability of the Inspire2Care programme in the pilot phase, extracts of which are given here:[8]

> This assessment has shown that the Inspire2Care program, implemented by Karuna Foundation Nepal during the period August 2011 to December 2013, was highly cost-effective according to the WHO benchmarks.

Side effects and cost reduction:

> Additionally, it is important to note that some of the major benefits or gains from the program – particularly the community mobilization around disability, improvements in attitudes of community members towards persons with disability and social cohesion – have not been measured or captured in the cost per DALY averted statistic. It is my opinion that the program was implemented in an efficient way during the period August 2011 to December 2013. Karuna Foundation Nepal has taken measures to cut costs wherever possible and frequently makes use of other existing resources (assistive devices funded by other organizations or programs and hospitals with their own funding for patient treatment).

With regard to sustainability of the programme, the report reads:

> This, combined with embedding the program fully within existing government structures and grass root structures, ensures no duplication. The program is designed to be sustainable, and shows strong signs of being so in Sunsari, where commitment to I2C appears to be high and local financial contributions are nearly on-par with those required in the first three years of implementation. In Rasuwa local financial contributions to the VDRC funds were much less, although non-financial commitment to the program appears to be significant. A proper sustainability assessment could be done in a minimum of two years in Sunsari and three in Rasuwa when Karuna's technical support is withdrawn as per the implementation agreement.

Impact study pilot communities after exit[9]

Since 2016, the communities where the Share&Care or Inspire2Care models were piloted have continued preventive mother and child care and integral care for children with a disability with their own resources. In 2017 it was time to look back and evaluate, so an external research team from Kathmandu executed an extensive impact study in these six villages. The most important findings can be summarised as follows:

8 Vaughan, 2015.
9 Phuyal, 2017.

The prevalence of birth defects and disabilities amongst children in their early years has decreased by 62%. This means that in the pilot villages the number of children born with a birth defect or disability has decreased from a total of 48 in the five years before the programme (2004-2008) to five in the years during the programme (2009-2013).

Seventy per cent of the children with a disability indicated that the quality of their lives had been improved relevantly or even significantly. This involves direct improvement in health, but also education, income and the attitude of people towards them. Approximately 80% of the children with a disability experienced that the attitude of fellow villagers towards them improved. According to 98% of the children in the research group, whereas formerly people labelled them by their disability, they now use friendly words or their names to call them. Among children in the research group, 93% said that other village inhabitants now think it is normal that children or adults with a disability participate in social activities.

Mid-term evaluation of the replication of Inspire2Care in Ilam district[10]

UBS Optimus Foundation – which contributed financially to Inspire2Care in the 15 villages of the second batch of the replication in the Ilam district that started in 2016 – commissioned an evaluation of the programme after 1½ years. The researchers focused on the relevance, effectiveness, efficiency, impact and sustainability of the programme.

The researchers concluded that:

> The Inspire2Care model was found to be a well-planned, coherent and relevant model that leverages on the existing human and financial resources and complements the conducive policy environment to work for persons and children with all kinds of disabilities in a well-rounded manner. The programme has a beginning to end model, with clear strategies in place for fund generation, access to resource and programme management structures. Within a very short period, it has been able to increase visibility of the issues faced by persons with disabilities and significantly improve maternal and child care in the project locations-thereby helping prevent avoidable disabilities. It provides almost a complete rehabilitative package for all persons identified with disabilities, which includes interventions along all parameters of quality of life, as per the WHO model. It has created linkages with all possible community level institutions and leverages support from every system/ structure that persons/ children with disabilities have any interface with.

With regard to further upscaling, the researchers from UBS Optimus Foundation concluded that:

> The I2C model was found to be scalable and replicable in any of Nepal's regions or other developing countries. In the absence of any other programme by the

10 Karaak Enterprise Development Service, 2017.

Government of Nepal for persons with disabilities, the success demonstrated by the programme, and willingness shown by the community and the government to incorporate it, can facilitate mainstreaming of this model into the existing administrative structure. Further, due to the overhauling of the political structure, and development of new strategies and programmes, I2C can establish itself from the beginning as an essential component.

Box III.1: Recognition for Inspire2Care

2018 Inspire2Care is in the top 10 'most scalable solutions' of the Zero Project Impact Transfer programme, a collaboration between Essl Foundation and Ashoka.
2018 Inspire2Care was selected as Innovative Practice on Accessibility during the Zero Project Conference 2018 in Vienna.
2017 Inspire2Care was selected as European Venture Philanthropy Association (EVPA) success story. The EVPA developed a webpage with 'Little funding stories, big social impact'.
2017 Best Wishes is one of eleven good practices in the book 'Everybody Matters' about inclusion of people with disabilities in sexual and reproductive health and rights programmes. Best Wishes is part of Inspire2Care.
2017 Inspire2Care was selected as Innovative Practice 2017 on Employment, Work and Vocational Education during the Zero Project Conference 2017 in Vienna.
2016 Inspire2Care was selected as a 'good example of a sustainable and innovative method' during the World Congress on Community Based Rehabilitation in Kuala Lumpur.
2015 Inspire2Care is one of the five best practices of integrating people with disabilities into their own communities, according to the Asian Pacific Centre for Development and Disability in an assessment among 37 Asian countries. In 2015, Karuna presented its results during an international congress in Tokyo by the World Health Organisation.
2012 Share&Care wins the Jobena Prize 2012 for the project with the most appealing practice for self-development as a method and goal. The Jobena Foundation supports cultural and development projects.
2011 Brilliant Failure award in 2011 by the Dutch Coalition of NGOs for the best learning moment 'Stopping is an option'. Karuna won the public's award in the category of development cooperation.

Going forward

For the coming years, replication of the model in two provinces in Nepal is planned with the aim of creating systemic change in the health system of the Nepalese government. Karuna Netherlands together with other like-minded social investors aligned in a consortium, supports this long-term plan financially and safeguards its cost-effectiveness and replicability. The ultimate ambition is that the Nepalese government is inspired and capable of implementing the model in the rest of the country.

The consortium consists of partners who are keen to learn but also to share their knowledge and technologies and who would like to contribute financially, but also strategically and creatively. Karuna Nepal assumes full responsibility for the implementation of this ambitious plan which will be carried out in partnership with the Government of Nepal.

One of the main challenges from the perspective of the social investors is to generate sufficient funds. In addition, it is crucial to create a diverse and stable consortium with partners who feel equally involved and responsible for the long-term support of the respective communities and the implementing partner, Karuna Nepal. The main challenge for Karuna Nepal is to find enough competent and passionate employees who are able and willing to make the needed social changes in their country.

A joint challenge is to generate further evidence through rigorous research through social impact assessment, as well as randomised control trial or other research methodologies. This evidence is crucial to be able to further scale up Inspire2Care, not only in Nepal, but also in other development contexts.

As long as all stakeholders (people with disabilities and their communities, political leaders, service providers, social investors and social entrepreneurs) are able to overcome internal and external challenges and have an equal partnership built on trust and mutual respect, the envisioned social changes can take place and will be long-lasting.

References

Karaak Enterprise Development Service Pvt Ltd, (2017), *Programme Evaluation of Karuna Foundation's Inspire2Care programme in Nepal.* (https://www.karunafoundation.nl/wp-content/uploads/2018/01/Final-Evaluation-Report_KFN_Kaarak_Dec-2017.pdf)

Phuyal, K., Bhattara A. & Prasad, A. & Khapung, S. (2017) *Impact Evaluation of Share&Care and Inspire2Care Project Evaluation* (https://www.karunafoundation.nl/wp-content/uploads/2017/09/Impact-Study-Sunsari-Executive-summary-FINAL.pdf)

Vaughan, K. (2015), *Cost-effectiveness and efficiency assessment of the Inspire2Care program, 2011-2013 FINAL REPORT* (https://www.karunafoundation.nl/wp-content/uploads/2017/06/KIT-final-report_Cost-effectiveness-Inspire2Care.pdf)

Website

https://www.karunafoundation.nl/en/

CHAPTER IV

Leadership in social business

Experiences from SNV's leadership development and support programme

Fons van der Velden & Worku Behonegne[I]

Leadership in social business

In her recent book *Who do we choose to be; Facing reality, claiming leadership, restoring sanity* (2017), management guru Margaret Wheatley convincingly argues that today's challenges call for what she labels 'sane leadership'. In her opinion, this centres around quality of relationships; love versus fear; quality of thinking; willingness to contribute; relationship with finance; ability to learn from experience.[2] Many chief executive officers from the corporate sector also acknowledge that a different quality of leadership is required. A recent Deloitte study indicates: 'leaders [need to] understand, manage, and respond to the complex social capital issues that organizations face, enabling them to tap opportunities, manage risks, and build relationships with internal and external stakeholders'.[3] Maira goes even further: 'Changing the world requires leaders, rather than merely managers. Leaders are those who take the first step towards a goal they care about deeply, and in ways that others wish to follow'.[4]

For social businesses, the challenge of retaining financial stability and utilising commercial practices to actively develop social impact in terms of blended value, brings about unique leadership and management challenges. Numerous researchers have explored the various traits, models and theories that shed light on a social entrepreneur's role as a social business leader. On the one hand, such a leader should lead with vision and guidance, and constantly reiterate the importance of social value institutionalisation. On the other hand, as the day-to-day running of a social business is based on sound business management principles, a social entrepreneur must master market competitiveness and risk-taking to ensure the sustained commercial viability of the business.

1 In the SNV leadership development and support programme (LEAP+), which is described in this chapter, Worku Behonenge was the programme manager and Fons van der Velden, from Context, international cooperation, was the lead consultant in supporting the programme. The authors want to express their gratitude to Mary Njuguna who provided feedback towards an earlier version of this chapter.

2 Wheatley, 2017 among others page 55 – 56.

3 Kaji et al, 2018. See also e.g.: Callanan et al. (2014).

4 Maira, 2011: 72.

Three roles of social business leadership[5]

The role of a social entrepreneur may be split into three core themes: societal leadership, strategic organisational management and personal leadership (see Diagram IV.1). Each of the three roles brings about unique challenges and considerations for the social entrepreneur as social business leader. The roles are of course interrelated; one must therefore not look at the roles as separate, but must consider them as a whole. Hence, a 'good' social entrepreneur strives to combine practices and personal qualities that optimally address each role.

Diagram IV.1: Three roles of leadership of social entrepreneurship

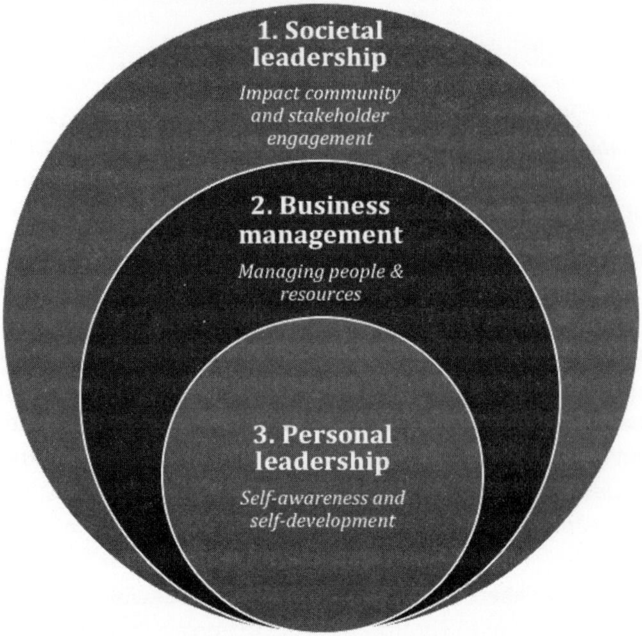

Source: Van der Spek, Schreven & Van der Velden, 2013.

Societal leadership

Societal leadership is concerned with the social entrepreneur's core commitment to bringing about socio-political change and how this commitment shapes his or her relationships with various social actors. Societal leadership is related to systemic change beyond the individual. It is a societal sphere, it is about creating an enabling environment. For example, the social entrepreneur is focused on making markets work or changing government policies.[6] In terms of engagement it implies reaching out to

5 This section (Three roles of social business leadership) is based on: Titus van der Spek, Anne-Marie Schreven & Fons van der Velden, 2013 and the article 'Three roles of social business leadership' that was co-authored by Titus van der Spek, Anne-Marie Schreven and Fons van der Velden, 2014.

6 Ref. e.g. the case descriptions of the Apple Project by Laxmi Prakash Semwal and Inspire2Care by Betteke de Gaay Fortman in this volume.

stakeholders from the private sector, the public sector, civil society and research. How can a social entrepreneur create a sense of shared commitment and co-ownership to a societal cause? This may be achieved by embedding the social objective in the hearts of relevant social actors. By practicing societal leadership, social entrepreneurs are able to foster active citizen involvement, and to encourage downward accountability and political transformation, and they can positively impact the rate and reach of their social vision. Societal leadership is about the ability to co-create and the ability to share commitment by nurturing and adopting various leadership styles including steward leadership, transformational leadership, servant leadership and responsible leadership.

Business management: Translating vision into action

In a social business, a distinction may be made between the social entrepreneur's role as mission-driven leader and his or her role at the strategic management level. The latter is about the social entrepreneur's responsibility to form business strategies and operational systems that will uphold the business's social vision. The importance of good leadership practice in business management is a crucial element in social business management. Vision-led strategies must be institutionalised in the culture and structure of a social business in order to avoid the social business from drifting away from its social mission. To achieve this, emphasis needs to be placed on exploring and adapting skills and traits as found within the theories of servant and steward leadership. It is important to emphasise the social entrepreneur's role as a leader who is able to constantly realign the strategic choices made at the commercial level with the social vision, while effectively utilising the social business' social capital (in terms of social networks) to this end.

Personal leadership: Self-awareness and self-development

The heart of a social business is formed by the social entrepreneur. Personal leadership, in this context, is concerned with the social entrepreneur's ability to drive forward the social objective and advocate the cause through a people's approach to doing business, while simultaneously reaching a point of financial sustainability. In terms of personality traits, the social entrepreneur's ability to be visionary and self-aware, and to learn and self-develop, is of crucial importance. A social entrepreneur should have change-making competencies, including the ability to change oneself.

However, as Margaret Wheatley would say 'there is no more need for heroes'.[7] In other words – as has already been argued in Chapter II of this volume – leadership does not relate to an individual person, but is an organisational function that can be carried out by more people (even teams) with complementary competencies.[8]

---

7 Wheatley, 2011.

8 In this context it may be observed that one of the biggest challenges for social businesses is succession planning. Hence working as a leadership team and mentoring successor(s) are quite critical matters.

Background of the programme[9]

Fostering and supporting the further development of endogenous competencies, capabilities and capacity is, and has always been, the core strategy of the Dutch development organisation SNV.[10] In many countries where SNV is present, the country offices have a long (sometimes decades) track record in supporting the further development of local capacities and working with local capacity-development support providers.[11] In SNV's strategy paper 2011-2015, it is stated that 'Due to the expanding and improving capacity-development market, local service providers (consultancy firms, training institutes, NGOs) will increasingly assume the prime responsibility for taking action and implementing interventions. SNV will intensify its focus on strengthening their capacities, facilitating the growth of local capacity building markets, providing backstopping and partnering with them in advisory services, knowledge networking and advocacy'.[12] Recognising 'the increasing importance and prominent role of local service providers (consultancy firms, training institutes, NGOs) in development interventions and projects implementation, SNV has opted for intensifying its efforts on strengthening their capacities in its strategy for 2011-2015'.[13]

Against this background, and as the leadership of SNV realised it is no secret that high-performing leadership is synonymous with the success of businesses, SNV decided in 2015 to organise a leadership development and support programme.[14] From literature it can be learned that leadership development is important to enhance relevance, competitiveness, performance, sustainability and increased learning of enterprises.[15] Leaders of social businesses need to have additional competencies in order to deal with challenges that are specifically related to social business, such as finding a proper balance between social orientation and financial sustainability (i.e. avoiding 'mission drift'); improving social impact through (community) participation; facilitating

---

9 SNV professionals and lead trainers, who participated in the programme design and implementation include, among others, Naa-aku Badoo, Jessie Bokhoven, Brigitte Dia, Sabdiyo Dido, Harm Duiker, Allert van den Ham, Phil Harman, Isaac Makanani, Henry Mugane, Mary Njuguna, Mary Njenga, Niko Pater, Margriet, Poel, Jeanette de Regt, Pamela Reynell, Faoussa Tadjou and Andy Wehkamp. Within Context Karine Godthelp, Carmen Kurvers, Margherita Scazza and Titus van der Spek provided support.

10 SNV is a not-for-profit international development organisation. Founded in the Netherlands in 1965, the organisation has built a long-term, local presence in over 26 countries in Asia, Africa, and Latin America. Its local and international advisors work with local partner organisations to support communities, (social) businesses and organisations with tools, knowledge and connections they need to increase their incomes and gain access to basic services – supporting them to break the cycle of poverty and guide their own development. Ref.www.snv.org

11 SNV works with these organisations as clients, subcontractors and partners. Clients are local partners that implement development activities and whose capacities are strengthened by SNV. In the day-to-day reality in the collaboration between SNV country offices and LCBs the main 'vehicle' is subcontracting. SNV is furthermore working with local organisations as partners around a shared agenda.

12 SNV, 2011: 10.

13 Ibid, page 10.

14 See among others: Laura Callanan et al., 2014.

15 Ibid. 'Given the positive return on leadership investment we've seen in the private sector, one might hypothesize that more systematic focus on, and investment in, leadership development in the social sector could pay off in more effective delivery of social interventions'

social impact assessment; obtaining access to patient ('social') capital[16]; finding the appropriate organisational form.[17]

The SNV Leadership Enhancement Programme was called LEAP+, and it was implemented by SNV in collaboration with Context, international cooperation (Utrecht, the Netherlands) in 2015–2016 in six cohorts with 150 participants in 19 countries across three continents (Africa, Asia, Latin America). It was the first programme of its kind that was being promoted and implemented by SNV.

Within the context of this programme, leadership was defined as an organisational function (at the level of collective capability and organisational capacity)[18] that needs to be performed by an organisation and not merely as an individual competency. The initiators of the programme realised that an adequate fulfilment of the leadership functions of a social business active in the area of capacity-development support (CDS) is an important precondition for a more sustainable business, for reinforced products and services and for contributions to an improved enabling environment geared towards systemic change.

The SNV Leadership programme was conceived and embedded within the broader localisation strategy adopted by SNV and aimed at contributing to the development of an endogenous capacity-development sector and to local ownership: local actors were being supported to shape and drive their own agendas.[19]

Objectives of the leadership programme

The overall objective of the programme was to strengthen the intrinsic capacity of local capacity-development support providers so that they can provide capacity-development support in a professional and financially sustainable manner. This was done through a leadership development and support programme with a rather practical orientation for professionals who are working in – or who work in the spirit of – a market-based social business,[20] and who have the potential to manage a local CDS provision. Hence, the programme was meant for leaders who are entrepreneurial by nature or intend to operate as social entrepreneurs. They do not focus only on shareholder satisfaction and/or profit maximising, rather they are focused on creating blended value (multiple

16 The concept of social capital is explained in Chapter II and refers here to patient capital that is provided by social investors to social businesses.

17 Ref. Van der Spek & Van der Velden, 2014.

18 Ref. Baser & Morgan, 2008.

19 Experiences and success factors of leadership programmes that have been implemented by SNV have informed the design of the programme. These include the Leadership for Change Programme of SNV West Africa that was implemented for staff members of client organisations, and experiences of other organisations active in leadership development.

20 Within this leadership programme the concept of social business was defined in line with the definition that has been provided in Chapter II: an organisation, which functions on the basis of business principles, that creates blended value in a (financially) sustainable manner in order to contribute to systemic change.

values that are relevant for themselves as the entrepreneur but also relevant for 'poor people' and the society at large)[21] in a financially sustainable manner.

As has been indicated in the beginning of this chapter, in the programme the role of a social entrepreneur was approached from three different perspectives: societal leadership, business management and personal leadership. These three roles were the thematic entry points for the curriculum.[22]

The intermediate level (organisation), where performance is understood in terms of sustainability and capacity to run a business case, received significant emphasis during the programme. The entry level (personal) was mostly dealt with in relation to the other dimensions: improving individual skills in order to improve the sustainability of the organisation and its contribution to the creation of societal value. The attention for the latter level (society) was included in order to contribute to systemic change (through evidence-based lobbying and advocacy, among other things).

Perceived outcomes of the programme

The perceived main outcomes of the programme were formulated as follows:

- *Business management*: managing a social business that provides capacity-development support with a social focus in a financially sustainable manner both at the strategic and operational level. Competencies and practical skills that are required to form and implement business strategies that will uphold the social vision and financial sustainability of the organisation. The ability to formulate a viable business proposition and to translate this into a concrete business plan.
- *Personal leadership*: ability to be visionary, to be self-aware and to learn and self-adapt; the agility to respond to changing circumstances. Focus is placed on change-making competencies and leading by example.
- *Societal leadership*: competency to facilitate the embedding of the social business within the respective society. The ability to position the organisation strategically in specific markets and to create blended value that goes beyond the immediate interests of the entrepreneur and remains focused on developmental objectives.

The strengthening of individual competencies was the principal objective to be attained during this programme in 2015-2016. Spin-offs originating from enhanced individual leadership are likely to be reflected in the participant's organisation and its surrounding environment beyond 2016.

Core process: Overview of the entire trajectory

The programme was implemented through a combination of interrelated creative and interactive methodologies.

21 Ref. for a more elaborate introduction of the concept of blended value, Chapter II.
22 Ref. Titus van der Spek, Anne-Marie Schreven & Fons van der Velden, 2014.

Two face-to-face learning workshops

Two five-day face-to-face *learning workshops* were organised: one at the beginning of the learning process, and a follow-up learning workshop after five months. During the face-to-face meetings the existing knowledge, experiences and skills of the participants was taken as a starting point and was then further deepened through an interactive training process. In the face-to-face meetings attention was given in an interrelated manner to business management, and to personal and societal leadership (see overall content of the curriculum).

In the second face-to-face meeting participants took the lead in deciding the focus and content of the programme and also took responsibility for sharing their experiences and learning questions. The emphasis was on deepening existing understanding of issues that were dealt with in the first learning workshop and subjects that emerged from the on-the-job support and coaching. New issues that had emerged (such as writing a business plan) were also covered.

External resource persons from the corporate sector, social business community, government agencies and civil society actors contributed to the programme. One of them was George Foot, director of the Zimbabwe Business Council, who stated: 'The knowledge gained and the determination to go forward with the programme has been very impressive. SNV has made a great leap forward'.

On-the-job accompaniment

'Most leadership development occurs on the job through assignments, relationships, and hardships. Formal development programs play an important and distinct role, but they are not a substitute for these other formal and informal experiences.'[23] Therefore, in between the face-to-face meetings, during a period of approximately five months, senior SNV advisors provided *on-the-job support* to participants of the programme, including sector technical support. This on-the-job support focused on enhancing the practical application of learnings that were dealt with during the face-to-face trainings, in day-to-day reality.

Coaching

In between the learning workshops, the participants had access to a *personal coach* (from outside SNV) in order to further foster personal leadership development. The coaching sessions were for 1.5 hours per month and in these sessions the participants mainly discussed issues related to their personal growth.

The quality of the relationship between the lead trainers of the six cohorts, SNV advisors who provided on-the-job support and coaches on the one hand and the trainees on the other, was based on reciprocity in terms of respect and learning. This was one of

---

23 llen van Velsor et al, 2010: xix.

the essential features of this programme. Moreover, the creation of a learning culture within the programme, in order to allow space for reflection and reciprocal learning, was important. Co-creation of individual and organisational learnings for the participants, coaches and staff members of SNV was one of the major opportunities pursued within the programme.

Peer support sessions at country level

At country and cohort level, participants provided peer support to each other in between the face-to-face meetings. For this peer support, the participants were in the driver's seat: the process was self-managed and often carried out with the support of social media (WhatsApp, Facebook, et cetera).

Methodology

The contents of the programme and the pedagogy used had a practical orientation: strengthening the leadership proficiencies of leaders of local organisations, as well as the collective capabilities and capacity of their organisations to run their social business in a professional and sustainable manner – through reinforced products and services.

Box IV.1: Competency, Capability and Capacity

Competency is defined as the mindsets, skills and motivations of individuals, which are an essential part of the broader concept of capacity.

Collective capabilities are the skills of a group of people, a team, or system, needed to carry out a particular organisational function or process. It is what enables an organisation to do things and sustain itself.

Capacity is the emergent combination of individual competencies, collective capabilities, assets and relationships, which enables a human system (organisations, businesses) to create value.[24]

The emphasis was on application of the learnings at individual, organisational and institutional (position of the organisation in the broader societal context) level.

The programme was based on principles of 'experience-based learning'. The link between practice (experience of the participants) and theory was a prominent element in the programme. Practical experiences from the daily work of the participants were used as input for the entire learning process (the two face-to-face learning workshops and on-the-job follow-up). This experience was linked to inputs (including concepts to be explored) that were provided by trainers and resource persons during the learning workshops, the support that was given by the senior SNV advisors, coaches and the peer support sessions. During the final workshop, participants visited social businesses and engaged with the leaders in these entities. In such a manner emphasis

24 Baser & Morgan, 2008: 3.

was placed on practical application of the contents of the trajectory in the daily work of the participants.

Hence the programme was 'process' rather than 'event' based. During the entire process a variety of interactive methods and participatory tools were used in order to enhance further development, foster the involvement of participants and maintain momentum. From day one, participants were requested to formulate a personal social business plan consisting of the three main foci of the programme.

Diagram IV.2: Social business action plan

Source: Van der Velden & Behonegne.

At the end of the second workshop, participants were provided with the opportunity to pitch their social business action plans, and received feedback from a panel consisting of social investors, entrepreneurs and representatives of civil society organisations.

In line with SNV's corporate values and strategy, the subject of leadership and gender received ample attention in the programme. There was a focus on leadership styles in general and differences in leadership styles between women and men in particular; there was also reflection on the question of how leadership by women can be fostered within organisations along with a request for participants to pay attention to this subject in their personal development plans.

Learning as a social process[25]

The learning workshops were organised as a social learning process: they had participatory, interactive sessions in which participants learned from each other, the lead trainer and resource persons. Around 25 participants worked together in groups, in a workshop venue with an environment conducive to learning.

The learning workshop days were organised in a particular rhythm: during the morning sessions, the emphasis was on conceptual/policy issues; in the afternoon sessions, the emphasis was on application in the everyday practice of the participants; in the evenings, the emphasis was on enhancing personal competencies in terms of skills (so-called 'skill clinics') and processing information.

During the week, the participants worked together in so-called 'Home Groups' of about five participants who came together several times according to their own choice, in order to process information, enhance application and follow-up, and support each other in general in the learning journey.[26]

The learning workshops also had an 'open space' session for sharing thoughts and practices which participants brought with them, which were not yet factored into the programme.

Overall content of the curriculum

The content of the curriculum was focused on leadership in a social business environment, where social value creation is driven by market competitiveness and where the organisation strives to grow through independent financial sustainability. The heart of the curriculum was formed on the basis of the competency, capability and capacity of participants to come up with a viable business proposition, to run a business case with a strong emphasis on sustainability and innovation. Attention was paid to managerial skills that are related to the main (perceived) outcomes of the programme: more sustainable businesses, reinforced products and services and an improved enabling environment.[27]

The personal and organisational formats of the Business Model Canvas[28] formed the personal and programmatic backdrop of the entire programme. A business model describes the rationale of how an organisation creates, delivers and captures value. The Business Model Canvas is a relative innovative approach and tool to design state of the

---

25 Ref. Wals, 2007.

26 The concept of home groups was developed by, and borrowed from, the Community Development Resource Association, Cape Town, South Africa. (http://www.cdra.org.za/)

27 Participants from public sector/government or from Non-Governmental Development Organisations, for whom it was not possible (not within their mandate) to establish a social business, still used the offerings of the programme as a thought discipline. The programme supported them to use, within their own institutional frameworks, a 'social business-ish' approach; to provide business development support to social entrepreneurs; to contribute to an enabling environment.

28 Osterwalder & Pigneur, 2010.

art, new business models through which value is created for companies, customers and society. The canvas is related to the concept of blended value as presented in Chapter II of this volume; multiple values that are created for the entrepreneur, the social business and society at large.

The main topics that received attention during LEAP+ were the following:

Business management

1. *Value proposition and the concept of blended value*: exploration of the concept of value creation by social entrepreneurs and the concept of blended value;
2. *Characteristics of a social business*: development of in-depth insights in characteristics of a social business and differences with other archetypes of businesses including social enterprise.[29] The participants were asked to carry out an analysis of the characteristics of the organisation where the participant was working;
3. *The Business Model Canvas*: introduction and practical application of the Business Model Canvas, which is a tool to design companies that generate blended value for the entrepreneur, company and society;
4. *Consulting Cycle*: introduction and practical application of Consulting Cycle from the participant's own perspective;
5. *Business plan development*: support with regard to the formulation of a full-fledged business plan for the participant's own organisation.

Personal leadership

1. *Traits of a social business leader*: introduction of the major traits of a social business leader;
2. *Self-assessment*: assessment of the own personal leadership style (using the DISC methodology[30]), in combination with reflection on the basis of tools that have been developed by Covey[31], among others;
3. *Self-management*: enhancing the art of self-management and balancing different spheres of live;
4. *Skills clinics*: a variety of different skill clinics such as speaking out, presenting yourself and listening;
5. *Personal development plan*: development of a personal action plan as per the personal Business Model Canvas approach.

---

29 Ref. Diagram II.3 in Chapter II.

30 For this purpose, the DISC methodology tool was used. Ref. among others: https://www.discprofile.com/what-is-disc/overview/

31 Covey, 1989.

Societal leadership

1. *Mapping the business environment*: sharing of practical approaches and tools to analyse the participant's own business environment;
2. *Positioning*: support with regard to strategic positioning of the participant's own organisation in multi-stakeholder settings such as value chains and public private partnerships and markets in general;
3. *Co-creation*: enhancing competencies to establish and maintain relationships; the art of co-creation;
4. *Networking*: enhancing competencies to establish and maintain links with relevant (knowledge) networks; managing relationships.

The Business Canvas Model formed the main backdrop of the programme; the three dimensions of social business leadership were not dealt with in a separate manner but in different interrelated sessions, and emphasised different dimensions of a social business leader (see Diagram IV.3).

Participants

The 150 participants of the programme represented a variety of organisations from the corporate sector (private limited companies, [aspiring] social entrepreneurs, and self-employed consultants), civil society (Non-Governmental Development Organisations [NGDOs] and community-based organisations, such as farmer organisations, women cooperatives) as well as government (varying from central government ministries to local government authorities). Participants were selected on the basis of a set of criteria. The final composition of each group of participants (cohort) was also analysed and taken into account, to ensure a harmonious and productive development of the programme.

The major outcomes of LEAP+

During the implementation of this programme a vibrant intercontinental community of practitioners emerged. Participants, lead trainers, resource persons and coaches found many creative ways to support and remain in contact with each other, exchange experiences and ideas, and share suggestions. The dropout rate of the programme was extremely low (only a few participants) and related to non-programme factors (such as participants' personal or family circumstances and people taking up new jobs).

Participants report that one of the main outcomes of the programme was a change in mindset: an eagerness to explore and apply the principles of social business. Sithembile Nyoni Mpofu (director Regional Centre for Social Responsibility, Zimbabwe) stated at the end of the programme:

> We are realising that we need to work on the financial sustainability of the organisation. We feel the pressure of having to blend values in the way we conduct our business. Although our work is social, we also need to be financially sustainable. It has been such a defining moment in many ways. The programme is helping us

Diagram IV.3: Business Model Canvas as the backdrop of the programme[32]

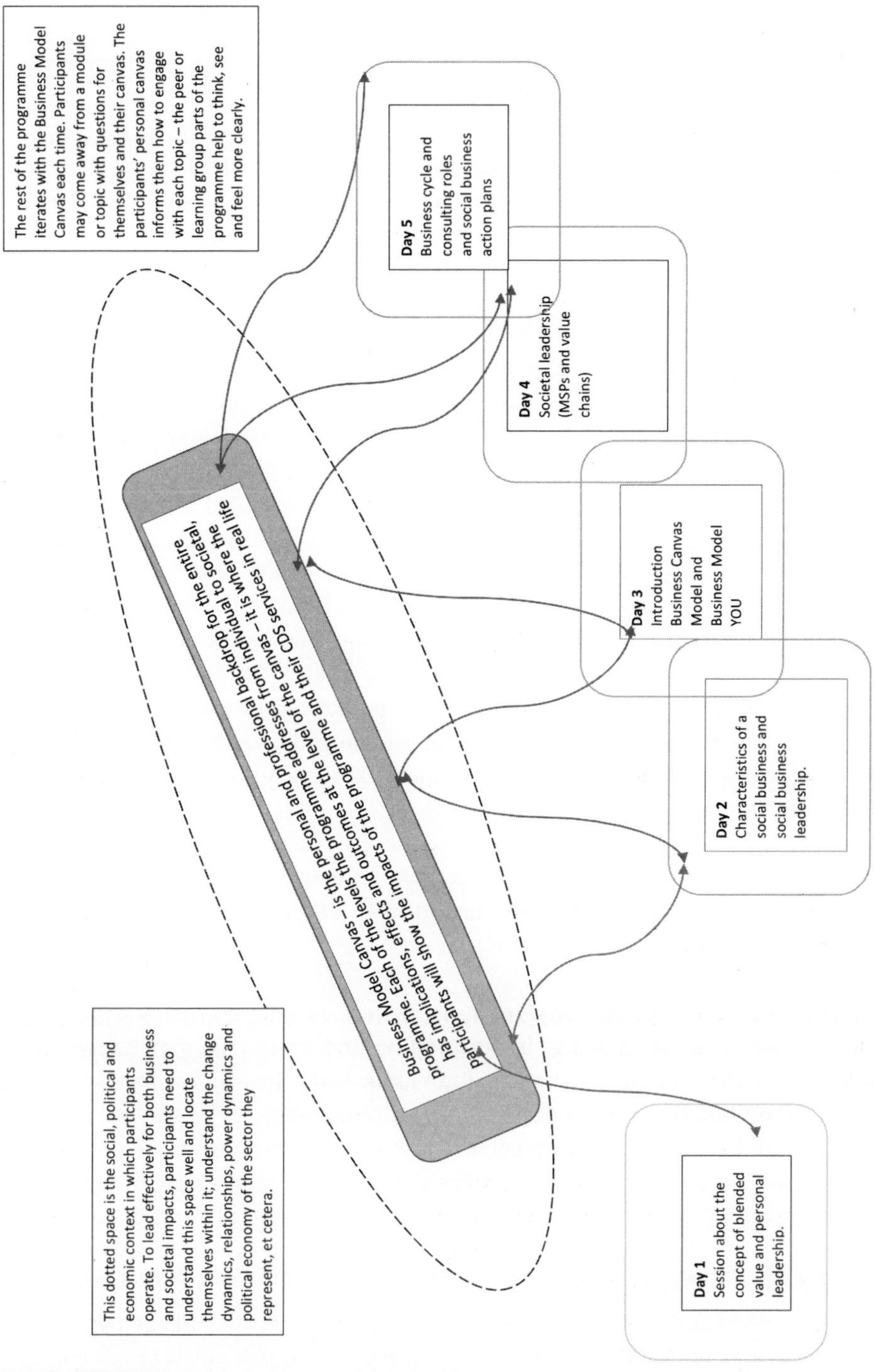

32 Naa-Aku Acquaye-Baddoo contributed to the design of this diagram.

address our challenges as an organisation, and become more relevant in our work helping the private sector integrate social values.[33]

Participants not only understood the main concepts of the programme, but internalised them in the process and started applying them at home. Rukaiyah Rafik reports:

> Social business is the new model and an alternative for social organisations to address the challenge of balancing financial sustainability with their social mission. Social business is our way of adapting and adjusting to market conditions in order to keep the organisation running in a financially sustainable manner while still focusing on its mission.

The timing and overall approach of the programme was appreciated as well, Peter Ndauti (Africa Turnaround Limited, Kenya) says:

> The partnership has enhanced and deepened our renewable energy profile in the market. Their approach to working with consultants is very empowering and mutually beneficial. The local capacity builder is given a free hand to implement projects, in a guided way. And LEAP+ couldn't have come at a better time. As a consulting company that targets development organisations and the government, LEAP+ has challenged me to consider a positioning where we trade directly with the market as a means to strengthening our financial sustainability. This is what our social business plan will be based on, and exciting ideas are already emerging.

The programme has not only strengthened competencies or collective capabilities but has also led to a complete make-over of some organisations (from Non-Governmental Development Organisation to a social business). Lina Moies (Indonesia) planned at the end of the programme:

> Investing in the enhancement of the leaders' capacity will increase the capacity of the organisation. My organisation has to become financially independent within the next three years. I take this learning opportunity very seriously as it will increase my organisation's survival possibilities.

Trainees report a steep personal learning process as well (operating differently as a social business leader and e.g. understanding and practicing that leadership is an organisational function and not an individual task). Jusceline Giringana (director National Youth Entrepreneurs Association, Mozambique):

> I am really excited about what is going to happen in my business in a few months or in a year. However, I am not very anxious about implementing everything straight away because I know it is a process. For instance, it is going to be a while before we get the blended value concept rolling in full swing as we are currently facing sustainability challenges.

---

33 The quotes of the participants are taken from an internal, SNV, after action review document.

Jane Walls (director My Pad, Zimbabwe):

> I learnt a lot and acquired proper processes to follow for managing a business, like putting together a business model and a mind map - unlike the haphazard approach I used to use. I also learnt what exactly a leader is and what characteristics they have, to be successful. So you see I got extremely practical knowledge on how to run my business.

Moreover, many organisations whose staff members participated in the leadership programme have started practicing major business management principles that characterise a social business: such as operating through the market with real products and real process; functioning on the basis of patient (social) capital (instead of grants); focusing on financial sustainability. One of the major outcomes of the programme is that organisations that previously worked using strategic plans made a shift to business plans that address revenue generation in a market-driven approach. Raul Gonzalo Valverde Mariaca (Organisational Consultant FEDECAAS, Bolivia) underlined his satisfaction as follows:

> Finally, I can make Gandhi's word 'be the change you want to see in the world' my own. It summarises the LEAP+ approach of improving people's lives and not just changing organisational forms and rules.

All the testimonies from different stakeholders, including those stated above, confirm the relevance of the social business approach, the crucial role of leadership in championing sustainable development and the value of the LEAP+ approach. SNV has realised that leadership is crucial in achieving this mission. The organisation continues integrating the lessons learned from the programme, to enhance the leadership capacity of its local partners.

Box IV.2: The story of Julius Awaregya from Ghana

'My dream about Africa's rural women and the environment is: putting value on our neglected and underutilised Sahel and Savannah wild fruits. So I set up ORGIIS Ghana[34], a Non-Governmental Development Organisation that promotes the value of natural resources.

In 2015, after a thorough selection process, I was invited to join SNV's programme LEAP+, with participants from Ghana and Kenya. This leadership programme offered me a great opportunity to practice and take action and move my ambition forward, as I acquired various skills and knowledge about social business from experienced trainers and facilitators from across the globe.

I learned about the concept of social entrepreneurship where social entrepreneurs do not only focus on shareholder satisfaction and/or profit maximising, but are focused on creating multiple values that are relevant for themselves as entrepreneurs, but also for 'poor people' and the society at large. I learned that social business operates in a financially sustainable manner and is not dependent on grants. The business model canvas and personal leadership training, both

34 http://orgiisghana.org

theoretical and with practical experiences, impacted on my life. This helped me to transform ORGIIS from a small organisation to a growing institution which started with 34 cooperative groups (before LEAP+) to 600 cooperatives today and the number is still growing. My skill and ability to motivate my team to work hard and my personal competency to strengthen the capacity of my team and stakeholders, have been enhanced by my participation in LEAP+.

After attending the leadership programme, I set-up a baobab social business unit, which started with a volume of 6 metric tons in 2014. We produced 23 metric tons in 2017 and for 2018 we have the ambition to produce 46 metric tons. We have access to a ready market through Aduna, a UK-based fair trade organisation[35], which is prepared and capable to buy any volumes we produce. We added shea in the enterprise stream and sold 400 metric tons to Olvea[36] in 2017. We are looking forward to sell more in 2018.

I was fortunate that both in LEAP+ and the further development of my social businesses, I met like-minded individuals and institutions who also believe in practising social business principles while using under-utilised resources, such as baobab and shea products, to create a sustainable income for small and marginal farmers.

With age-long challenges in Africa, such as lack of access to micro loans, high interest rates and currency depreciation, we need innovative capacity strengthening programmes like LEAP+'.

References

Heather Baser and Peter Morgan (2008), *Capacity, change and performance; study report*, Maastricht, ECDPM.

Laura Callanan et al. (2014), What social – sector leaders need to succeed, *McKinsey on line*, November.

Brigitte Dia & Eggink Jan Willem (2010), Leadership, the hidden factor in capacity development: a West Africa experience, in: Ubels, J., Acquaye-Baddoo, N. & Fowler, A., *Capacity Development in practice*, London/Washington: Earthscan.

Covey, S. (1989), *The seven habits of highly effective people*, London, Simon & Schuster.

Kaji. J. et al, (2018), *The rise of the social enterprise,* 2018 Deloitte Global Human Capital Trends, Deloitte Insights.

Maira, A. (2011), *Transforming capitalism; Improving the world for everyone*, New Delhi, NIMBY books.

Osterwalder, A. & Pigneur, Y. (2010), *Business model generation*, Hoboken, John Wiley & Sons.

Senge, Peter, Hal Hamilton & John Kania (2015), The Dawn of System Leadership, *Stanford Social Innovation Review*, Winter.

SNV (2011), *SNV Strategy Paper 2011 – 2015*, The Hague: SNV, November 2011.

SNV (2015 – 2016), various internal documents related to the leadership development and support programme (Leadership Enhancement Action Programme, LEAP+).

35 The mission of Aduna is to bring the natural vitality of Africa's superfoods to customers, while creating sustainable livelihoods for small-scale producers. (https://aduna.com/)

36 The OLVEA Group states to be a leading supplier of vegetable and fish oils. OLVEA has a long-term commitment with suppliers, promotes natural products with exceptional properties, while guaranteeing total traceability, controlled quality, and contribution to sustainable development. (https://www.olvea.com/en)

Van der Spek, T., Schreven, A. & Van der Velden, F. (2013), *Leadership in Social Business*, Utrecht (Context, international cooperation) (Contextual 11).

Van der Spek, T., Schreven, A. & Van der Velden, F. (2014), The three roles of Social Business leadership, in: *The Broker online* 23 October 2017.

Van Velsor, E, McCauley, C & Ruderman, M. (2010), *Handbook leadership development*, San Francisco (Jossey-Bass/Center for Creative Leadership).

Wals, A. (ed.) (2007), *Social learning; towards a sustainable world*, Wageningen, Wageningen Academic Publishers.

Wheatley, M. (2011), Leadership in the age of complexity: from hero to host, *Resurgence Magazine*, Winter 2011.

Wheatley, M. (2017), Who do we choose to be; *Facing reality, claiming leadership, restoring sanity*, Oakland: Berret-Koehler Publishers.

Webpages

www.cdra.org.za

https://margaretwheatley.com/

http://www.3nv.org/

CHAPTER V

Shared value creation

The inside story of Pactics in Cambodia

Jack van Dokkum[1]

Introduction

The Pactics Group runs a factory in Siem Reap, Cambodia, in the shadows of the mighty temples of Angkor. With 350 employees, it is one of the larger non-hospitality businesses in the town. Unlike Phnom Penh, with its extensive garment industry, Siem Reap hardly has any industrial activity, except for souvenir and handicraft workshops. Siem Reap province, though harbouring the famed temples that attract millions of visitors from East and West each year, is still the second poorest province in Cambodia. Employment is scarce and seasonal, since the tourist season, economically the most important one, runs only from November to February. Public facilities like health care and education lack consistent quality.

At the edge of Siem Reap town, the Pactics factory churns out cleaning cloths and pouches for sunglasses for a range of high-end brands. Millions of products leave the factory every month, and are shipped to Europe, North-America and China. The production process of these very basic products can be described as low-cost and labour-intensive. This is the key reason for Pactics' presence in Cambodia: producing products with a value of next to zero, cost control is of the essence. And since labour comprises about 40% of the cost, it is one of the essential cost factors. The lower wages and beneficial trade regulations of Cambodia have been the main pull factors for Pactics' move from Shanghai in China to Siem Reap in Cambodia. There were, however, other important reasons.

Pactics as a company, based in both Shanghai and Siem Reap, has always tried to take care of its employees, acknowledging that good people make good products. This programme, which started as basic corporate social responsibility (CSR), has been gradually developed and with the SA8000 certification it is now deeply rooted in the

1 The author wants to express his thanks to Boris Ploum, former General Manager of Pactics Cambodia, for reviewing this contribution on clarity and readability. The ideas expressed in this chapter are the author's ideas alone, though the practices at Pactics' factories are fully supported by the whole Pactics Group management.

company culture. Over time, the CSR programme has deepened to a business philosophy of reviewing the company's local impact; reduce negative and enhance positive impact. This philosophy now contains many elements of shared value creation. This chapter intends to share the development of the programme that led from basic corporate social responsibility to shared value creation.[2]

Pactics Shanghai: Migrant workers

At the inception of the idea of a factory in Cambodia, corporate social responsibility was already at its core. The idea of creating a responsible factory was a response to the situation in the textile factories in Shanghai and to the increasing difficulties in keeping the Shanghai factory profitable. The CSR package was at that time based on alignment with the Cambodian national Labour Law and International Labour Standards.[3]

The Pactics factory in Shanghai started off on similar conditions: fair wages, decent working environment and good health & safety regulations. After working with other local producers, Pactics decided that working conditions could be much better, if managed properly. The workforce in Shanghai, though, proved to be of a different nature than what management was used to in the Netherlands. Most of them were girls in their early twenties, who lived together in rooms on the industrial estate, far away from their families: they were typical migrant workers. They complained that they had nothing to do in the evenings and would prefer to do some extra hours of work. Their idea of life in Shanghai was: 'work now, live later', and take as much money home as you can. The Pactics management did not allow more than 10 hours of work per day (eight normal hours plus two hours overtime), and thus staff turnover was high, forcing the Pactics factory to increase the wages to match the 14-hour workdays of neighbouring plants to retain workers.

The factories in China and Cambodia have both been working with piece rates, rewarding employees with productivity bonuses for every product finished, on top of a standard guaranteed wage. The drive for maximisation of income by the migrant workers, consequently led to them disabling safety equipment on machines in order to produce faster, or skipping lunch breaks to increase production. Over the years, labour costs have risen dramatically in Shanghai, and the pressure on Pactics to retain its key employees was high. Market prices for finished products remained low, and an alternative was needed for this business environment in which a socially responsible factory basically gets doubly charged for labour costs.

2 Pactics believes that as a non-native element in the local society, it holds responsibility for the impact it has on this society and an obligation to minimise negative consequences of its presence, while increasing positive consequences. All this is done low-cost, since the sunglass accessory business does not create huge profits.

3 The Labour Law of Cambodia was re-written in 1997 and embodies all modern labour conventions, like paid leave, maternity leave, overtime premiums, termination regulations and prevention of forced and child labour. In the garment industry in Phnom Penh, this same law is not being followed and government is unable (and sometimes unwilling) to enforce the law upon local and (especially) foreign investors.

Pactics Cambodia: Building the right environment

In 2010, Pactics started in Cambodia with 15 employees on one floor of a shop house in Siem Reap, with 10 sewing machines. Their objective was to make pouches for sunglasses, the same as in Shanghai. It was an experiment to see whether production in Cambodia was possible, from the perspective of logistics (all raw materials had to come from Shanghai), quality (for the high-end brands, only high quality was acceptable) and productivity (in the textile industry there is a common perception that Cambodians are only half as productive as the Chinese). Setting up a company in Cambodia proved not too difficult, and the logistical issues were very soon sorted out.

Finding a decent existing location came with some key problems, as the work space needed to have emergency exits and sufficient windows for ventilation. Basic wages were low, but in line with minimum wages. Working conditions were reasonable and team spirit was high. Soon productivity passed the 50% line (compared with Shanghai) and Pactics noticed that there was more improvement possible. The team grew to fill a double shop house with 75 employees.

When production kept on improving, logistics were under control and quality was consistently high, it was time for the next step: building a facility in Siem Reap. The generally deplorable situation in the garment industry combined with the consistent negative media attention, led Pactics to apply for a grant from the Dutch Private Sector Investment fund to build a 'good' factory. The company was granted enough capital to create the first real factory in Siem Reap. An architect was commissioned with the task to create a compound that complied with all internationally agreed suggestions for good working conditions[4] and was energy-efficient: natural daylight, cross-ventilation, outdoor space. Instead of building a big hall, Pactics chose to build several smaller buildings with windows all around and gardens in between. Additionally, environmental impact was further considered and reduced by including rainwater harvesting and solar energy in its design.

When the compound was ready, the Pactics payroll had grown to 125 people, and migration to the new facility started in March 2014. As of June 2018, 450 people work in the factory, which is practically its maximum capacity. All production has moved from Shanghai to Siem Reap. The Siem Reap facility is running like a charm. On top of that, Pactics achieved SA8000 certification in July 2015 and ISO9001 certification in June 2016. Working towards certification, Pactics needed to implement a management system for social responsibility. Pactics has taken this opportunity to create a system that incorporates social, environmental and governance responsibilities, and converted the original corporate social responsibility programme into a wider programme, which

4 These conditions are set down in the Better Factories Cambodia regulations. The document gives a list of recommendations to garment factories to improve the working conditions. This list was taken as a bare minimum for the Pactics factory, and the architect was given the liberty to add both environmental and social improvements as long as the costs were not soaring. After all, it had to be a relatively low-cost building.

could be called corporate responsibility. This programme is basically a system that enables shared value creation (although at the time that term was unknown to Pactics management).

Taking responsibility at Pactics

In Cambodia, Pactics saw the opportunity to create a new factory that would have lower wages (since the cost of living was much lower in Cambodia than in China) and only local staff, as opposed to migrant workers. This would relieve the stress on wages, hopefully also decrease staff turnover and allow management to actually start managing production according to international standards.

The strength of the responsibility programme is that it was not a separate project within the company, but a core value to which, gradually, the whole management team subscribed.[5] There was no need for a separate CSR manager, or similar position, as corporate responsibility was the 'story' all senior management carried out.[6]

Five pillars of responsibility

Pactics' corporate responsibility is based on five pillars: Employee Care, Customer Care, Environmental Awareness, Good Governance and Community Involvement.

- *Employee Care* focuses on the employees and their working conditions. Pactics adheres strictly to the Labour Law and to international regulations (as prescribed by the International Labour Office). This includes decent minimum wages, correct overtime payments and working hours and high-level health & safety rules, but also health insurance, subsidised lunch and saving programmes. The whole package is designed to provide employees with a minimum standard of living (for them and their families, since they can choose to insure family members as well).
- *Customer Care* materialises in customer services like on-time delivery, near-zero defect rates, cost-free defects replacement, extended quality management and supplier-managed inventory. Pactics prides itself in being a preferred supplier due to an excellent quality record. Another part of customer care is continuously searching for new materials that are less harmful, for both people and planet, and have better qualities.
- *Environmental Awareness* aims at reducing the environmental impact of the company and is guided by ISO14001. This includes training of employees on the use of plastics, electricity and fuel, which not only has an environmental impact, but also a financial one (fuel and electricity are expensive in Cambodia).
- *Good Governance* deals with the way the company acts within the business community and interacts with the government (a strict zero-tolerance on corruption, in a collaboration project with Transparency International), and with how the

5 For the Cambodian managers, the open and communicative management style was rather new and unknown, but they gradually grew into it.

6 In the first two years from 2013 to 2015 though, Pactics Siem Reap did have a CSR manager. This manager was tasked with preparing and setting up the system to manage SA8000 certification.

company is managed. Transparency is crucial in the latter, as management believes that explaining decisions to people will create more support.
- *Community Involvement* builds on activities within the local community: support of charity initiatives, involvement in street cleaning programmes, and support for families of employees who suffered severe stresses like flooding or heavy storms. It also includes communication to the business community at large that low-cost production can be done in a responsible way.

These five pillars have been coming together for the last four years and have resulted in some amazing interrelated results:[7]
- Turnover is below 10% annually, which, compared with the garment industry average of 15% monthly, is extraordinary.
- Sick leave is below 1%, which is far lower than for instance in the Netherlands (around 4-5%). Sick leave rates in Cambodia are difficult to obtain, as in many factories sick leave is not granted or is only granted on condition that workers give up their entire monthly 'attendance bonus'.[8] It is generally assumed that the health of Cambodian garment workers is relatively poor, due to poor lunches at work with low nutritional value and unfavourable working conditions (bad ventilation, high temperatures, lack of water).[9]
- Productivity is 80-100% compared with China, which disproves the common perception that Cambodians are unable (or unwilling) to reach average Chinese productivity levels (the general consensus in the garment industry).[10]
- People line up to work for Pactics, from operator to management level and even expats.

All in all, Pactics' approach to its responsibility has yielded many advantages for both the company and the employees. It shows that value creation is not a one-sided process: Pactics actively tries to create more value for the employees (and for the community). In return, the employees create more value for the company. Pactics believes that this shared value creation has delivered a very solid base for mutual responsibility, and a very good foundation for production.

---

7 Basic statistics on the Cambodian garment industry are difficult to retrieve. The industry has a bad image and reports confirming this image are generally suppressed by the government, through the local ILO office and the Better Factories Cambodia organisation (comprised of industry, ILO and government). The statistics mentioned here are based on informal exchanges with current and former researchers, policy workers and managers of garments factories.

8 Human Rights Watch, 2015.

9 Dasgupta, Poutiainen & Williams, 2011.

10 This is one of the main reasons Vietnam, with slightly higher minimum wages and social security taxes, is still comparatively competitive: productivity levels are around 80% compared with China. The fact that productivity in Pactics is not 100% compared with China is not a matter of culture, or aptitude. It is most probably based on the fact that the majority of Chinese labour force in factories are migrant workers, who have no other prospect, for the couple of years that they work in the industrial zones in eastern China, then to just work and earn money. They have no or very little social life and care for nothing but extra hours and extra salary. In Pactics, all employees live with their families in town or in the surrounding villages and have many other things in their lives that concern them.

Creating a corporate culture of responsibility

One of the key concepts at the inception of the new factory in Siem Reap, was to create a strong company culture. Key elements of that culture were going to be 'responsibility' and 'transparency'; responsibility of everyone working at the site and transparency with regard to decision-making by the company.

The objective was to set a company culture as strong as one can experience in a hospital. When entering hospitals, people consciously and subconsciously adjust their behaviour: they lower their voices, switch off phones or keep calls very short, refrain from littering, speak respectfully to people in white clothes, and so on. The strong identity and culture of a hospital forces us to behave in a certain manner. That was exactly the aim of the company: when entering through the company gates, local people become employees and display a professional behaviour suitable for a high-quality responsible factory.

One of the driving forces for company culture is proper inducement of employees. At Pactics, all new employees go through a six-day full-time training. The objective of the training is to create awareness of the responsibilities of management (the worker's rights and the company's duty) and of workers (company rules and regulations and expectations from management towards the employees). With most employees having enjoyed little formal education, this training is not a classical classroom exercise, instead it is highly interactive and relies almost solely on spoken and sign language (in fact, even deaf employees go through the training).

With a workforce that has between three and twelve years of formal education, creating a shared culture starts at the entrance gates. On average, Pactics employees have worked with no other formal employer and are therefore not used to duties such as announcing leave, filling out forms and requests and suggestion boxes. The training programme facilitates this integration into company culture.

The high intensity of interaction and communication in the initial training has three major results:

- Employees understand that this is not a common factory. Even though not all of them have full reference or understanding of the concepts of rights and duties, they do understand that the factory values employees in a more positive way than traditionally in businesses in Cambodia.
- Trainees bond strongly and the training groups create relations across functions and stations in the factory. This results in more and open communication across the factory.
- Initial shyness and inhibitions to communicate are drastically reduced, which facilitates on-the-job training, but also results in more feedback to supervisors and management.

All elements result in a sense of participation, belonging and responsibility at the factory. By doing the training and with the current workforce all following this culture, new employees quickly assimilate and 'do as the others do'. This reduces training time and increases the productivity of new employees. Together with reinforcing training (follow-up training), Pactics has been successful in creating a 'culture of responsibility' within its factory walls.

Having a home base

A rule of thumb for Pactics recruitment is that employees come from communities around the factory. In Shanghai this was not possible: all factories are filled with migrants, as residents from Shanghai do not work in the factories.[11] This created the problems mentioned at the beginning of this chapter. In Siem Reap, it was decided not to hire 'migrants', but only employees living in the area where the factory is located.[12] This has several advantages:

- Their travel time would be short, since they live in villages around the factory.
- There is no need to rent employee accommodation near the factory, saving the employees money and also saving the factory the expense and management of running any kind of housing allowance scheme or dormitory.
- Employees have a social life outside the factory, which means they need to fit their work in with their other responsibilities. There is no pressure from employees to work more, longer or harder (in fact, there are clear limitations to requests for overtime from employees who have duties at home after work, which forces the factory to improve its planning and level out the workload).

Up to now, this has proven to be a successful approach. The only limitation is that locally there are very few people with technical or production knowledge or experience. These people are still recruited from the capital of Cambodia, Phnom Penh, but are often local people who studied there and want to return to their family home.

Steady income

Of course, in all of Cambodia, salary is still perceived as the most important element of employment. At Pactics, this is no different. Therefore, a lot of attention is being paid to the correct wage and incentive structure. In Cambodia there is no legal minimum wage outside the garment and footwear industry. Still, at inception, Pactics used the garment and footwear minimum wage as a guideline for setting the salary system.

11 The main reason for this is the salary structure: taxes are based on the hometown of people, and therefore migrants from rural areas are much cheaper than local Shanghai people.

12 There has never been a selection instrument for filtering out migrant workers. Pactics simply doesn't provide any allowances for housing or transportation, instead it pays higher wages (making it relatively unattractive for migrants from faraway provinces to move to Siem Reap). Siem Reap town has migrants mainly from the surrounding provinces, who are happily part of the Pactics workforce.

In early 2014, Pactics invited a local NGO to conduct a study into the 'living wage'[13] in Siem Reap. Pactics did not want to conduct this study itself, since it wanted to know what a realistic estimate was across multiple sectors with many less-educated employees, like construction and hospitality. The results of this study, adjusted for inflation, served as a benchmark for salaries in 2015 and 2016, and are known within the company as the Pactics Guaranteed Wage.

Basically, nobody in Pactics will earn less than the Pactics Guaranteed Wage, which is updated annually to reflect the increases in the minimum wage, set only for the garment industry in Phnom Penh. On top of that, employees are paid a top-up amount, depending on whether they are on a piece rate system, or on an hourly system. Since workers who work on the basis of a piece rate have a higher risk of 'a bad month',[14] their top-up amount is higher than that of employees who work on an hourly basis. In total this amounts to around minimum wage for the lowest incomes, and minimum wage plus 15% on average.[15]

The piece rate system calculates a fixed price for each item produced by the employee, with no upper limit. This means that if people become good at their work, they can increase their income to around 160% of minimum wage. Compared with wages in the hospitality industry, which hover around 75-90% of minimum wage depending on the business, that is a decent income. Moreover, employees can rest assured that they will at least earn their Pactics Guaranteed Wage in the next month, but will generally earn more.

Growth with a human face

Of course, productivity growth will have to be levelled out in the factory. At each increase of the legal minimum wage, Pactics revisits the calculation of the Pactics Guaranteed Wage and the piece rate system. This is done on a shared risk basis: an increase in minimum wage will lead to a smaller increase in the targets required for the piece rate. This means in practice, that Pactics will pay half of the increase, and the workforce will pay half by increasing its productivity.[16] This model is sustainable for the business and has led to steadily increased wages in the factory, without endangering the competitive position of Pactics in the market, and without disenfranchising the employees.

---

13 According to SA8000, Living Wage is the remuneration received for a standard workweek by a worker in a particular place sufficient to afford a decent standard of living for the worker and her or his family. Elements of a decent standard of living include food, water, housing, education, health care, transport, clothing, and other essential needs including provision for unexpected events.

14 Not in terms of business, but in terms of slow work due to sickness from seasonal weather changes or family and relational stresses.

15 At the time of writing (2017) the Legal Minimum Wage in the Phnom Penh garment industry was 153 USD per month. In Siem Reap, the cost of living is considerably lower, but Pactics has kept the Pactics Guaranteed Wage at 145 USD. Average salaries for production people in the factory were between 160 USD and 190 USD per month.

16 Productivity gains are always shared between the company and the employees, since productivity increases are the results of combined efforts by the company and the employees. With every productivity correction, management presents a package of improvement measures that should allow employees to increase productivity.

Changes in salaries are always a meticulous process, in which the whole management team is involved. Results are presented and explained to the Worker Representative Group. Challenges to the changes, brought forward by individual employees, supervisors and the Worker Representative Group, are usually acknowledged and implemented according to the comments of the workers. This shared revision process has so far led to a workforce that earns an above-average salary with annual increases. Since the production process is still very repetitive and sometimes mind-numbing, Pactics is always searching for ways to make work easier or more fun and to provide alternatives during lunch breaks. The company has added a library to its facilities, supported by the local NGO Sipar, and has set up a jeu-de-boules track, volleyball courts and relaxation areas.

Efficiency with decency

In a low-cost labour-intensive environment, efficiency is vital. At Pactics, efficiency is never more important than the rules set by the Labour Law and the company's own health & safety programme. If a machine is not safe, it cannot be used. This mentality needed some reiteration with production management and supervisors, for it is not the normal practice in Cambodian companies.[17] Training programmes in Phnom Penh and in the Pactics factory in Shanghai have made sure that the production department will not compromise on employee safety.

To Pactics, this is 'business as usual', but to local people, this is an exception. Still, Pactics believes that decency is a key ingredient in delivering high-quality products on time, in the right amounts. Only trained and motivated employees will be able to create a factory that can compete in international business.

Creating shared value: Profit – people – planet

Pactics is a business, it exists to satisfy its stakeholders and make profits. The more profit it makes, the more it can invest in growth. Growth means more jobs available and more opportunities for people. Pactics believes that creating value for employees encourages employees to create value for the company. And it is proving that this is working. Decisions are based on considering the impact on the business, as well as on the employees and on the community it operates in. Shared value creation has been a natural way for Pactics to grow; it felt right, it proved right.

Creating opportunities

Siem Reap is a province lacking income opportunities. Many families send their children, once they are old enough, to Thailand to work in factories or construction

17 The general attitude of factory management in many factories in Cambodia is: never compromise on customer orders. This includes breaking the law (if needed), unsafe environments and illegal payments in order to get customer orders out on time. Threatened with losing their single biggest customer (often Western brands) factories often see no other way out.

work. The monthly wages there of around 200 USD[18] are attractive when a seasonal job as maid in the local hotels only yields 80-100 USD per month. The cross-border labour migration is thriving and, on both sides, 'job brokers' earn lots of money facilitating employment.

With monthly wages of 150-180 USD Pactics Siem Reap offers a realistic alternative to Thailand, keeping children with their families. The additional training employees receive, allows them to try for better jobs in town. Whenever an employee manages to secure a better job, Pactics sees that as a small success. A loss for the company, of course, but a huge improvement for the employee. Mostly office employees get the opportunity of a better job outside the factory. Pactics encourages and favours internal recruitment among factory and office workers to fill the vacant position in the office and on the management team.

No give-aways

Although Pactics seems to provide a lot of extras to employees, almost nothing is completely free. Pactics works with subsidies to make choices for responsible behaviour affordable. Helmets, lunches, driving licences, work permits, are all paid for 50% by the company, 50% by the employee.[19] Since many regulations are by law required of all Cambodians, Pactics employees have to contribute to basic compliance rules. Lunches are treated in the same manner. Healthy food is basically a responsibility of employees themselves, not of the employer, but Pactics can make the choice for healthy lunches affordable. Currently, for quite a number of employees, the work lunch is the most 'decent meal' (in terms of nutrients) they get daily.

Taking responsibility as a company

A company operating in a foreign country should take its responsibility as a local stakeholder. Running a factory is more than just churning out products. The management of Pactics believes that every business should take responsibility for its employees, for the environment and for the community they operate in. Only that will create sustainable relations that will benefit both the company and the community. It will facilitate creating shared value within the company walls, and outside in the community. In this way a sound company can be built that can be profitable and flexible enough to adjust to changes in the environment. And likewise, it can provide its employees with that key factor of development: decent work and a sustainable source of income.

18 The 10 USD per day are often promised, but not always fully received. Usually there are hidden costs, like housing, transport, food, taxes that must be paid back to the company. Apart from that, the employment brokers often demand a share of the salary, or a payback of the loan. And since families abroad demand a certain amount to be sent home, the life of these migrant workers in Thailand is often rather harsh.

19 The most dangerous part of working at Pactics is the commute from home to the factory and back. Cambodian traffic is notoriously dangerous, especially for those on bicycles and motorbikes.

Box V.1: The Pactics Menu, a selection of what's on offer

- *Training on company culture*
  Training on social responsibility, first aid, occupational health & safety, quality management, environmental awareness, health & hygiene. This includes training on the Labour Law and on mutual responsibilities of employer and employee.
- *Educational training*
  English classes for managers, supervisors and team leaders, and Khmer classes for anyone who has problems reading or writing (about 50% of the workforce). Apart from that, Pactics repeats training on sensitive issues like household finances, health and environment. Pactics also runs anti-plastic workshops and supplies aluminium drinking bottles to staff to prevent them buying new plastics water bottles.
- *Subsidised lunch*
  During the trial period of the factory in the shop house, it became clear that the lunches that people bring from home or buy on the street was far from nutritious. It consisted mainly of rice, with a small amount of dried fish or grilled meat and barely any vegetables. According to nutrition standards that can hardly give people enough energy to work. In the new factory, Pactics started a lunch programme, to provide everyone with the opportunity to have a decent lunch, with at least 80 grams of protein (meat, fish or egg) and 200 grams of vegetables per meal. About 70% of all employees participate. The main reason for not participating is that employees have to make breakfast for their family and can easily bring some for lunch at work, or that they receive lunch from their families and cannot reject it.
- *Subsidised helmets*
  Helmets are essential in Cambodia. Looking at the sickness statistics, it can be observed that most work-related accidents are actually traffic accidents during the commute: the most dangerous part of working at Pactics is the commute. Since most employees do not see the value of a helmet (15 USD for a decent helmet), Pactics subsidises helmets and offers the employees a decent helmet for 6.50 USD, and made them mandatory for anyone wanting to drive to/from work on a motorbike.
- *Pleasant work place and gardens*
  The Pactics compound has a big pond and several buildings, surrounded by lush bushes, flowers and other plants. Based on the idea that green leaves do not heat up and actually create cool air, Pactics aims to keep the air around the buildings relatively cool, so that any air going into the buildings is not hot (design to create natural ventilation).
- *Driving instruction and subsidised driving licences*
  Since driving licences are obliged by law, all employees need to have one, even though it is not common to comply with this law. This is part of the Good Governance programme and of the company's responsibility. Pactics subsidies 50% of the driving licence and pays the driving classes (2 days) in full.[20]
- *Banking and savings programme*
  In any Western company, one would not think of paying out salaries in cash anymore. In Cambodia, this is still largely the case. Pactics has gone through two stages of creating safe salary payments for its employees. The first phase was using a local payment system called WING, a local money transfer system using local shops and mobile phone text messages. The system did not have any savings options and with the stability of income, more employees started to take out loans to finance family investments like house improvements, motorbikes or education. This led to discussions with a microfinance institution about opening bank accounts with savings options and starting a savings plan (in which the bank provides the saving percentage, and the company a bonus after a fixed term of continued saving). Apart from that, Pactics negotiated reasonable repayment schemes for small loans, to prevent employees from falling victim to local loan sharks.

20 As per 2016, driving license for motorbikes up to 125cc have been abolished.

- *Money Management*
  In addition to the bank accounts, Pactics invited a Cambodian Non-Governmental Development Organisation (NGDO) to provide training to all employees on money management. This includes savings, loans, but also insurances. Many people have little understanding of banks, loan sharks, interests and savings and often accept debts to acquire modern facilities like mobile phones or motorbikes.
- *Company nurse and contracted health clinic*
  Pactics has a full-time nurse on site to deal with occupational accidents, but also to provide basic assistance and advice to sick employees or employees with sick relatives. Besides the nurse, Pactics has contracted (and fully pays for) the services of a local clinic (after an extensive vetting process) to provide second opinions for cases where local doctors have limited experience and knowledge.
- *Day care and nursing facilities*
  A simple solution for turnover among employees returning from maternity leave. For most female employees, the first pregnancy is an uncertain period and especially the first months after delivery there is pressure from the family and a strong desire from the employee to stay with the child and not go back to work. As a solution to not losing valuable, trained personnel, Pactics decided to open a day care on the premises, allowing young mothers to bring their new-borns and have them on site, almost within arm's reach. Initially, this was regarded with some suspicion (people did not know the concept or how it would work, nor what to expect), until an older employee had her third child and started using the day care immediately after her maternity leave. She created a positive perception of the service, and soon more mothers started to bring their children.
  Currently, the day care is part of an integrated maternity programme, consisting of early follow-ups by the onsite nurse, re-assessment of the risks of the job and work station of pregnant employees, maternity training and training on post-delivery issues. Most of these elements have been established in collaboration with local NDGOs and have been relatively low-cost. The returns for the company are almost 100% retention after maternity leave. For the mothers, it provides valuable insights into their pregnancy, *delivery and first weeks as new mothers.*
- Library and educational videos
  In collaboration with NGO Sipar, Pactics has established a library on the factory premises with books ranging from novels and picture stories to gardening, livestock rearing and maternal health. Sipar also installed tablets with a range of educational and instructional videos. Employees use the library mainly during their lunch break.
- *Renewable energy*
  Pactics generates around 20% of its electricity use through solar panels. Besides that, it runs the generators (in cases of power breaks) on bio-diesel made from cooking oil from the large hotels in town.
- *Community volunteering and involvement*
  In a community like Siem Reap, with many foreign visitors, there are many NGDOs. They run schools, training programmes, safe houses, agricultural projects and many more. Where possible, Pactics engages the NGDOs for training and awareness, in order to profit from the knowledge of the NGDOs and to invest in the local community through these same NGDOs. Apart from that, Pactics actively participates in several community charity programmes, like the annual Giant Puppet parade where local children engage in an arts project by drawing and building huge puppets of (often) endangered local animals. These puppets are paraded around the town with Pactics employees volunteering to supply the security on the road and accompany the puppets. In turn, Pactics treats them to a nice evening of food and drinks.
- *Company activities and team building*
  Pactics values commitment and loyalty and on several occasions throughout the year it treats its employees, supervisors and management staff to company outings, parties, BBQs, and (traditional) ceremonies.

References

Human Rights Watch, (2015), *Work faster or get out; Labor Rights Abuses in Cambodia's Garment Industry*, Human Rights, March 11. (https://www.hrw.org/report/2015/03/11/work-faster-or-get-out/labor-rights-abuses-cambodias-garment-industry

Natsuda, K., Goto, K. & John Thoburn, J. (2009), *Challenges to the Cambodian Garment Industry in the Global Garment Value Chain*, RCAPS Working Paper No. 09 - 3 July 2009, Ritsumeikan Center for Asia Pacific Studies (RCAPS), Ritsumeikan Asia Pacific University.

Anonymous, *The Cambodian garment industry: A case study.*

(https://garmentworkersunited.wordpress.com/2014/09/05/382/)

Gillian ,K. (2015), *Cambodia Factsheet, Facts on Cambodia's Garment Industry.* (https:// cleanclothes.org/resources/publications/factsheets/cambodia-factsheet-february-2015.pdf)

Dasgupta, S., Poutiainen, T. & Williams, D. (2011), *From downturn to recovery: Cambodia's garment sector in transition*, Phnom Penh, ILO Country Office for Thailand, Cambodia and Lao People's Democratic Republic.

Ministry of Labour and Vocational Training (MoVLT) (1997), Royal Decree No CS/RKM/0397/01 of March 13, 1997: Labour Law, Royal Government of Cambodia.

CHAPTER VI

Measuring performance and impact of a social business

Reflections from practice

Eric Roetman & Pol De Greve[1]

Introduction

Performance measurement is thoroughly embedded in business management. Knowing how well an enterprise performs is crucial for managing the business and key to keeping shareholders informed and satisfied. This, in principle, is not any different for social businesses: social businesses that aim at creating blended social and financial values also need to measure performance to stay on track and be accountable. Whereas in financial management the measuring of business performance is fairly straightforward with a wide choice of methods available, it is much harder to find companies that are interested in and able to systematically measure their social performance and impact. Investors and managers may find existing methods for measuring social change too complex or bothersome and rather prefer simple unimpressive proxies, such as customer satisfaction and financial results that do not touch upon core outcomes in terms of social change.

In this chapter, we focus on performance measurement of social businesses and make an argument for a more widely scoped measurement approach. Such an approach would not only serve as a management tool, but also as an assessment system to measure and summarise the results of blended value creation. Instead of just focusing on financial indicators and customer satisfaction, we challenge social business managers and investors to assess their business case from three points of view: financial, customer and social aspects. In this approach, it is recognised that not every aspect of performance and impact can or needs to be measured. The focus in performance measurement lies on what the company considers to be important in reaching its strategic objectives. In an ever-changing business environment, the model will need to be adjusted to ensure that the company stays focused on its objectives and that measurement tools truly capture what matters to the company and its shareholders.

1 With contributions by Laila Bouallouch. This chapter was peer reviewed by André de Jager.

Exploring social impact measurement

In the last decade, Context, international cooperation collaborated with ICS[2] and a number of other client organisations in areas related to social business development. This happened in the Netherlands and different countries in Africa and Asia.[3] The collaboration included hands-on support to social business development in, action research on the interface between child well-being and social business; action research on the role and function of International Non-Governmental Organisations (INGOs) in social business development and capacity-development support for international and national staff. A last domain of action research concerned an exploration of social impact assessment approaches, methods and tools with special (but not exclusive) focus on Social Return on Investment (SROI) as a multi-stakeholder collaborative approach that captures economic as well as social (and environmental) impacts.

Box VI.1: Social Return on Investment[4]

Social Return on Investment (SROI) is an innovative approach to incorporating social, environmental, financial and economic values into impact assessment of social businesses. SROI acknowledges that social change may be experienced in a subjective way by different stakeholders with different realities and that mapping insights together with them leads to the most instructive and objective insights. SROI is a participatory approach for impact assessment, involving stakeholders during the whole process. By using participatory methods, the changes that people experience (subjective rating) are systematically mapped. This clarifies where, when, how, how much, and what sort of values are created. It has the potential to bring values to the surface which seem difficult to trace at first. In SROI monetary values are assigned to outcomes and benefits. These are combined with a strong narrative that explains the story behind change. Hence, by combining a quantitative measurement ratio with a narrative, SROI provides a framework that can be used for measuring and accounting the broader concept of value. It can thus put a value on issues that truly matter.

Context's work in this field was aimed at contributing to a better understanding and more widespread recognition of the need for appropriate impact assessment approaches and methods that can be used by social enterprises.[5]

Throughout our exploration it became clear that social entrepreneurs and social investors share a general recognition of the relevance and need of social impact measurement for social business for various reasons, such as:

- enhancing business performance by improving the quality of products and service delivery to clients;
- improving planning, learning and strategic steering in business management;

2 http://www.contextinternationalcooperation.org/ and https://www.ics.nl/en/home/
3 Including Burundi, Cambodia, DRC, Ghana, Kenya, Nigeria, Tanzania.
4 For more coverage of SROI, see: De Greve et al, 2013.
5 Brandenburger & Nalebuff, 1997.

- assessing opportunities for replication and scaling-up of specific business models, and;
- being accountable to shareholders, investors and other stakeholders.[6]

Positioning social impact assessment

Over the last decade, many INGOs have gradually been exploring more business-like orientations towards addressing social challenges. They have done so through a collaborative learning trajectory on social business development which from the start focused, among others, on social impact assessment.

Impact assessment is indeed a 'classic' feature of monitoring and evaluation approaches of development organisations. The OECD[7] has defined impact assessment in very general terms as an 'approach for exploring the combined economic, environmental and social impacts of a range of proposed policies, programmes, strategies and action plans', underlining that such 'assessments can also assist decision making and strategic planning throughout the entire policy cycle'. A more operational definition is provided by the International Federation of Red Cross and Red Crescent IFRC stating that impact assessment is a means 'of measuring the effectiveness of organisational activities and judging the significance of changes brought about by those activities'[8]. For development organisations, impact assessment is intimately linked to the mission of the organisation, and, in that sense, ripples through the organisation. Being able to assess and articulate impact is a powerful means of communicating, internally and externally, the contribution of activities in realising the mandate and mission of the organisation. Impact is seen as the positive and negative, intended or unintended long-term results produced by the organisation, either directly or indirectly. It reflects the contribution of the intervention to the overall goal.

Shifting the lens from a purely 'classic' development perspective to the blended approach of social business development necessarily required a rethinking of the way in which monitoring of progress and assessment of impacts are conceived and organised. As will be argued in more detail in the section *Spotlights on performance measurement*, the nature and purpose of a social business demands an approach that not only aims to capture the social dimension (as in a classic development settings) but also incorporates management tools to follow and guide business performance.

Performance measurement thus becomes part and parcel of a comprehensive management information system. The contribution of performance measurement will be to:[9]

---

6 Bugg-Levine & Emerson, 2011.

7 OECD, 2010: 4.

8 Definition by International Federation of Red Cross in http://www.ifrc.org/docs/evaluations/impact-handbook.pdf

9 Adapted from an unpublished internal memo on performance measurement by Prof. Alan Shepard for the OMASI Initiative of Stichting Het Groene Woudt.

a. provide timely and reliable information on performance, focusing on the relationship between business investments and socio-economic changes experienced by direct stakeholders and the wider community;
b. provide timely and reliable information on the intended and unanticipated impacts of business as well as non-business investments; and
c. enhance the quality of decision-making and the accountabilities that go with it.

The design and application of social impact assessment methods for social businesses is not an easy feat. Whereas in financial management there are ample ways of measuring business performance, it is much harder to find practical and versatile methods to systematically measure both financial performance (Return on Investment – ROI) and results at socio-political level. Many (social) investors and entrepreneurs appear to find existing methods for measuring social change – such as Social Return on Investment (SROI) – rather complex and demanding (in terms of resource use). Often, they rather resort to simpler and easier proxies, such as market share and customer satisfaction. Such proxies, unfortunately, do not touch upon core aspects of social change that one wants to capture.

Challenges in social impact assessment

Common challenges in social impact assessment that were encountered along the collaborative learning trajectory included:

1. *Intangible nature of outcomes*: a core challenge in impact assessment for development is that many of the outcomes (read: blended values) that are created through programme investments are intangible but - at the same time - very authentic to beneficiaries. Think for example of increased self-esteem, changes in power relations, or improved family harmony. Their value is incontestable but also highly determined by the perceptions of those affected. Such outcomes cannot easily be captured in prevailing quantitative monitoring and evaluation (M&E) methodologies. They would then risk being disregarded when assessing the effects and impacts of a programme. In terms of accountability to stakeholders (donors and beneficiaries), one would then fail to capture and report on the actual impact or to assess the true effectiveness of a programme. Conversely, in the initial design and assessment of the feasibility of a proposed programme, it is of crucial importance to capture and integrate blended value creation in the (cost-benefit) equation that constitutes the basis for decision-making. If not, key factors that may contribute to a programme's likely impact and effectiveness might be overlooked.
2. *Social businesses typically create blended values*: values, however, are intrinsically subjective, i.e. different individuals perceive values differently. In some cases, a specific outcome that is perceived positively by some people, may be perceived negatively by others.[10] Values thus reflect multiple realities.

10 For instance, empowerment of marginalised people may be perceived negatively by those who hold power and exploit the less powerful.

3. *The challenge of monetising non-marketed social returns*: whereas the mechanisms for calculating financial returns are well-known and straightforward (input data are all numbers), it is often very difficult, and sometimes impossible, to calculate quantified and monetised social returns. The latter would require that social outcomes are quantified and that a unit monetary value is determined for each specific outcome. But what is it worth in Rupees when a girl in India is no longer harassed while fetching water at a faraway public pond? And what is the Zambian Kwacha value of a little boy no longer suffering from diarrhoea thanks to clean water? Daunting questions indeed.
4. *Time period*: social impact is generated over longer periods of time. In many – if not most – cases, social impact is realised after a considerable time period, possibly even decades. For example: a social business that offers skills training for marginalised youth, intends to have a positive effect on the livelihood, social status and economic well-being (improved income) of the trainees for the rest of their lives. The longer it takes until a social impact is achieved, the more difficult it becomes to attribute these long-term outcomes to a skills programme, as the participants will be influenced by many other factors as well.
5. *Aggregating blended values*: this blend does not only relate to a mix of financial and non-financial values, but a single business may create very different social and environmental values simultaneously. Think of a social business that provides people with access to clean water: in the short run it will impact on health and hygiene; in the longer run it may have effects on e.g. food safety, environment, educational performance, safety of women, and/or social integration and empowerment of people. The challenge that a social entrepreneur faces is often less in identifying likely outcomes in the short and longer run, and more in the complexity and (technical) difficulty of measuring, quantifying and (depending on the assessment approach used) monetising a multitude of outcomes (see Point 7 of this list).
6. *Different levels of impact*: impacts can occur at individual level, at community level, at corporate level, or at societal level. Experience shows that public toilet service delivery in shantytowns can be set up in an entrepreneurial and commercially viable manner. Social impacts of such services relate to individual benefits (health, hygiene, safety) as well as benefits for society (reduced cost of health services, less crime, positive environmental effects, and social changes). Bringing all these levels together into a single impact measurement standard necessitates the use of mixed methods: as there are multiple values, often a combination of quantitative and qualitative methods is needed to assess impact.
7. *The cost of measuring impact*: finally, NGOs that support social business development are accountable towards their stakeholders, including their donors and sponsors. Monitoring and evaluation systems are typically funded through grants. Social businesses, on the contrary, earn their money through market-based operations and often do not have access to grants to cover the cost of elaborate performance measurement systems as argued in the previous point. This leads to the question: to

what extent and in what form do impact investors expect performance measurement to cover social impact and are they willing to include the cost of such measurement systems in their investment?

Some principles and assumptions for assessment

The process of establishing and testing appropriate methods for measuring social business performance stemmed from six assumptions:

1. In principle, every business creates blended value.
2. Blended value creation concerns a mix of financial, social, environmental and possibly other values.
3. A social entrepreneur manages the business along three dynamic pathways: optimising business performance, realising client satisfaction and assuring social value creation.
4. In strategic decision-making, the social entrepreneur considers the nature of the values that are (to be) created.
5. The outcome of this decision-making should be reflected in the business model.
6. The challenge in impact measurement then becomes: what values did my business create, for whom and how can one measure these values and their impacts at different levels and for different stakeholders?

Consequently, performance measurement and social impact assessment for a business should be guided by and linked to an embedded business strategy that is balancing these three perspectives: the business itself, the market and customers it serves, and the society it influences and affects. This is not an input-output-like entity nor is it a static cause-effect setting such as in a Logical Framework Approach which is used by many organisations that operate within the (grant-based) development sector. On the contrary, business performance measurement in the suggested perspectives concerns a complex and non-linear balancing between three dynamics, as reflected in Diagram VI.1.

Within such a setting, it is suggested that performance be measured by highlighting three types of value creation:

- *Customer results*: creating value for customers by delivering unique products and services that meet the customers' overt and latent needs;
- *Business results*: creating business value in the market while establishing a profitable and viable business and realising adequate financial returns (profit) for investors and shareholders;
- *Social results*: creating value for society by contributing to distinctive solutions for social problems or resolving social challenges.[11]

11 Roetman, 2014.

Diagram VI.1: Result areas for a social business

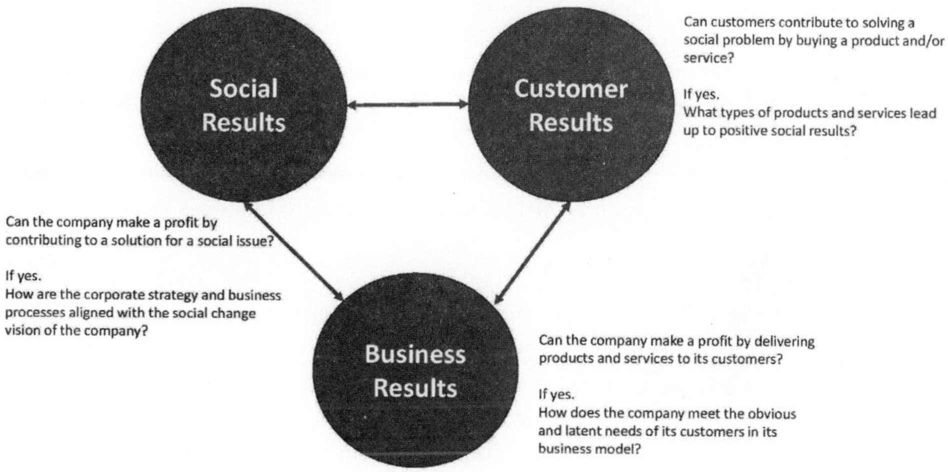

Source: Roetman and De Greve.

Diagram VI.2: The interrelatedness of three types of business results

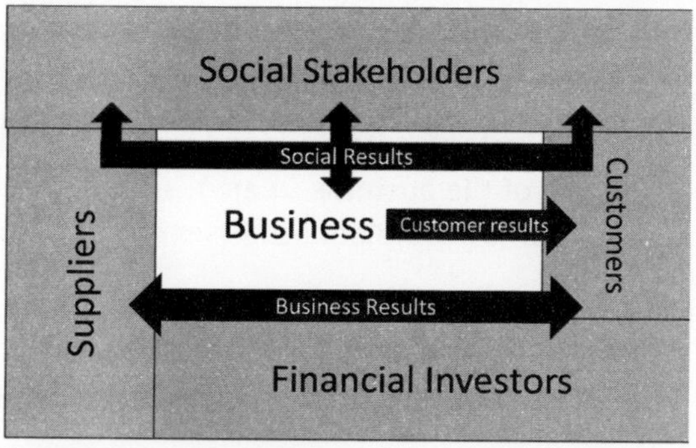

Source: Roetman and De Greve.

These three types of results ideally strengthen each other in a social business: customers contribute to resolving social problems by buying specific products or services; these products or services cater for (unmet) needs or wishes of customers; the business makes financial profit by selling these products or services; and finally, the business creates social value. Admittedly, in most cases (some of) these different categories are strongly interrelated; notably in for-profit companies, business results are closely linked to market results. However, in a social enterprise, the link between business results and customer satisfaction may be less evident, especially so in cases where the core business is related to social service delivery[12] or related products.

12 Reference is made to Chapter II where the challenge of mission drift is presented.

The three groups that experience the different result categories and enjoy the different kinds of value creation are:

1. Business clientele, i.e. those individuals that buy the products or use the services offered by the business – for customer results;
2. All actors directly involved in business operations, e.g. upstream and downstream primary value chain actors, business service providers, and most specifically the managers, investors and shareholders – for business results;
3. Societal actors, including those mentioned in the two earlier categories, but possibly many others that are directly or indirectly affected by business operations – for social results.

In many cases, the company's customers will not only enjoy intrinsic product or service values, but also social benefits derived from the products or services. For instance, the people who buy clean water or use the hygienic public toilet services offered by a social enterprise, are both the company's commercial customers (group 1) and part of the social beneficiaries (group 3). In addition to the direct use value of the water or public toilet, they may also enjoy indirect benefits in terms of improved hygiene, reduced morbidity, improved human security, self-respect, and so on.

In other cases, customers may not be the social beneficiaries. Take the example of the 'Friends' restaurant in Siem Reap, which employs street youth as cooks and waiters and is serving tourists and local inhabitants from middle- and high-class income segments. Here the three groups are fairly distinct: customers will not truly gain social benefits (apart from the satisfaction of supporting a good cause); social values are generated for the street youth who are given the opportunity to acquire skills and experience on-the-job and earn a living; the financial return of the business (if any) is used by the investor – an INGO in this case – to reinvest in this or similar businesses or to support other social projects.

Another example: by providing small and medium farmers in rural Africa an opportunity to become engaged in an (inclusive) value chain and sell their products at a fair price, social and economic benefits are created for them. In this case, social impact is realised not for the end-customers in the value chain, but rather for the company's suppliers, i.e. the farmers and their families. A similar case is the SJS Apple Project (see Chapter I), where apple farmers are the suppliers in the value chain and the farmers' families are the beneficiaries of the social business.

In practice, these three categories of customers and results cannot be completely separated. Besides, in many cases, there will be trade-offs between direct and indirect costs and benefits, e.g. employing marginalised youngsters to teach them a skill may come at the expense of lower profitability because of the incremental costs and possibly lower efficiency of staff (as compared with a business employing people with ready skills for the job). However, the specific character of the social enterprise can be used to position the company in the high-end market segment.[13] In that case, higher costs do not necessarily imply lower profits.

Spotlights on performance measurement

As argued above, the drive to establish and manage a sustained blend of social, customer and business results calls for a performance measurement system that is not over-complex yet able to capture key elements of value creation in all three domains. Beating this challenge necessitates a design that meets the following requirements:

- Impact & Performance Indicators (IPIs) reflect entrepreneurial vision and are informed by the business model;
- Selection and use of a limited manageable number of IPIs[14];
- Covering three perspectives, i.e. customer satisfaction, financial business performance and social outcomes;
- Possibly a mix of outcome indicators (e.g. number of youth trained as cook who find employment in the hospitality sector) and/or process-related performance indicators (e.g. level of community participation in management of public toilet business).

The desired model of performance measurement that emerged from our experiences is figuratively presented as a 'spotlight model' whereby the social enterprise is illuminated by the three different spotlights (customer satisfaction, business financial performance and social value creation).

Diagram VI.3: Performance measurement system in a spotlight configuration

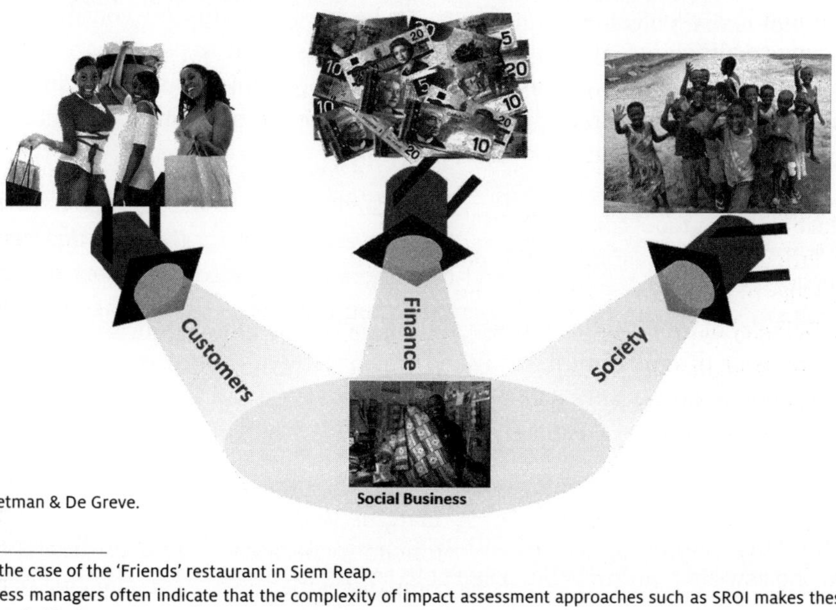

Source: Roetman & De Greve.

13 As in the case of the 'Friends' restaurant in Siem Reap.

14 Business managers often indicate that the complexity of impact assessment approaches such as SROI makes these methods unsuitable for management purposes. They rather manage businesses on the basis of a small number of well selected IPIs.

The spotlights thus capture aspects of performance from three different angles, with a number of overall specifications as follows:

1. *Layers of information*: a first layer concerns measures to assess market performance. A second layer covers measures related to the strategy, content and operational performance of a social investment as to guide management in operations and assure financial viability and profitability. A third layer concerns measures of what changes matter to the stakeholders, their communities and society at large. This should enable the assessment of different types of socio-economic change over different time frames.[15]
2. *Focus*: selection of key outcome areas within each of the three perspectives. These relate to how to identify what outcomes to consider in terms of customer satisfaction, financial business performance and social change.
3. *Intensity*: the identification of indicators and level of detail in measurement for key outcome areas at the different layers.
4. *Timing*: frequency and duration of measurement which may vary according to the nature of the outcome, e.g. business and market performance will need to be followed regularly in order to allow for timely corrections in business strategies, while social performance requires a longer timespan (e.g. every 4-5 years) to allow for meaningful assessment of progress and impact.

Case illustration of performance measurement framework

The following is an example of a framework for performance measurement based on a real case: a social business focused on relieving poverty rates among smallholder farmers. Limited availability of quality agrarian inputs and a lack of modern agronomic knowledge are considered to be main reasons for continuing poverty among smallholders. Therefore, the social business aims to provide access to quality farm inputs for as many smallholder farmers as possible. This should increase their yields and secure food for farming families for subsistence or income generation, and thus realise improved livelihoods.

The business model consists of:

1. Procurement of agricultural inputs in bulk;
2. Sales of inputs to smallholders on credit;
3. Delivery of inputs to the farmers at the onset of the production season;
4. Provision of agronomic training and other services to optimise yields;
5. Support to farmers in establishing market linkages; and
6. Maintaining strong customer relations through a network of community facilitators.

---

15 A fourth possible layer could be the corporate level for the (social) investor who engages in multiple investments as he/she may wish to compare performances across these investments and may wish to optimise the overall impact and effectiveness of the investment portfolio and guide decision-making on resource allocation to alternative investment options. This layer was not considered in this context.

Table VI.1: Indicative framework for performance measurement of a social business

	Customer	Business	Social
Layers:	Smallholder farmers in the area. The company's client base consists of marginalised farmers with poor access to the supply chain.	Company level. Procurement in bulk, storage, sales on credit, delivery of extension services, link farmers to markets.	Farmers and their families getting out of poverty and realising improved livelihoods.
	Key is customer profile and diversification. Customer data disaggregated for aspects like gender, age, farm size, and family composition.	Key is description of the business processes. Description of business processes with operational details.	Key is impact beyond customer group. Narrative on beneficiaries of social value creation, mainly farmers and their families.
Focus	Establishing the range of products and services that smallholders acquire or make use of. What is key to the value proposition?	The range of products and services offered through various market channels.	The social problem/challenge that is addressed. The desired and actual social change the business is pursuing (and the possible undesired social outcomes)?
	Key is customer satisfaction with the range of products and services. KPIs: sales figures by product (input) over time (quarterly, yearly); number of trainees and farmers reached in extension over time; contact statistics of the community facilitators.	Key is good operational performance in the market. KPIs: revenue flows from sales of inputs by product/ service; profit-loss account ratios; balance sheet ratios.	Key is desired social effect: food security and income. KPIs: long-term impact to be measured by: changes in dietary diversity and intake at household level; household income from farming; household income from off-farm activities.
Intensity	Established data formats to determine market performance and level of satisfaction of customers.	Established data formats (ratios) to determine level of financial business performance.	Methods to assess social impact?
	Surveys, different scores, social media, face-to-face interactions to gather information on perceived quality, reliability and needs fulfilled (how satisfied are you with the services), loyalty measurement (will you recommend the business services to others), satisfaction (how important is the business to you).	Standard financial KPIs – see previous line.	Elaborate social impact assessment – via SROI or similar method. Alternatively: limited number pre-established indicators for family livelihood status.
Timing	How frequently do you want to be updated on customer satisfaction, taking into consideration the time, costs and energy it takes to generate this information?	How frequently do you measure the different KPIs?	How often do you want to assess your social impact, taking into consideration the time, costs and energy it takes to generate this information?
	Regular updates on sales performance during farming season. Annual reviews of training coverage.	Quarterly or semi-annual financial reporting. Annual financial report.	Annual review of farm productivity (yield) and income realisation. Social impact assessment with time intervals of 3-5 years – poverty assessment.

Source: Roetman & De Greve.

The key stakeholders are:
- The social business, its management and staff;
- Community facilitators who link the business with the farmers and provide training to farmers;
- Smallholder farmers who are the customers of the company;
- The farmers' households who are the main beneficiaries of expected social impact;
- Service providers (e.g. bank) and input suppliers.

Concluding remarks

Some (but still limited) innovative research and development is taking place on approaches, methods and tools for business performance measurement of social businesses. A number of challenges remain and require further reflection, experimenting and learning. Some methods, such as SROI, offer comprehensive coverage for assessing value creation but are often considered to be complex and demanding in terms of resources and time requirements. The social business community is still exploring and searching for lean, manageable and user-friendly methodologies of impact and performance measurement that capture social, customer and business-related value creation in a social business setting. Questions remain, for instance on the possible alignment and interaction between social, customer and business results, the nature of such interactions and their implications: can they be complementary and reinforcing or are they more often than not counterproductive?

Development and roll-out of comprehensive, yet practical and adaptive, methods of performance measurement is only the beginning. Next is the need to link performance measurement and reporting to organisational characteristics such as staff competencies, instruments and reporting formats and procedures.

Even more so than in commercial businesses and development organisations, social businesses are accountable to many different stakeholders. The results of social businesses affect shareholders, (impact) investors, customers and communities that eventually benefit from the social value created. Social businesses have to be accountable to all these stakeholders, showing the different types of results that are being achieved.

It is undeniable that there is no one-size-fits-all approach in business performance measurement. Whereas financial performance systems for profit-seeking companies are well-known and fairly uniform, performance measurement for social business cannot be standardised. Each social business creates its own specific blend of different values, financial as well as non-financial, tangible and intangible.

Some areas for further research and learning include:

- Continuous business and organisational development exploring mutual reinforcement, interaction between, integration of and possible conflict between social, customer and business results;[16]
- Investing in development of lean and cost-efficient methodologies that allow one to capture the social, customer and business value creation;
- The development and use of mixed methods that capture both quantitative and qualitative aspects and whether and how this can be captured in a single impact measurement standard.

References

Alnoor E. & Rangan K. (2010), *The limint to nonprofit impact: A contingency framework for measuring social performance*, Cambridge USA, Working paper 10-099, Harvard Business School.

Brandenburger A.M. & Nalebuff B. (1997), The added-value theory of business, Strategy+Business. October 1, Fourth Quarter 1997 Issue 9 (originally published by Booz & Company).

Bugg-Levine, A. & Emerson, J. (2011), *Impact investing; Transforming how we make money while making a difference*, San Francisco, John Wiley & Sons.

De Greve P., Lont H. & Van der Velden F. (2013), *Narrative numeracy: social impact assessment; A brief guide to Social Return on Investment*, Utrecht, Context, international cooperation (Contextual No. 10).

Maas K. & Liket K. (2014), *Social impact measurement: classification of methods*, Rotterdam, Erasmus University Rotterdam.

Messelink, R. & Van der Spek, T. (2015), *Supporting social enterprises from pre-start-up to scalability: challenging the status-quo*, Context & ICS, Symposium Scaling Social Business in East Africa, Kampala.

Roetman E. (2014), *Bricolage; Spotting business opportunities by creating an environment for entrepreneurship*, Leuven (Thesis for Vlerick Business School).

Tuan M.T. (2008), *Measuring and estimating social value creation: Insights into eight integrated cost approaches*, Seattle, Bill& Melinda Gates Foundation.

Van der Meij M. & Scholten P. (2014), *Dan ga ik liever op vakantie ... over de zin en onzin van maatschappelijke interventies*, Peter Scholte en Lenthe Publishers, Amsterdam.

Van der Velden, F. & De Greve, P. (2016), *De stille revolutie van sociaal ondernemers*, MO Paper 99, Brussel, Wereldmediahuis vzw.

Van der Velden, F. (2011), *Social business: a novel approach to socio-political change*, in: Velden, van der F. (ed.) (2011), New approaches to international development cooperation, Utrecht, Context, international cooperation, (2nd ed.), pp. 69 – 87.

16 See Chapter II: on mission drift.

CHAPTER VII

Strategic reflections on social business development

The case of Internet Now!

Pol De Greve[1]

Introduction

In the first half of 2016, Context, international cooperation teamed up with ACE Europe for the evaluation of the Oxfam Novib project Internet Now! (INOW!) over the period 2012-2015. The project was geared towards the establishment of a social business that would provide internet connectivity to rural areas in Northern Uganda. The role of the Context consultant was to strategically reflect on the process and dynamics of social business development. This was to be done within the context of the INOW! project and at a wider level: in relation to Oxfam Novib's overall strategy and efforts to adopt and integrate social business development principles into its programme. This chapter summarises some of the major considerations and findings of this analysis.[2]

Background information

The Internet Now! project (2012-2016) is an ICT for Development project of Oxfam Novib funded through the Dutch National Postcode Lottery.[3] The project was implemented in Northern Uganda, a region that has known little or no infrastructure investments over the past decades because of civil war. The region faces very high levels of unemployment, especially among the youth. As a matter of fact, over 80% of youth aged between 18 and 30 are unemployed and not easily employable due to a lack of advanced education (on account of the war).

The INOW! project aimed at generating income and employment for communities in Northern Uganda through the establishment of a social business, SINFA.[4] The intention

1 The author is grateful to Laurens Coeveld and Felicia Huding for feedback towards an earlier draft of this chapter.

2 Note: this chapter is based on research in the context of the 2016 Mid-Term Evaluation of the INOW! project as commissioned by Oxfam-Novib. Later developments of the project, the company SINFA and its partners, i.e. from 2016 onwards till date, are not covered in this chapter.

3 Nationale Postcodeloterij – https://www.postcodeloterij.nl/

4 'Stichting Internet Now Foundation for Africa'.

was to provide a variety of e-products and services via a network of 100 internet centres at rural villages. SINFA had different business units, offering different internet-based services, namely:

- *Business Process Outsourcing* (BPO) – employing individuals (so-called micro-workers) with limited opportunity for employment as e-workers to provide high-quality, information-based services to domestic and international clients;
- *Wireless Internet Service Provider* (WISP) – broadband internet service offering high-quality, affordable reliable internet access via a robust wireless infrastructure;
- *OctionX Commodity Resource Platform* (CRP) – an online platform that connects various actors in agricultural value chains and allows them to trade and share (offer & receive) different types of information (market, product, price, weather, agro-technical, et cetera);
- *Mobile Money and secretarial services* – providing mobile money services to the local communities via the community centres.

Achievements

The targets set for the employment of micro-workers and the training of community members in ICT literacy were largely achieved. Earnings for the micro-workers varied between 5 and 10 USD per day. This depended on the number of BPO tasks that they could perform (capacity) and the volume of work (demand). The project succeeded in realising changes in the lives of youth, mainly students. On the other hand, the number of users of services in the community centres and those using the Commodity Resource Platform remained below expectations.

The BPO work has brought about some important changes in the lives of the micro-workers. The most important changes for them were gaining work experience and being able to live independently thanks to their salary. The work experience gave them specific skills and widened their social network. For the micro-workers interviewed, SINFA was a training ground, preparing them for other livelihood opportunities, either as employee with e-companies, or by becoming self-employed. SINFA offered regular job positions to 40-50 fixed staff members and at peak times to up to 75 micro-workers (on variable contracts) of which 33% women.

Outcomes from the community centres related to ICT literacy training, access to internet and other services, and the Commodity Resource Platform were below initial expectations. The business model especially was not sufficiently robust and should have been pre-tested more thoroughly.

Free ICT literacy training attracted community members, in particular youth, and provided them with a first introduction to ICT. ICT literacy training followed an adapted approach (comparable to functional literacy training) targeting groups with their specific needs and developing tailored products and services.

The project was an interesting and useful learning experience for Oxfam and partners and created space for innovative and relevant learning experiences for all stakeholders. It demonstrated that low-cost technology can work to connect people in rural areas to the internet. Involving community members and local government in management and operations provided opportunities for embedding the centres in communities. Outreach and extension services are needed to strengthen the capacity of communities and ensure viability and sustainability of the ICT centres.

Experiences and lessons learned from Internet Now!

The evaluation of INOW! revealed several challenges. In the following sections, these findings will be brought to a strategic level, seeking answers to some questions with respect to Oxfam Novib's strategy and approach to social business development. They are presented as reflections on nine selected thematic areas:[5]

Diagram VII.1: Areas for strategic reflection

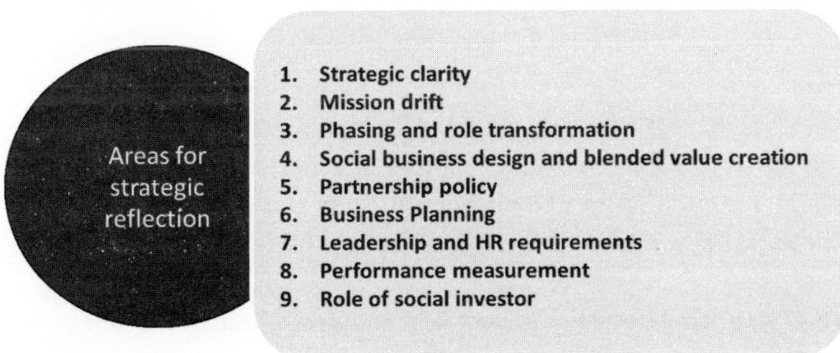

Source: De Greve.

Strategic clarity

The INOW! project was a first of its kind for Oxfam Novib. The organisation had hardly ever worked with an explicit market-based social business approach whereby a central role was played by an enterprise (and not by partner organisations as in Oxfam Novib's 'regular' development programme which works mainly on the basis of grants). Because the project was a pilot, it was not grounded in an established organisational strategy for social business development (which did not exist at that time). The questions as to why Oxfam Novib wanted to venture into a social business as a strategic approach and how this was aligned with the overarching mission of Oxfam Novib were not explicitly addressed at the start. The donor's funding line ('Dream Fund') was explicitly meant for innovative projects, which INOW! certainly was for Oxfam Novib. Due to the fact that this was a pilot, Oxfam Novib may not have been fully prepared in organisational or operational terms to implement such a social business project.

5 Selection of areas was based on an analytic framework developed and applied by Context, international cooperation.

Indeed, the intention was to learn from practice and thus implicitly to test the planned approach. As a consequence, one had to be prepared for and accept shortcomings and failures in some aspects of the project. Oxfam Novib thus acknowledged or at least was aware of the high-risk nature of the project. On the other hand, the size of the project, its prestigious character and the importance of maintaining good relationships with an important back-donor demanded vigorous control and management and timely corrections in the business model in case problems occurred.

Eventually, the evaluation team recommended that Oxfam Novib should develop an organisational strategy on social business development. Such a strategy clarifies the goal, objectives, boundaries and approaches that the organisation will follow. The strategy highlights the role and place of social business development within the organisation, what forms it may take and how this aligns with Oxfam Novib's overall vision and mission. The sequential approach to follow is that clarity in vision is first translated into a project strategy and subsequently into operational and organisational terms.

Mission drift

Social businesses set out to create social impact, but, in order to do so the business would need to be financially viable.[6] Balancing between social and commercial objectives may potentially give rise to conflicts as the social entrepreneur aims to translate the social vision into executable and commercially viable strategies.[7]

Diagram VII.2: Balancing between impact first and profit first

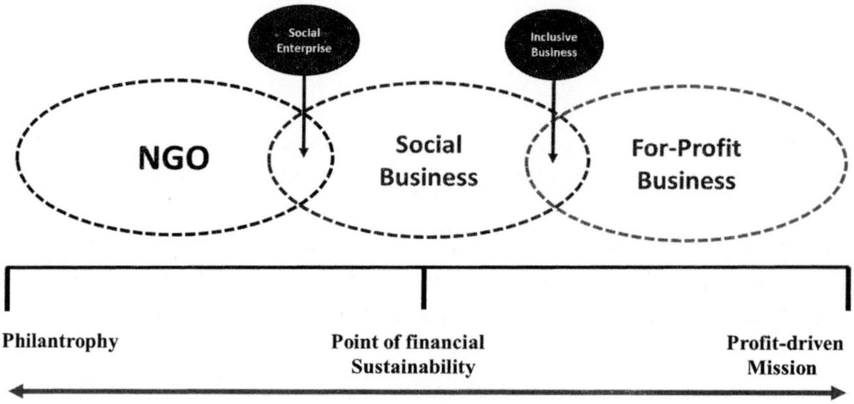

Adapted from presentation by Dr. John Hoffmire

6 Bull & Crampton, 2005.

7 See also Diagram II.3 with typology of businesses presented in Chapter II by Fons van der Velden.

The friction caused during this process is referred to as mission drift.[8] In practice, a social business aims to generate both social and financial value. This duality in value orientation means that sometimes decisions and actions may be in conflict and cause friction. This is the point at which a social business may face an existentialist challenge which is almost inevitable as social entrepreneurs progress towards commercial viability and possibly expansion. Mission drift entails the struggle of holding on to one's core objective (in this case social change) while trying to satisfy other value objectives including financial sustainability of the enterprise.

SINFA faced this challenge while searching for a sustainable balance between social objectives and financial viability. Initially, social objectives were very prominent in the design and business model. Gradually, because commercial performance was weak, more attention had to be paid to improving commercial and financial performance. Nevertheless, Oxfam Novib's management continued to emphasise that the 'raison d'être' of the company firmly remained the creation of social impact with SINFA as 'a for-profit social enterprise, providing commercial services that address the needs of the local communities'.[9] In business practice, SINFA thus adopted a hybrid model whereby it was accepted that the company may not be able to sustain itself financially, and that some form of subsidised support would be required to continue delivering (certain elements of) its social services.

Phasing of the project and role transformation

Like any (social) business, SINFA has gone through different phases from a design phase (pre-start-up) via start-up phase to where it is now: entering the growth stage.

Diagram VII.3: Social business life cycle

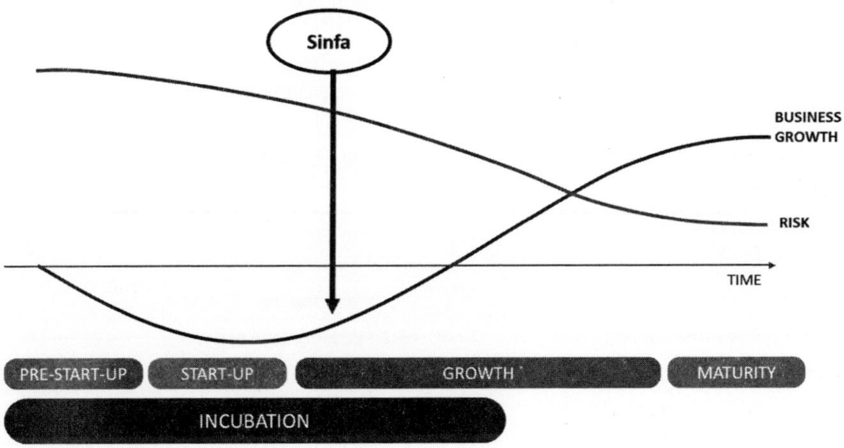

Source: Messelink & Van der Spek, 2015.

8 In Chapter II the issue of mission drift is explained.

9 As stated in the project proposal of INOW!.

Admittedly, several issues still need to be addressed before maturity, scalability and replicability is reached. In social business, each phase comes with specific challenges that require appropriate management decision-making and support. In INOW! some of these early challenges included logistics of infrastructure deployment, the deployment of local management, and the roll-out of CRP and of BPO service delivery. Transformative changes may, as in the case of INOW!, also involve that roles and responsibilities of partners and other actors will change. New actors and business service providers may enter the stage while others withdraw. For example, a social business with a strong social mandate may receive funding from a Non-Governmental Development Organisation (NGDO) at the early stages, but then may find itself without the necessary business and financial support in its growth phase, as potential impact investors fear that the business model behind the social mandate is not robust enough.[10]

Table VII.1: Support to business[11]

Pre-start-up & Start-up	Growth stage
Support providers	
- NGOs	- NGOs
- QuANGOs	- Impact investors
- Social investors	- Banks
- Angel Investors	
- Incubators	
- Accelerators	
- Et cetera	
Nature of support	
- Grant structure	- Loan/Equity structure
- Less governance and control issues	- Increased governance and control issues
- Basic business acumen training	- Financial and technical reporting
- Support awarded on basis of social cause and impact	- Support awarded on basis of risk versus return
- Risk is relatively unimportant	- Risk-sensitive investors step in
Types of support	
- Grants and funding	- Equity financing
- Repayable (low interest) loans	- Debt financing
- Leadership	- Technical support
- Basic business acumen training	- Market-entry support
Reporting culture	
- Social orientation of concept priority	- Technical financial
- Terminology NGO-ish	- Use of Key Performance Indicators (KPIs)

10 Messelink & Van der Spek, 2015

11 Ibid.

Some observations on timing and phasing that may apply to start-ups in general:

- The roll-out within the project, both in terms of geographic/market coverage and of different value propositions (services), is situation-specific. A massive one-go roll-out hinders learning. In a more gradual build-up of service delivery a business can learn from what goes right and wrong and adapt its management and operational approach accordingly.
- Each business line has its own phasing and its performance can be monitored in terms of a combination of financial returns (commercial success) and social returns (social impact). This balance will be different for each business line.

Social business model design and blended value creation

Social business model design is focused on blended value creation. In other words, social businesses are designed not only to create financial returns, but also to generate other values such as social values, environmental values, economic values, political values, or gender equity. Values are essentially subjective in nature and will be perceived differently by different stakeholders. Take the value of internet connectivity: for an individual, the value will depend on the use she is able and willing to make of a specific functionality. So, even for one specific service value, perception will be markedly different between individuals.

The initial set-up and role of SINFA as a social business was based on social value creation in a business-like ecosystem. A conclusion was therefore that managing mission drift required adapting existing business lines or even introducing new lines in the search for a sustainable balance between social impact and commercial viability. Hence, a creative and flexible management approach is a precondition for success. Managing mission drift is a process of trial and error, learning and adjusting. Therefore, flexibility and creativity in management is a must.

Partnership model

In 'normal' commercial settings, there are no 'partner' organisations involved when setting up a business. In the INOW! project, Oxfam did use a partnership concept in their collaboration with local NGOs to implement some activities, and with business partners being local or foreign private sector agencies that collaborate with SINFA in business development and service delivery. A question that was raised in this case was: is having four partners involved in setting up a company a good and workable model? The conclusion of the evaluation team was that this constellation was indeed complex in terms of management and alignment with all partners and that ideally a leaner set-up would have been preferable.

The lessons that can be drawn from INOW! experiences in terms of partnership approach for social business development, are:

- Selection of (business) partners must be done in order to fill gaps in technical and managerial capabilities of major stakeholders involved with a view to achieve complementarity;
- In comparison with 'regular' development programmes, partnership relations with companies in social business programmes must be based on business-like contract arrangements (SLA – service level agreements);
- Longer-term agreements can be in the form of a memorandum of understanding that specifies the overall principles and rules of the game for multi-year collaboration;
- SLAs must include clearly specified benchmarks, deadlines and targets and have built-in flexibility that allows for revision of specific elements based on actual performance and achievements;
- Likewise, financial commitments ideally contain subsequent allotments that are conditional upon achieving contractual targets and deadlines;
- Partner contracts must clearly spell out roles and responsibilities while benchmarks and targets for each partner must be agreed upon and laid down in the business plan.

Business planning and organisation

Social business development starts with clarity in vision. This is translated into a business investment strategy that constitutes the basis for developing a business model, followed by operational business planning. INOW! experiences demonstrated that business planning must be a recurrent iterative process that allows for adjustments in design and operations. Responsibilities for specific tasks and benchmarks in the business plan must be assigned to partners. Even though the end responsibility for realising the plan was with SINFA, stronger accountability could have been built in for partners to deliver. This would equally apply to managerial and technical aspects as well as to the realisation of social objectives and monitoring thereof.

The Business Model Canvas can be used as a practical and systematic tool to develop and present a first outline of a business model and its constituting elements, like value propositions, customer segments, partners, communication, and so on. The canvas also allows the development of building blocks for financial planning, both in terms of expenditure and revenue streams. Finally, in updated versions of the model, the social aspects of business design can also be incorporated. By using the model, a well-structured discussion could be conducted about the strengths and weaknesses in the performance of social businesses. The canvas would then be used as the starting point for developing a fully-fledged business model and financial plan.

Diagram VII.4: Social Business Model Canvas[12]

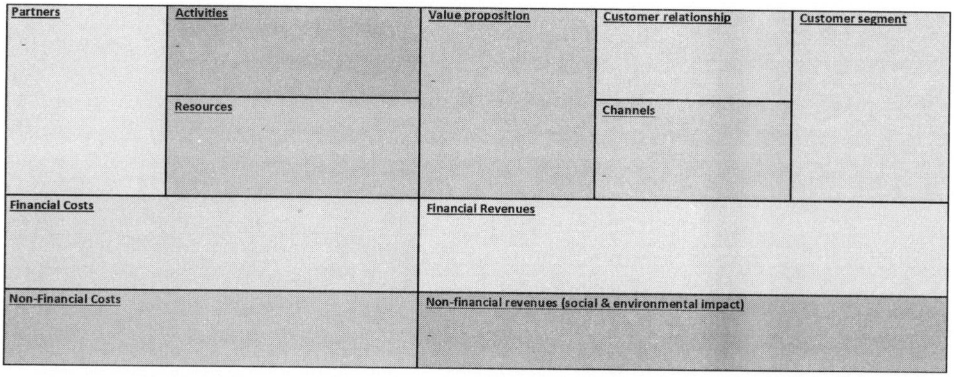

Leadership and HR requirements

Within a social business approach, the leadership is tasked with blending commercial value creation with social value creation.[13] This challenge of driving forward a commercial business while actively creating social impact brings about unique leadership and management challenges. To better understand the challenge of social business, one may break leadership down into three roles: (1) entrepreneurial and business management skills, (2) social vision and leadership drive, and (3) strong personal skills. This mix of leadership qualities is needed if only to establish and maintain the business in a complex ecosystem with private market-based operators (including competitors), social actors with whom one may want to cooperate (e.g. communities, CBOs, CSOs, NGDOs) and institutional actors like local authorities, regulatory bodies and agencies and alike. It is therefore important to ensure that managers and key actors at different levels and positions within a social business set-up have or acquire a balanced set of competencies that cover these aforementioned areas (business, social, personal).

Throughout the years, turnover of staff and management at SINFA was high. This was at times challenging for the continuity in operations, management and leadership. At the start of INOW!, Oxfam Novib had little in-house expertise on business development and management, and key positions in the project were held by staff with a strong background in social development. In later years, Oxfam Novib sought to establish a better alignment of staff competencies with the requirements of a social business programme, notably by posting staff with stronger entrepreneurial and financial competencies. Business performance is all about having the right people in the right spot. A key lesson from INOW! is the critical need to ensure that a correct mix of entrepreneurial, social and personal competencies are in place at different positions; and where needed to offer coaching and business development support to fill in specific gaps.

12 Adapted from: Osterwalder & Pigneur, 2010.

13 Van der Spek, Schreven & Van der Velden, 2013.

In a final observation, it is noted that not all of the required competencies or knowledge can or should be provided by and within Oxfam Novib/SINFA only, but that it is normal practice in business to link with partners and other business service providers to bring in specific capacities and expertise.

Performance measurement

As indicated in the previous chapter, performance measurement is thoroughly embedded in regular businesses. This is no different for social businesses: social businesses that aim at creating blended values need to institutionalise performance measurement to stay on track and be accountable. Performance measurement is important for steering and enhancing business performance, for planning, learning, assessing opportunities for replication or upscaling, and last but not least for ensuring accountability to (social) investors, back-donors, and other stakeholders.

Operational project monitoring (on activities and outcomes) and, to a limited extent, business performance measurement, were in place in INOW! from the beginning. However, performance measurement was weak on social value creation and/or social impact assessment. Identifying and, where possible, measuring social results of the business is necessary for all the same reasons that commercial performance measurement is needed in business management. Accounting for social impacts can be complicated because social results are often intangible and difficult to grasp (say, self-esteem from IT literacy). Social impacts emerge often after the medium or long term (say, benefits of IT education), they are often of a diverse nature and cannot be aggregated (employment, access to information, education), and finally they are subjective (as value is subjective).[14]

Putting in place adequate performance measurement systems to capture the blended value creation was a strong recommendation in this evaluation of SINFA/INOW!, but is equally relevant for any possible replication of this model by Oxfam Novib.

The back-donor of INOW! is not a typical social investor, as the investor provides funding on a grant basis. However, in a setting like INOW! that has a business set-up and involves a substantial amount of funding, close follow-up of different aspects of the programme (financial, commercial, social) is a prerequisite, if not for accountability than certainly for steering and controlling the business operations. This requires appropriate mechanisms for business management as well as mechanisms to monitor financial, commercial and social results. An impact investor does not only demand some financial returns on investments but rather accepts that returns are less rewarding, often slower to be realised and may be comprised of a mix of financial and social returns and impacts.

14 For further discussion on performance management and measurement, see Chapter VI.

In conclusion: Reflections on the INOW! business model

Even though a social business development strategy for Oxfam Novib may not need to be in place to allow for piloting and learning, even pilot business ventures must nevertheless be firmly designed based on adequate market research and a well-thought-out business model.

It is crucial to be very clear on the commercial and social objectives of the social business and to design the business model and value propositions accordingly. A theory of change may help in guiding the design process, especially in handling the delicate balance between social and financial objectives and in making underlying assumptions about social change more explicit. The INOW! model was deliberately experimental and may have had some shortcomings.

Adaptations and corrections to business planning are bound to happen. These will lead to learning. For this to happen, vigorous management and follow-up of business performance and results are required and necessary performance measurement tools and methods must be established from the beginning. This concerns financial, commercial, operational as well as social performance measurement (including collection of gender disaggregated data in relation to outcomes).

Likewise, the governance and management set-up must allow for flexibility and adaptability but also for effective and adequate decision-making processes, in response to (positive as well as negative) developments.

Programme planning (including social business start-up) must be realistic and pragmatic in terms of scope and timing. Operational phasing of start-up and growth cannot be completely predetermined, but needs to be adjusted as the business matures. Learning takes time.

Managing mission drift is critical in social business development. Social entrepreneurs and impact investors typically face challenges of mission drift such as in:

- Handling human resources (address limitations in capacities, skills, competencies);
- The need for multiple performance measures (see above);
- Managing multi-stakeholder dependencies and engagements;
- Handling market competitiveness;
- Adjusting mindset and organisational culture;
- Phasing of the start-up and growth of the business with changing roles and responsibilities;
- Flexibility and adaptability, but also decisiveness in management;
- Leadership challenges in terms of individual competencies and organisational capacities, but also in positioning and recognition of leadership.

Suggestions for grant makers

The previous sections demonstrated that INOW! brought ample learning to Oxfam Novib. These lessons are obviously mostly related to the approach that Oxfam Novib applied in this specific case, whereby Oxfam Novib was involved directly in the start-up, management and ownership of a social business. This, however, is just one of the possible approaches to social business development.

A key question here was: if a grant maker intends to further pursue a social business development agenda, what kind of approach should it follow?
The point is that different approaches are possible,[15] such as:

- To be directly involved in the establishment, management, and possibly ownership of social businesses, i.e. very much as in the INOW! model;
- To promote and support social business start-up (incubator) through various activities, ranging from offering access to start-up capital, business development support, strengthening networks of business support service providers, provision of market intelligence, promoting knowledge exchange, and many more;
- Support social business development after start-up through similar service delivery systems as mentioned in the previous point;
- Strengthen social business ecosystems, i.e. ensure that the necessary institutional, policy regulatory, finance and/or market settings are in place so that social businesses (as pre-start-ups, start-ups or in growth stage) can indeed develop and upscale their investments;
- Promote business models whereby for-profit companies are supported in developing a strong social orientation (such as strong corporate social responsibility, shared value creation or social business), or a mix of some of the above models.

Every option has its merits and its challenges. The choice of which social business model to pursue is highly contextual and very much depends on the vision and mission of the agency and social investor; the opportunities to create blended values; external factors that motivate (or demotivate) potential social entrepreneurs and investors; market conditions and opportunities to penetrate specific niches for blended value; and many other factors. The decision whether to pursue social business, and if so, which model to adopt, is a strategic choice for management and investors. After all, it is the mandate of management to decide on the course to follow. The judgement on an appropriate 'strategy fit' is in their hands. Lessons learned in the INOW! project may inform such decision-making.

15 It is worth noting that Oxfam has indeed worked with most of these approaches in other programme settings.

References

Bull, M. & Crampton, H. (2005), *Business practice in Social Enterprise*, Manchester, Metropolitan University Business School.

Dhaene, C., Kasumba , G. & De Greve, P. (2016), *Evaluation report Internet NOW!*. for Oxfam Novib & Nationale Postcode Loterij, ACE Europe, Mechelen.

Doherty. B., et al. (2009), *Management for Social Enterprise*, London, SAGE Publications Ltd.

Hoffmire, J. (2012) *Social Finance: Power Point presentation* Said Social Business School

Messelink, R. & Van der Spek, T. (2015), *Supporting social enterprises from pre-start-up to scalability: challenging the status-quo*, Context & ICS, Symposium Scaling Social Business in East Africa, Kampala.

Osterwalder, A. & Pigneur, Y. (2010), *Business Model Generation: A Handbook for Visionaries*, Game Changers, and Challengers, Hoboken, John Wiley & Sons.

Oxfam Novib (2013-2016), Various project-related documents of INOW! Project, The Hague, Oxfam Novib.

Van der Spek, T., Schreven, A-M & Van der Velden, F. (2013), *Leadership in social business*, Utrecht, Context, international cooperation (Contextual 11).

Van der Velden, F. & De Greve, P. (2016), *De stille revolutie van sociaal ondernemers*, MO Paper 99, Brussel, Wereldmediahuis vzw.

Van der Velden, F., (2011), Social business: a novel approach to socio-political change. In: Velden, van der F. (ed.) (2011) *New approaches to international development cooperation*. 2nd ed., Utrecht, Context, international cooperation, pp. 69 – 87.

CHAPTER VIII

Mentoring and coaching of social entrepreneurs

A UK perspective

Uday Thakkar[1]

Introduction

Mentoring has been considered a vital support mechanism to start, grow and make successful social enterprises in the United Kingdom (UK). The majority of support programmes and support agencies encourage and promote mentoring. The available evidence points to the fact that much of the mentoring support is not ideally structured with clear understanding of the roles, responsibilities and engagement terms for both parties to the process.

Though anecdotal evidence confirms that mentees benefit from the process and also that volunteer mentors improve their soft skills, there is little empirical evidence to demonstrate the impact of mentoring on social entrepreneurs in the long term. This is true of mentoring programmes that are part of the support programmes for small and medium enterprises and charities in the UK. A considerable amount of structured mentoring takes place which is not publicly acknowledged and once again anecdotal evidence indicates that the mentees benefit from being mentored.

This chapter is based on Red Ochre's own experience of participating in social enterprise support programmes for over 15 years and 'mentoring' over 1,000 social entrepreneurs; discussions and interviews with other mentors, mentees, programme managers and support organisations.

1 Uday Thakkar founded and leads Red Ochre. Red Ochre is a social enterprise that was launched in 2002. It is a specialist support organisation for social enterprises, community businesses, ethical and green businesses and not-for-profit organisations. Red Ochre operates primarily in the UK but has provided social enterprise support and workshops in sixteen other countries. Members of the team have won awards for their work, developed many tools and manuals for social entrepreneurs, contribute articles and regularly speak at conferences globally. Red Ochre has participated in over 25 social enterprise support programmes, delivering mentoring and training. Red Ochre has also trained over 100 consultants in social enterprise skills in five countries. Red Ochre is a panel consultant for the majority of social economy membership and support organisations in the UK and in particular Social Enterprise UK.

We have found some literature from the corporate social responsibility (CSR) sector but not much else that has been published and made available in the public realm to support our own evidence and reviews.

Mentoring and coaching

Mentoring and coaching are well-regarded mechanisms for improving management performance. Within the UK various social enterprise support networks, initiatives and programmes have enthusiastically encouraged the mentoring of founders and chief executives of social enterprises. There have been numerous support programmes since 2000 where mentoring support has been a key element of the support programme.

Social enterprise support agencies, such as Unltd and the School for Social Enterprise, have also consistently encouraged their award winners/students to participate in the mentoring process. We are aware that many individuals participate in mentoring arrangements, but there is currently no data available on the extent of this activity or on the results of the ongoing support. Where we discuss engagement and outcomes below, the information is based on our own experience and from interviews we have undertaken with mentors and mentees.

Coaching on the other hand, receives little or no publicity and there is a dearth of evidence and statistics on this activity as well. However, it is likely that the 'mentoring' activities include elements of coaching and our experience has been that all stakeholders regularly use either term to define the engagement. There are some published reports on mentoring in practice, but none that we have been able to find on coaching. For this reason, this chapter will refer primarily to mentoring activities.

Background

Social enterprise in the UK enjoyed considerable statutory support in its early history, from circa 2000 to 2010. Numerous support programmes for start-ups and scale-ups were launched. Funding for these came from local, regional and central government and often also from European Social Funding (ESF). The programmes required that participants received a set amount of mentoring support. These were discreet time allocations, with limited choices regarding mentors for mentees and the timing of the support.

Statutory support initiatives for social enterprise are now rare. There are a number of business-support programmes supported by European Regional Development Funding (ERDF) which include elements of support for social enterprise and may or may not include mentoring support.

Current support programmes for social enterprise are funded through a number of commercial players through their corporate social responsibility programmes. These programmes continue to offer mentoring as part of the support package. They retain the drawbacks of limited choice of mentors and proscribed times for meetings.

Founders and chief executives of social enterprises do also engage with mentors directly on a paid-for as well as a pro bono basis, but there is limited data available on this in terms of numbers, relevance, outcomes etc.

Mentoring input

Academic literature and best practice distinguish mentoring from coaching. In terms of the mentoring programmes that we have reviewed and participated in, 'mentoring' has been used as a generic term to encompass any activity that involved one-to-one engagement. It is rare that the mentoring activity is defined or explained. We have not come across any examples where there is a contract between mentors and mentees setting out what is expected from each party, the time input, termination etc. Consequently, the engagement is often driven by the mentee's immediate requirements or the mentor's expertise and experience.

Statutory funded programmes

For statutory ESF/ERDF programmes, there is a formal engagement process for mentors. They have to meet criteria that encompass experience and knowledge and possibly a track record in mentoring. There are no criteria for judging quality. Our experience with many of the early support programmes was that the quality of the mentors was variable with some mentors known to give incorrect legal or tax advice.

The mentors for these programmes are paid under a contract and are expected to deliver a set number of hours of mentoring per mentee. The sheer volume of the support programmes required the recruitment of many mentors who only had a tangential understanding of social enterprise or enterprise. Where they were there for their specialist skills, their impact on new start-ups and immature social enterprises was limited. For instance, a number of legal experts were able to assist with legal structures but struggled with guidance on strategy, finance, marketing and team recruitment. Specialist skills benefited the more mature social enterprises.

Unfortunately, as mentors get paid for their time input, some of the less professional mentors tended to keep the engagement with the mentee to themselves throughout the mentoring process, even when they were not necessarily the best support for the mentee. Programme managers struggling with ensuring a sufficient throughput of mentees through the programme battled with the logistics of allocating mentees to two or more mentors and so allowed the monopolisation of the mentee to go unchallenged.

This issue had improved considerably towards the latter period of the support programmes with programme managers contracting experienced mentors and social entrepreneurs and having a better understanding of the requirements of the mentees.

Start-ups

The majority of mentees had started or intended to start social enterprises because they were cause-motivated. That is, they wanted to make some social or environmental change. We defined these people as being relational players. The majority (>80%) had no or little managerial or entrepreneurial experience. There has been an appreciable increase in participants with some prior experience in management and enterprise now entering the social enterprise sector.

Those that are cause-motivated were reluctant to be challenged on the problem and solution that they were proposing. Often, they wanted to avoid measuring impact, despite being alerted to the importance of this evidence for funding and obtaining contracts. These people are driven by emotion and personal experience and are focused on their own solution without undertaking any objective marketing. For many mentors these areas were the ones that needed challenging and clearer definition prior to engaging on the areas that the mentees were demanding assistance on. The most common areas of assistance requested include:

- funding;
- strategy;
- business planning; and
- legal structures.

A majority (>90%) wanted help with (grant) funding. There was a reluctance to seek loan finance for two reasons: no prior experience of enterprise and the use of loan finance, and the reluctance to give personal commitments to secure the finance. The poor market research (including customer research and long-term income generation), strategy, business models and lack of financial understanding and reporting would in any case have made the majority of social enterprises ineligible for loan finance. This is despite the availability of loan finance from a growing body of specialist social investors.

We reiterate that the majority of participants did not understand the importance of impact measurement and reporting at this stage in their organisational life cycle.

Grant finance from local authorities, support organisations (Unltd) and grant-making trusts enabled many social enterprises to start up because there was a poor understanding by the funders of the requirements of sustainability. The majority of funded social enterprises have subsequently failed and the funders have become much better at supporting those that have a more sustainable approach. Mentoring success was therefore initially judged on the fact that the social enterprises accessed grant funding. Whereas for many the best advice should have been to close down or to consider operating as a charity if a market need could be identified.

A small percentage (10-15%) had identified a need but had an approach that was outcome-driven rather than linked to a sustainable business model. They, however, were prepared to be challenged and to modify the strategy and business model. Our limited review of these participants indicates that these mentees had a better than average survival rate and were still operational two to three years after the mentoring programme was completed.

One of the key benefits of participating in a mentoring programme is the introductions the mentor can make. Our own experience is that numerous mentees benefited through being introduced to partners, potential customers, potential employees and managers, specialists, funders and investors. However, this benefit is rarely mentioned by mentees and appears to be overlooked as being part of a successful mentoring engagement.

Scale-ups

There were fewer programmes supporting scale-ups. Many of the participants were from charities seeking to diversify income streams or considering establishing captive social enterprises.

The most important support requirements for the charity managers were:

- establishing a market need for the proposed service (marketing);
- understanding whether the service would be sustainable (income generation);
- establishing whether the service could generate sufficient profits to justify the parent charity investing in the service or the social enterprise;
- demonstrating entrepreneurial skills; and
- understanding of finance.

A series of separate initiatives were launched from approximately 2009 by the National Health Service, the probation service, local and regional authorities and some government departments to explore the possibility of 'spinning out' operational units as stand-alone social enterprises. The support programmes included assisting the management teams with the process and also with mentoring the senior management team.

The spin-offs from the statutory sectors' requirements were:

- business planning;
- entrepreneurial skills;
- negotiation skills and legal support to undertake the legal separation; and
- the financial function.

The majority of managers (>90%) had never had to worry about cash flow (they worked to an allocated budget), banking arrangements, supplier contracts such as IT, HR, legal and accountancy support, rent and lease arrangements.

The business opportunity was there but the managers lacked sufficient confidence and skills to set up new structures and make the new organisations financially self-sufficient. The main driver for many of them was the survival of the operating units into the future, as often the alternative was the closure of these units. They required transactional rather than relational support. The social outcomes were secondary, or taken as given, to the need to become financially sustainable as soon as possible.

Success is again difficult to measure. The majority of the larger and mid-size charities now have trading activities if not captive social enterprises and the support programmes will have had a positive impact on this. The spin-offs, if they happened, usually came with a contract guarantee for service delivery to the parent statutory body. There is anecdotal evidence (Red Ochre interviews with chief executives and senior management) that many of the managers benefited from the mentoring and guidance received to prepare them for the transition and in ensuring the longer-term viability of the social enterprise.

CSR-supported programmes

Initially the CSR-supported programmes were poorly designed and delivered. Mentors were recruited from within the middle management ranks of very large businesses. The mentors did not understand small businesses or the entrepreneurial culture, let alone social enterprise. The mentors were encouraged by the higher echelons to volunteer into these programmes and many did so not out of commitment, but because it was expected of them. They volunteered reluctantly and often with poor commitment and limited engagement. Mentors driven by performance targets and profit struggled to comprehend social outcome drivers and imperatives.

Mentors also struggled to comprehend the limited resources available to mentees. An example was where a mature social enterprise that wanted to replicate its successful model for rescuing and positively engaging with children at risk, approached a multinational insurance company for a marketing mentor. At the first meeting the mentor asked for the social enterprise's marketing budget. When informed it was limited to £5,000 he stormed out of the meeting claiming it was not possible to undertake anything useful if you did not have at least £5 million in the marketing budget. To that date the social enterprise had not spent any money directly on marketing, yet it had achieved considerable success.

The corporate mentors have moved on from this. They are better prepared and often their employers ensure that there is some pre-training and commitment, as the mentoring is offered on a voluntary basis. The corporates have also looked at the mentoring process as improving the mentors' soft skills, and it is hoped, strategic and entrepreneurial skills which will benefit the corporate's own development. The soft skills impact has been justified (see below), but there is little evidence that the engagements have benefited managers in other aspects.

Reviews of these programmes showed that the benefits claimed by mentees were limited to assistance with certain business areas only. Consistently, these programmes were more poorly rated then those that involved seasoned and knowledgeable mentors from the social enterprise or small business sector (Red Ochre reviews and data collection 2004 to 2017).

PricewaterhouseCoopers (PwC), a professional service firm, has been actively involved in supporting social enterprises for a number of years. PwC published a paper on outcomes from a social enterprise mentoring programme that they participated in.[2] The 16 mentees were participants of a programme of the School for Social Entrepreneurs (SSE). The background of the mentees was not disclosed but historically the intake for the SSE has been a mix of existing social entrepreneurs and those seeking to become social entrepreneurs. The mentors were from a variety of grades and from across different departments. There was no fixed agenda and meetings took place as required. Topics covered included:

- business plans;
- fundraising and revenue generation;
- growth and expansion; and
- strategy development.

The PwC paper reviewed the benefits to the mentors but did not mention benefits to the mentees.

The benefits to the mentors were mainly around soft skills, with the skills identified being ones that PwC encourages staff to develop, namely:

- development of self and others through coaching (confusion about whether this was mentoring or coaching);
- building and developing relationships;
- demonstrate courage and integrity;
- be open-minded, agile with change and practice;
- communicating with impact and empathy; and
- be curious, learn, share and innovate.

The impact on hard skills, defined by PwC as team success, project management, decision-making, planning and leadership, were not enhanced. It appears that PwC were using internal development matrices to an external programme where many of the Key Performance Indicators (KPIs) were not really being tested. This reflects our findings that the majority of mentoring programmes are poorly thought-through, structured and delivered. It is unclear whether the mentees benefited more from engaging with managers from large corporates than they would have from engagement with experienced social enterprise practitioners.

2 PricewaterhouseCoopers, 2011.

There is a major ongoing programme operated by Business in the Community[3] where social enterprises receive workshops from specialists, but mentoring from managers from a variety of large business such as BP (energy company), Freshfields (legal company), Interserve (design and construction), ASDA (supermarket chain) and ExterionMedia. A report published in 2015[4] gave considerable commentary on the benefits to the social enterprises but it was difficult to ascertain which benefits can be directly attributed to the mentoring part of the programme. The main benefits that the participants claimed they received from the mentor engagement were:

- improved understanding of risk management;
- business strategy; and
- marketing and brand development.

All of these areas are also part of the workshop programme and it may well be that the mentoring and workshops reinforced these skills developments. The mentees appear again to have benefited in developing their soft skills from the mentoring programme, the three skills most affected being:

- adapting communications styles;
- challenge effectively; and
- relationship building.

Unltd, which was established in 2000, has long encouraged its award winners to be mentored. It is reliant in this on CSR programmes and so the mentees face similar issues as mentioned above. Unltd provides a continuous support programme that assists award winners through their growth journey, so once again it may be difficult to separate the benefits of the mentoring process from the benefits of the overall support programme. We have not been able to access any other literature on mentoring programmes for social entrepreneurs.

Mentees

One of the barriers to creating an effective mentoring programme has been that for the mentees the offering has come at no cost. This applies to both the statutory programmes and the CSR programmes. For many participants this has led to a diminished perception of the value of the mentoring engagement. As a consequence, a number of participants missed appointments or did not follow up on agreed action points.

The poor engagement of between 10-15% of participants tended to involve those that had poorly developed strategies and business plans and were not happy to be challenged about this, or those that had such conviction in their own abilities that they were dismissive of the mentors' input. Our questioning of other mentors and programme managers reinforced our own findings that over 90% of cases of those that had total

3 Ref. https://www.bitc.org.uk/campaigns-programmes/communities/arc – the ARC programme.

4 ARC 2015 impact report.

self-belief were more likely to fail because of their refusal to engage in any meaningful way with individual mentors or the mentoring programme. There was no justification to their self-belief. The self-belief was often a cover for the absence of knowledge, skills and the willingness to learn – fatal qualities for any potential entrepreneur.

As the programmes were concerned with maximising the numbers of potential/existing social entrepreneurs (with rapid throughput into and exit out of the programmes) it has proved difficult to follow up with mentees in any meaningful way as to the benefits, if any, that they received from the mentoring. Later programmes measured success on the number of new jobs created (e.g. the ARC programme). Undoubtedly the mentoring programme assisted, but again no direct link can be ascertained between the mentoring and job creation.

The ones that were successful in launching or scaling up their social enterprises tended to keep in touch intermittently requesting follow-up meetings. They were also the participants who derived the most from the initial mentoring, as they ensured that they obtained the maximum support in the areas where they were weak. This has perpetuated the belief that on the whole the mentoring process does benefit the mentees.

From the mentees that did keep up contact with mentors and reverted to them on a regular basis, the areas that they expressed the greatest derived benefit were:
strategy;
- business modelling;
- business planning;
- impact measurement;
- fundraising/finance;
- trading/income generation/sustainability;
- developing personal leadership and management skills;
- recruitment and team building; and
- operations and systems development.

In our observation with supporting start-up social enterprises in the UK and many other countries, there are a number of areas in which many (60-75%) of social enterprises are weak:
- Market analysis – is there a real problem and have you got a solution that meets the requirements of the majority of stakeholders in an efficient and effective way?
- Impact measurement – knowing what it is that you want to change, how you will do it and how you will know that you are bringing about the change and finally how you will report it.
- Finance – very poor financial understanding, so there is poor understanding of funding requirements, budgets, future cash requirements, pricing and cost control.

- Managing growing teams – poor understanding of skills requirements, recruitment, delegation and management.
- Operating systems – creating structures and information flows.

The scale-ups have the following issues:
- sustainability – income generation beyond the immediate (6 months – 18 months);
- understanding of finance;
- marketing – poor trend analysis, customer focus and customer diversification;
- succession planning; and
- poor governance.

Both types of social entrepreneurs are known to have benefited considerably from the contacts and networks facilitated by mentors. Yet this is a benefit that is rarely if at all mentioned by the mentees.

Direct mentoring/coaching

Unstructured mentoring/coaching of social entrepreneurs takes place infrequently. This is inevitably because of the cost and to a lesser extent the time commitment. The monetary cost consideration means that it is usually only the chief executive, though occasionally members of the senior management team of a social enterprise who participate in this activity.

Our experience indicates that the trigger for seeking mentoring assistance is event-related. Common reasons for engaging a mentor are:
- strategic re-evaluation of the social enterprise;
- income diversification/potential loss of major contract;
- exploring investment opportunities (to drive growth/seize potential opportunities);
- financial problems;
- existential crisis (potential closure);
- impending promotion; and
- governance (problems with chair and/or board).

Many of these topics are subsets of strategic change.

Invariably the engagement is triggered by the mentee approaching the mentor (through a personal recommendation). In a few cases, the referrer will ask the mentor to contact the potential mentee.

Given the driver for engagement, which is assistance with navigating major change, implementing change or confronting change, and given the urgency associated with the event, the engagements are more in the nature of coaching than mentoring (as described for the structured engagements discussed in this chapter).

The engagement has a finite life, usually between four to eight sessions. The sessions are driven by the mentees' requirements. They are initially at short intervals and intensive. A few further sessions may take place – these are more spread out and are more in the nature of a review of progress and for minor iterations of the agreed action plan.

As the relationship is to run over a number of sessions and over a period of weeks, there is a necessity to formalise the engagement. Many mentors have templated agreements that can be easily altered to meet individual requirements. In our experience, the mentees usually ask for a very simple agreement that sets out the roles and responsibilities of each party as well as the rules governing information exchange. The cost and payment schedules are also agreed on. The mentor/coach has to ensure that the relationship does not cause the mentor to be regarded as a shadow director. This has legal implications, particularly when dealing with investment or where the social enterprise is in a financially vulnerable state. The support should allow the mentor to explore suggestions and decide on a course of action rather than being directive.

The engagement proceeds in a well-recognised cycle. Initially the mentee is reluctant to be open about the extent of the personal or organisational problems. A combination of astute questioning by the mentor (based on experience) as well as an increase in trust from the mentee leads to better transparency of the problems. It also allows the mentor to help the mentee objectively prioritise the solutions.

The sessions develop a close and intense partnership, often with Skype or phone conversations to supplement face-to-face sessions. In many cases, once the agreed actions have been implemented there is a gradual wind-down in intensity and disengagement from the openness by the mentees. The mentoring sessions are usually terminated by the mentee. Approximately a third of mentoring engagements are terminated by the mentor due to a decrease in positive and constructive engagement. Some mentees will ask for a few follow-up sessions at monthly or fortnightly breaks as they still perceive that value can be gained from the mentoring sessions.

Our own research indicates that a very small proportion of former mentees will contact the mentor after a break of two to three years. Again, the driver is event-based and these sessions are of a very short duration. Mentees will however refer other potential mentees.

Mentees have indicated when prompted that they have chosen to limit the time with mentors for two major reasons, firstly having to justify the cost and secondly (for a reasonably large number) the embarrassment of having to seek assistance to tackle a perceived crisis. This is regarded as a failure of leadership and the mentoring assistance is often kept hidden except with their most trusted peers.

What all but a very small minority of mentees agree on is that the mentoring experience has been positive. It has improved skills and most importantly increased confidence in their own abilities, which is sometimes cited as a reason not to continue with the mentoring sessions. The other positive is that mentoring from someone with the appropriate personal experience of having managed a social enterprise, or commercial enterprise, is of greater benefit than assistance from managers of large corporations who experientially cannot empathise with the particular situation and do not have the experience to identify appropriate solutions.

Conclusion

There is anecdotal evidence that social entrepreneurs do benefit from mentoring (this has been a consistent finding in end of project reviews, follow-ups and interviews immediately after and at timed intervals after the completion of various support programmes).

The more targeted the match and the availability of appropriate mentors, the more likely it is that this results in successful outcomes, even if at this stage the measure is subjective or tangential. The way support programmes are structured – to meet political or CSR targets where numbers of participants engaged with takes precedence – makes it difficult to measure the true benefit of the mentoring process.

The evidence of outcomes for mentees who engage directly with mentors has been derived through evaluations, interviews and questionnaires; there does not appear to be any empirical research available. The mentees on the whole found the mentoring process to be beneficial as it assisted them to work through event-based problems. The outcomes were enhanced if the mentor had a similar background and a great deal more experience in managing social enterprises or small businesses.

References

PricewaterhouseCoopers (2011), *Corporate Sustainability Lessons Learned - The business benefits of mentoring Social Entrepreneurs*, UK PricewaterhouseCoopers.

CHAPTER IX

Intrapreneurship

The case of SOS Children's Villages

David Katzlinger[1]

Introduction: Intrapreneurship

In the preceding chapters, attention has been paid to social business as a transformative approach to facilitating the emergence of a social and solidarity economy. Special attention has been given to the rationale of such an approach, characteristics of a social business, and specific approaches and methods – such as leadership in social business development, business performance measurement, and mentoring of social entrepreneurs.

This chapter presents a slightly different perspective. Today, both in the corporate as well as the development sector, companies and organisations are extremely large, which means it is not always necessary to initiate a new business in order to manifest and entrepreneurial spirit as this can be done within existing organisations. Furthermore, those who manifest their entrepreneurial capacities in an existing company bring about innovation from within.[2] This is called intrapreneurship: 'successful adaptation of entrepreneurial attitudes and strategies inside of a bureaucratic organisation and/or implementation of start-up practices within a large organisation producing valued innovation.'[3]

People involved in these activities cannot be called entrepreneurs in the proper sense of the word. Rather, they are specialists with exceptional training, who are able to use the knowledge they have accumulated in order to innovate successfully. Such people are called social intrapreneurs.[4] For instance, Guy Kawasaki was an early employee at

1 This chapter is mainly based on the learning document that was written by staff members of Context, international cooperation in 2015 on the basis of interactions and interviews with SOS staff members and SOS partner organisations about the experiences of SOS Children's Villages and related organisations with regard to civic driven change and social business. (Ref. De Greve et al. 2015.) Pol De Greve, Anthony Gyamfi, Mark Nwakaudu, Annemarie Ojunga, Margherita Scazza, Titus van der Spek, Stefan van der Swaluw, Fons van der Velden were among those who participated in this endeavour. The text was updated by David Katzlinger in collaboration with Fons van der Velden.

2 Cadar & Badulescu, 2015.

3 https://www.techchange.org/2013/09/30/what-is-intrapreneurship/

4 Grayson, McLaren & Spitzeck, 2014.

Apple and a 'chief evangelist' at the company for years. With his 2004 book The Art of the Start, Kawasaki began making direct references to intrapreneurs and has recently become a more vocal advocate on the subject. He wrote:

> There are lots of guys and gals inside established companies who are as innovative and revolutionary as their bootstrapping, soy-sauce-and-rice-subsisting, external entrepreneur counterparts. This is for these brave souls who face a different kind of reality and must practice the art of entrepreneurship inside a company—or intrapreneurship'.[5] In literature, intrapreneurship has been conceptualised as a cause of innovativeness, competitiveness and organisational renewal.[6]

SOS Children's Villages

What does it take to change in order to foster change within entrenched organisations? What does it take to change existing organisations from within? This chapter describes the case of SOS Children's Villages International (SOS CVI).

SOS CV International is a federation of independent SOS Children's Villages Associations operating in 135 countries and territories.[7] When children can no longer live with their families, SOS Children's Villages Federation gives them the support they need by providing quality alternative care; and when families are at risk of separation, it provides family strengthening services to prevent loss of care. Such care programmes transform the lives of close to 600,000 children and youth every year. Through educational programmes in over 250 kindergartens, schools and vocational training centres more than 150,000 children and youth are being skilled to succeed in life. Sixty-four medical centres, 38 social centres and emergency response programmes act wherever the need occurs, with the organisation well placed to service more than one million people with tailored support in broad-spectrum distress. Lifesaving and life-transforming medical services are delivered approximately 2 million times every year.

In 2017 the Federation and its members partnered with public and private actors to leverage the resources entrusted to the organisation into a programme investment worth more than €1.2-bn. Approximately 40,000 staff are running 2,500 programmes in all regions of the world in order to support realising the frameworks of the UN Convention of the Rights of the Child, the UN Guidelines for the Alternative Care of Children and Sustainable Development Goals.[8]

Exploration of civic driven change and social business

In 2009 the Dutch Ministry of Foreign Affairs invited civil society organisations to propose large social innovation programmes, geared at serving the Millennium Development

5 July 2013 blog post on LinkedIn on 'The Art of Intrapreneurship'.
6 Koleva & Azam Roomi, 2015.
7 Figures in this paragraph are taken from the SOS Children's Villages International Annual Report 2017.
8 In particular the following SDGs: SDG 1 'no poverty'; SDG 4 'quality education,'; SDG 8 'decent work and economic growth'; SDG10 'reduced inequalities and SDG 16 'peace, justice and strong institutions'.

Goals. One of the preconditions was that such programmes should be established through alliances between various Non-Governmental Development Organisations (NGDOs). SOS Children's Villages the Netherlands joined forces with three other organisations: ICS (Investing in Children and their Societies), Wilde Ganzen (accompanying local initiatives in setting up support networks abroad) and Wereldkinderen (a Dutch development organisation moving from international adoption to other forms of alternative care). They jointly organised the Together4Change (T4C) Alliance. The organisations shared the desire to explore civic driven change (CDC) as an approach to increase the effectiveness of development cooperation initiatives.[9] Within the SOS Children's Villages Federation, a pilot programme was started in Ghana, Kenya and Nigeria.

Box IX.1: Civic driven change: Changing the way we see change

CDC offers a novel lens to look at social change as the result of self-driven actions by citizens, rather than by states or markets. Development and social change are no longer perceived as linear processes that can be engineered from outside but rather as complex and universal phenomena that must emerge from within society.

A CDC approach emphasises the importance of co-creation by stakeholders and of organising communities, rather than mobilising them. Consequently, it supports communities to develop into key change agents that drive their own processes of development, set their own goals and as much as possible rely on local resources as opposed to external resource provision.

Furthermore, CDC helps to overcome the North-South dichotomy by promoting a more integrated concept of development, whereby social change is generated through civic energy operating across all sectors of society (state, market, family and civil society).

A CDC approach for SOS Children's Villages meant inviting communities to define and take responsibility for the change they want to bring about for child well-being, thereby shifting the role of International Non-Governmental Development Organisations (INGDOs), such as SOS CV from that of implementers to facilitators of the change processes. This was of particular interest to SOS CV, which had already started increasing its preventive work with communities, expanding from its curative work in their traditional intervention, i.e. the SOS Children's Villages, through which they implement the UN Guidelines for Alternative Care.

While the Together4Change Alliance partners were applying the CDC approach in their everyday practice in countries in Africa and Asia, they slowly but steadily realised that the economic dimension of child and family well-being and change processes in general, were underrepresented in the discourse at conceptual and operational level: livelihood, access to productive assets, employment and income had not been receiving sufficient attention. This triggered interest in a social business approach to change processes: the T4C partners recognised that all organisations have the potential to generate a blend

9 Fowler & Biekart 2008; Fowler & Biekart, 2013.

of economic, social and environmental value. Most for-profit corporations, however, have historically underperformed socially and environmentally and most non-profit organisations (such as SOS CV) have underperformed economically.

Box IX.2: What is social business?[10]

An 'ideal' social business has the following ten characteristics:

1. Its primary purpose is systematic social and political change;
2. It operates through the market;
3. It is financially sustainable;
4. It operates in multi-actor environments and manages interests of various groups in the social power equation;
5. It is run by a social entrepreneur;
6. It operates on the basis of social (patient) capital, provided by social investors who are driven by a clear vision on solving societal issues and a dedicated worldview;
7. It is socially accountable, as it accounts for what has been achieved beyond financial returns;
8. It has active citizen involvement in all stages;
9. It engages in innovation;
10. It engages in lobby and advocacy, to promote awareness, create a conducive environment and support systemic changes.

Over time, the T4C partners came to realise that – in the words of Nobel Prize laureate Mohammad Yunus:

> The future of the world lies in the hands of these market-based social entrepreneurs. We cannot combat poverty within the orthodoxy of capitalism practiced today. Economic theory has not provided us with any alternative to this familiar model but I argue that we can create a powerful alternative: a social consciousness-driven private sector, created by social entrepreneurs.[11]

SOS CV staff members in Ghana, Kenya and Nigeria and at the SOS CV headquarters in Innsbruck, as well as staff members of other T4C Alliance members (especially ICS), consultants, academics and policy makers who collaborated in the T4C programme, then engaged in a process of co-creation. The notion emerged that it is not so much about needing to 'think outside the box' - there is a need to 'shape a new box'. These practitioners realised that CDC is in fact a crosscutting issue that needs to be integrated and mainstreamed in other approaches to change processes, and that social entrepreneurship may be one of these new approaches to international solidarity.

Such an approach is distinctly different from 'traditional', 'dominant' development approaches in terms of putting people first. It forces practitioners to acknowledge that change processes are complex, non-linear affairs and that the traditional North-South dichotomy is no longer helpful. We live in a highly interconnected 'One World' (Peter

---

10 The ten characteristics of a social business are further explained in Chapter II of this volume.

11 Yunus, 2010.

Singer).[12] The world can only become a better place through processes of co-creation; and home-grown solutions are most probably the best. Furthermore, the emphasis is on financial and economic issues: job creation, enhancement of income and sustainable development in an attempt to take back the economy – as described in the Introduction of this volume.

Box IX.3: The maize and rice mill in Kaduna, Ghana

One of the social businesses that have emerged with the support of SOS is a maize and rice mill in Kaduna, Ghana. The business follows a commercial market-based social business model, providing milling services to the community. The mill was constructed in 2014. Commercial operations are satisfactory so far, with maize milling already reaching a level of turnover ahead of projections. Rice milling results are modest, so far. Initial performance targets are still within reach, but require some technical adaptations (to process the supply of non-parboiled rice) and strong managerial efforts to be achieved.

Community engagement is realised through ownership by a community-based organisation. Social return is realised through generating employment opportunities for community members, providing access to affordable milling services for households, improving access to quality staple food (maize meal) and improving nutrition and dietary diversity at household level. Potential profit will be reinvested in the community.

Why are civic driven change and social business relevant for SOS CV?

When using civic driven change and social business, the scope for fostering socio-political and economic change becomes more nuanced; agencies must 'navigate complexity' and deal with unpredictable developments. They can no longer steer development, but instead they must play a facilitating role. The emphasis lies on organising people to claim their rights and fulfil their responsibilities, and on establishing changes in the social and economic domain. The focus is therefore not only on project implementation at child, family and community level, but also on making a contribution to systemic change. It can be noted that, by 2018, modalities of official development assistance were beginning to provide elements for facilitating social entrepreneurial approaches to development. Still, the majority of these modalities could do more to foster 'eye level partnerships'[13] between actors from various societal sectors, such as civil society and private enterprises.

Many changes that occurred in the past nine years, in respect of experimenting with and replicating a CDC and social business approach, had not been anticipated at the community level, the organisational level nor within organisational practices. Within the SOS Children's Villages programmes, an emergence of civic driven change and social business influence can be observed, beyond the levels that were originally expected. Currently, the organisation is ready to build on the learnings from the past.

12 Singer, 2002.

13 Partnerships characterised by values such as equality, mutuality and reciprocity.

This can clearly be seen in SOS CV's latest strategic plans, which allow for potential replication of the approach, objectives and methodology of the T4C programme in the 135 countries and territories where the Federation is active, and therefore has the potential to dramatically increase the impact initially agreed upon. The organisation has shifted much of its aid-induced operation[14] towards more locally-driven projects, moving away from traditional handouts towards modern social work with larger impact objectives that support communities to become more child and family friendly and independent.

Box IX.4: From mobilising to organising

'The emphasis shifted from mobilising communities towards organising communities. This was an important paradigm shift. Organising people means bringing people together, helping them to organise collaboration and making sure that once together they are able to create a community structure. This then constitutes a foundation for them to start looking at and addressing other issues that they themselves identify. The difference from before was that it became an inclusive process, i.e. the entire community was brought in and participated'.
Mark Nwakaudu, staff member SOS Nigeria

Piloting and mainstreaming civic driven change and social business

Since 2009, various trainings, workshops and support services have been developed and implemented by SOS CV in collaboration with the T4C Alliance members and Context, international cooperation. The aim was to explore the feasibility and viability of a 'CDC-ish' approach and social business principles within the specific programme activities of SOS CV in three countries: Ghana, Nigeria and Kenya.

It is obvious that such an approach has radical implications, not only for the 'doing' (programmes) of organisations that have the ambition to contribute to pro-poor change processes, but also for the 'being', i.e. organisational characteristics (shared values, strategy, systems, structure, style and leadership), and for their network of relationships. Hence, during the course of the programme implementation, it became clear that the introduction of civic driven change and social business had inevitable consequences for SOS CV as an institution.

14 Which may also be labelled as 'externally', 'donor', 'top-down' or expert-driven operations, depending on context.

Box IX.5: Implications of CDC and social business for SOS Children's Villages[15]

1. Strategic clarity and its direction
2. Mindset change
3. Contextualisation
4. Fostering ownership from within
5. Re-examining organisational culture and leadership
6. A multi-model approach of development
7. The degree of facilitation may vary
8. Ensuring the right competencies are in place
9. Exploring and using local resources
10. Reconsidering communication and M&E systems
11. Accessing social investment capital for SB development
12. Reflecting on change in structures, systems & processes
13. Packaging the transformation process
14. Considering SOS CV's role in lobby and advocacy
15. Change takes time

For SOS CV to adopt a CDC and social business approach meant, first and foremost, letting go of programme control. Putting people in charge of defining the change they want to achieve to enable their community to realise the rights of the child, means a shift from delivering services towards facilitating the realisation of results by the local community. The T4C programme was able to allow for some room to experiment with locally-driven interventions. Accommodating such programmatic flexibility within a rigorous framework of operational control and accountability, was by no means an easy process. Trust between staff and community workers, volunteers and local change makers had to be built. At all levels of the organisation, management was facing challenges, as guidelines and procedures did not always cater for unforeseen or unprecedented programme development. Allowing space for experimentation creativity does carry some risk, and the management of these risks needed to happen in a professional manner that could withstand scrutiny by international audit standards.

A decade after the CDC and social business approach was first conceptualised within SOS CV, a multidimensional organisational change has started to materialise. Result areas are being redefined from outputs at the level of facilities (such as schools, health facilities and hospitals) towards social-change results (such as reduction of child abuse; improvement with regard to gender issues, youth employability programmes, policy development support for alternative care). Furthermore, the whole organisation is starting to fully mainstream a related management approach; the policy landscape of the organisation has reached an unprecedented level of universality and the strategic orientation of SOS CV has now embraced international frameworks (such as the UN Convention of the Rights of the Child, the UN Guidelines for the alternative Care of Children and the UN Sustainable Development Goals). The CDC drive has triggered the formation of staff councils across several levels of the organisation, stimulating

15 Ref. De Greve et al, 2015: 17 – 30.

the participation of co-workers in many parts of the world in the operational and entrepreneurial orientation of the organisation. The adoption of market-based solutions to societal challenges and a more positive attitude that focuses on realisation of opportunities rather than seeing things in terms of problems are emerging phenomena in the SOS CV programme landscape. This change of emphasis has derived much of its inspiration and energy from the five years of T4C experimentation and the subsequent learnings from 2010-2015.

Box IX.6: Cassava-processing Owu-Ijebu Nigeria

One of the major deliverables of the Family Strengthening Programmes of SOS is to support families to become self-reliant in the care of their children. The cassava-processing project is a social business initiative of SOS Children's Villages Nigeria under its Family Strengthening Programme, and is managed as a group income-generating activity. The overall goal of the project is improving and leveraging the rural economy by driving innovations in agri-food value chains through cassava-processing in combination with animal husbandry (piggery). The ultimate aims are to reduce poverty, increase food security and reduce unemployment. Five acres of land within the SOS village Owu-Ijebu are cultivated with cassava, which is then processed into garri (cassava flakes) at the factory. Cassava waste is used as fodder for the pigs, while piggery waste is used as manure on the farm.

Objectives and beneficiaries:
Create employment opportunities for 5 caregivers and 10 community members;
Improve household income for 30 caregivers;
Improve savings culture among caregivers;
Improve food security of caregivers' families.

The caregivers were supported to form a cooperative group (Isokan Agric Cooperative Society) with a membership of 30 caregivers. The project encourages caregivers to save for future re-investment and security. The management is done by a project management committee which is made up of representatives from SOS CV, FCDI (partner CSO) and Isokan Agric Cooperative Society. The project pays a monthly allowance to staff working at the piggery. Provision is made for a reward system for cooperative members who voluntarily work in the garri factory and the farm. SOS Children's Village's investment in the project is recouped in two years.

Profit sharing:
- 20% of yearly income is paid to SOS to offset the investment cost;
- 40% of the yearly income is paid into an endowment fund for care of vulnerable children in the community, managed by CFDI;
- 20% of yearly income is set aside for re-investment;
- 20% of yearly income is shared by members as dividend.

Enablers, hindrances and lessons learned

The Together4Change programme within SOS CV dedicated 7.5% of the entire programme budget to developing the capacity of the SOS CV federal secretariat and its shared services department. This department provides specialised services such as capacity development, finance management, development of standards, maintenance of integrity and compliance support. The programme included theoretical and practical workshops on civic driven change and social business throughout the programme period, which resulted in preparing the ground for scaling up the approach and objectives of the T4C programme far beyond the span of this programme. The achievements of the T4C Alliance for SOS CV global operations will only become clear in the years to come. The real impact of the investment by the Dutch tax payers starts to become visible through replications of the approach in programmes of SOS in other countries (such as Burundi and the Democratic Republic of Congo),[16] and within the general approaches of SOS CV. The organisation is currently reviewing its operational activities worldwide. Stronger local ownership is being sought, broader impact solutions are supported, and sustainable local funding bases are successfully being built, particularly through the organisations' 'sustainable path' objective, which aims to make national SOS Associations financially self-reliant within an agreed number of years.

Social business is a practice-oriented approach that obviates CDC's limited focus on economic development and especially livelihood. Civic driven change reminds us that communities and citizens should be involved in every step of the development of a social venture – as producers, consumers and guardians of the natural environment.

So far, SOS CV has been the largest organisation ever to engage in piloting CDC and social business throughout their systems. The T4C programme represented approximately 3% of the annual turn-over, but demanded high flexibility in every dimension from SOS as an institution. Accommodating these requirements was a formidable challenge to the organisation and its operational practices. It meant letting go of programmatic control, which included a shift in power from global North to South. The management can only be congratulated for having allowed space for this experiment. The staff, across all levels of the organisation, showed the courage to engage their superiors in programme development beyond agreed work plans, strategies and habits.

In this particular case, CDC originally was an externally-induced programme innovation that raised many questions within the project teams in SOS CV. At first everybody thought that SOS CV would now run 'T4C programmes' instead of their community intervention 'Family Strengthening Programme'. Only through intensive training, reflection and familiarisation curricula about civic driven change and social business, did SOS staff members start realising that the time had come to change from delivering a predefined set of social work interventions to facilitating solutions defined by the local population themselves. This entailed acquisition of new skill sets, as social workers do not normally possess the skills of a business developer. It is also not in everybody's nature to become an entrepreneur, but unleashing the energy and creativity that lies within members of every community, including the less privileged ones, to turn their challenges into opportunities was a strong accelerator of programmatic change.

16 Initiated by SOS Burundi and DR Congo in collaboration with SOS Belgium and with the support of the Government of Belgium through the Belgian Development Directorate (DGD).

Running the new approach in three different African countries has allowed for the observation of different coping mechanisms and different speeds of process change, as well as various degrees of success over time. Whereas colleagues in one country initially struggled to adopt a civic driven change and social business approach and could only demonstrate limited project progress, they made up for this initial weakness by showing the most beautiful and successful programme innovations of the whole project. Other regions performed diametrically differently and had an easy start but faced bigger challenges in the middle of the project period. All in all, it was dedicated programme staff in the communities (who did not give up when they started hitting the wrong staff-beneficiary ratios) combined with people in middle management (who demonstrated courage when projected budget burn rates would not realise as per rigid guidelines) who made the project into a success. Determination of project management to deliver over the full five-year project period and the readiness of top management to adopt new programme strategies and to develop high-level organisational guidelines, contributed immensely to making the programme a success. The results constitute a lasting transformative effect for programme participants, their communities, families and for SOS Children's Villages as a whole.

References

Agoada J. and Estevez, J. (2013), *What is intrapreneurship*, September 30. (*https://www.techchange.org/2013/09/30/what-is-intrapreneurship/*)

Berkhout, R., de Koster, K., Kieboom, M., Pieper, I., Fernando, U., Ruijmschoot, L. (2011) *Civic Driven Change: synthesising implications for policy and practice*, Utrecht, DPRN.

Biekart K., Fowler, A. (2012), *Civic Driven Change: An update on the basics*, ISS, The Hague, the Netherlands.

Biekart K., Fowler, A. (2008), *Introducing Civic-Driven Change*, ISS-CDC (Policy Brief #1), October, ISS, The Hague, the Netherlands.

Cadar O. & Badulescu, D. (2015), Entrepreneur, Entrepreneurship and intrapreneurship, A literature review, *The Annals of the University of Oradea*, Economic Sciences XXIV (2):658-664·December.

De Graaff, D., Rijneveld, W., Tijkotte, E., 2014. *"It takes a community to strengthen a family". Synthesis of evaluations of Family Strengthening Program in Ghana, Kenya and Nigeria*. SOS Kinderdorpen Nederland – Avance. Amsterdam, the Netherlands.

De Graaff, D., Rijneveld, W., Tijkotte, E., 2015. *"It takes a community to strengthen a family". Ten rules of thumb for Family Strengthening Programmes*. SOS Kinderdorpen Nederland – Avance. Amsterdam, the Netherlands.

De Greve, P., Van der Velden, F., Scazza, M. & Van der Spek, T. (2015), *Moving forward with Civic Driven Change and social Business*, Innsbruck/Utrecht, SOS Children's Villages International/Context, international cooperation

Fowler, A. & Biekart, K. eds. (2008), *Civic Driven Change; Citizen's Imagination in Action*, The Hague, Institute of Social Studies.

Fowler, A. & Biekart, K. (2013), Relocating Civil Society in a Politics of Civic-Driven Change, *Development Policy Review*, 2013, 31 (4), pp. 463 – 483.

Grayson D., McLaren, M. & Spitzeck, H. (2014), *Social intrapreneurism and all that jazz: How business innovators are helping to build a more sustainable world*, London, Routledge.

Koleva, P. & Azam Roomi, M. (2015), Social Intrapreneurism and All That Jazz, How business innovators are helping to build a more sustainable world, *Society and Business Review*, Vol. 10, No. 2, 2015 pp. 194 – 199.

Singer, P. (2002), *One world; The ethics of globalization*, Yale, Tale University Press.

Van der Velden, F., 2011. Social business: a novel approach to socio-political change? In *New approaches to development cooperation*. Context, international cooperation. Utrecht, the Netherlands.

Yunus, M. (2010), *Building Social Business; The new Kind of Capitalism that Serves Humanity's Most Pressing Needs*, New York, Public Affairs.

Websites

https://www.iss.nl/en/research/research-projects/civic-driven-change

https://www.sos-childrensvillages.org/

Box IX.7: Dialogue between traditional development and social business[17]

This poem is based on a conversation between Traditional Development (TD) and Social Business (SB).

By Chantel Sharon Kennedy

TD: I come into your community
Assuming what you need
That education is a problem
And that I know what's best for you indeed

SB: See
I come from the community
I'm part of the speed
I do not work on assumptions
Cause I am part of that need

TD: See
I get the money
I know that my aim is on social issues
I can always give you a tissue

SB: Whoow whoow whoow!
The aim is more than just a financial gain
It is to sustain the environment,
The blended values that you cannot see
So please keep your tissue for another social issue

TD: So where do you get your funding?

17 This poem was written by Chantel Sharon Kennedy and presented as a rap during the module about social business and social and solidarity economy of the diploma course of Training for Transformation in Kleinmond (South Africa) March 2018. (The module was facilitated by Jumana Eltigani (Training for Transformation) and Fons van der Velden (Context, international cooperation).

SB: See without money your projects end
Leaving the people in the mist of their storms
But me, I'm independent
I live on sustainability
For you the funder determines your aim
But for me, my funding does not restrict me in any way
I determine what I bring to the floor
What I want to explore

TD: Well, what's wrong being driven by funding?

SB: And that's your biggest mistake
Your heart should play the biggest part
Curiosity, the will to change

TD: You know what Social Business, just stop!
Cause I've got great leadership skills
No teamwork needed
I think for the people
And have my restrictions

SB: Leadership skills? Really?
It's an individual thing
It's about taking risks
Being flexible, creative
Bringing new ideas, a new way of thinking
But most importantly, involving the community

TD: And how can you measure that?
I educate 50 people in one day on Human Rights
The change is visible over 10 years

SB: Really?
The change I see is in the community jives
The well-being, and unemployment taking a hike
It does not come easily
But in slow motion you can see their smiles

And that's the conclusion of this illusion!

CHAPTER X

Social business

A new mode of production?

Zunaid Moolla & Fons van der Velden[1]

'We have two choices. We can be pessimistic, give up, and help ensure that the worst will happen. Or we can be optimistic, grasp opportunities that surely exist, and maybe help make the world a better place. Not much of a choice'.

NOAM CHOMSKY[2]

Introduction

In the preceding chapters a few case descriptions of social businesses and outcomes of action research with regard to social business have been presented. In the Introduction to this volume and the second chapter some conceptual issues have been dealt with. The main message of this book is that social business is a radical transformative approach to fostering the emergence of a social and solidarity economy. Furthermore, it is argued that it is useful to come up with very practical experiments and examples that provide insights into the fundamental transition processes; and that such an approach needs to be enabled through combined and interrelated local and global action.

The conceptual notions offered in the Introduction and Chapter II are important in order to demarcate the difference between the transformative agenda of a social business approach to change processes and the a-political, technocratic approaches – such as corporate social responsibility, shared value creation and social enterprise – which promote only marginal changes within the boundaries of the dominant, neo-liberal development paradigm.

However, the concepts of social business and a social and solidarity economy are still a 'work in progress'. They are heavily constrained by structural contexts and the absence of comprehensive conceptual and political frameworks. In order to contribute to the

1 The authors want to express their gratitude to Hans Beerends, Pradeep Esteves, Ted van Hees and Jyotsna Roy for reviewing an earlier version of this text.

2 Chomsky, 2017: 196.

further development of these concepts, this concluding chapter presents an attempt to explore the degree to which a social business approach to change processes can contribute to systemic change in terms of the emergence of a new mode of production, i.e. a social and solidarity economy.

The approach to political economy of Karl Marx and neo-Marxists is taken as an entry point, as Marx's conceptual framework of the capitalist mode of production offers a comprehensive, fundamental and adequate framework for exploration.

The function of profit in capitalism

Over the past 50 years capitalism has become stronger. Yes, there have been many body blows and crises during this period. And yes, the grounds on which it stands are wobbly but there are no signs of its imminent collapse. There are now fewer countries with alternative economic systems in place. With the rise of China and India as unambiguous capitalist systems, the countries of the world, it seems, are firmly fixed into the capitalist orbit.

What, if anything, does this say about the future of the capitalist system? That it will get stronger? Possibly, but perhaps also more unstable if its underbelly is examined. As has been indicated in the Introduction and Chapter II, inequality has increased as accumulation has proceeded. Piketty's data leaves no doubt about that. Unemployment is critically high in most of the less-industrialised countries. Even in countries belonging to the OECD, the 'new normal' for the rate of unemployment averages 6%.[3] As the fourth industrial revolution looms, and artificial intelligence enters the realm of production, this is not likely to improve. As if none of this is bad enough, the earth's natural systems are suffocating under the relentless drive for profits. A system of production thus exists which simultaneously creates wealth and misery; provides an array of new products while denuding the natural environment. Furthermore, democracy is in crisis, not only in a number of low- and medium-income countries, but especially in a number of high-income countries. Is capitalism so entrenched that even under such deplorable conditions it seems unshakeable? Is there a way out?

The tension between labour and capital has erupted into numerous struggles but has not resulted in a fundamental change. Movements for change rise and wane (such as the Lula da Silva government in Brazil), chip away at the capitalist edifice but stay confined to the periphery. On trade, minimum wages, conditions of work, the ecological crisis, housing and many other fronts, some battles are won but so far, the victory is never far-reaching enough to alter the balance of power in any given society.

The power of profit, the life blood of capitalism, needs to be acknowledged. It is through profit that more markets are created; production is expanded; the division of

3 https://data.oecd.org/unemp/unemployment-rate.htm

labour is made more complex; more labour-displacing technologies are introduced; politicians are bought; housing, health care, education and culture are exchanged as goods; and wars are created and fought. If the profit motive were removed, it stands to reason that a very different society from what is known today might be created. It may be possible to imagine life in a profitless world as the way some of our ancestors lived, but is this possible in a world so steeped in the capitalist modes of production? Will such a world be qualitatively and ethically different from the system that defines life in the contemporary world? Is it possible to build an economy without profit being appropriated by the owners and managers who run enterprises and would this lead to the eventual demise of capitalism? Would such an economy be able to end the ever-widening inequality in wealth and income distribution?

Social business is a system of production and distribution with the objective of not only rewarding the entrepreneur's talents and hard work but also finding solutions to many societal problems. It does this by factoring in the cost of materials and labour, then selling at a margin that enables the enterprise to create 'blended value'[4] for society, and at the same time recoup its costs in order to safeguard financial sustainability and repeat the cycle. This is not restricted to physical goods but can include a range of social services that communities require. As elaborated in the Introduction and Chapter II of this volume, the primary purpose of a social business is creating blended value for society in a financially sustainable manner. There is much discussion on whether such a system, even if it were to grow exponentially, could replace capitalism as it presently exists.

Social enterprises and social business: (Neo-) Marxist views

For neo-Marxists, social business, and for that matter social enterprise, does not eliminate the inherent tension in the relations between labour, capital and state; and between market and civil society. Rather, it ameliorates some of the socially harmful effects associated with capitalism. By virtue of the power it wields, the market remains the dominant institution and is able to structure the relations between the state and civil society in ways that perpetuate its dominance.

There are not many comprehensive (neo-) Marxist critiques of the concept of social business and social enterprise. The argument of some of the critiques that can be found can be summarised as follows. For Chik Ho Ning, there are many benefits of social businesses and social enterprises when compared with conventional businesses.

> Firstly, the welfare of workers can be better protected, in terms of working conditions and a fairer distribution of surplus value produced. Secondly, through employment and training opportunities, vulnerable groups in society can be aided. Thirdly,

4 As has been elaborated in Chapter II the concept of blended value has been developed by Jed Emerson and is 'a conceptual framework for advancing a vision of value creation which is not based upon a bifurcated understanding of the nature of value (either financial/or societal value), but rather a unified, holistic understanding of value as "both/and," integrated and non-divisible'. (http://www.blendedvalue.org/framework/)

> common good can be achieved: social harmony through understanding and respect for the vulnerable; and social justice through preventing exploitation of workers and promoting equality among workers.[5]

Even though social business and enterprise provide a different working environment, which possibly provides more protection from exploitation, it does not solve the fundamental problem of alienation. This is because workers still fall under the power of capital and sustain themselves through capital. Though, endeavouring to achieve the common good, social businesses still bear the characteristics of a capitalistic business, and are inevitably affected by objective situations such as market dynamics and competition. Overcoming the alienation of labour requires an inversion of the capitalistic mechanism, which is far beyond the power of social businesses.[6]

Marxists are more severe in their criticism of social enterprises and businesses. The defining point for them is whether there is a fundamental change in ownership of the means of production from private to public hands. Daniel Greener expresses the Marxist view succinctly:

> While social enterprises on the surface represent a break from the conventional business model, these enterprises still depend on and profit from a capitalist system: the means of production continue to be privately owned and exchange takes place in the free market. Seen from a Gramscian perspective, the social elite are simply developing a new system while retaining many of the old system's features. As a result, people are still self-interested yet bourgeoisie desire is concealed as social concern. Consumers are demanding a holistic value proposition from their purchases and hence businesses stand to gain privately from investing in social causes.[7]

JooHwan Kim[8] (2016) is much stronger in his criticism of social enterprises and businesses. In his PhD dissertation he argues 'that the promotion of social enterprises operates as a new neoliberal government strategy that captures anti-neoliberal progressive social movements and shifts the responsibilities of the state for solving particularly problems of poverty and unemployment on to civil society and social activists.'[9]

In a contribution to the Stanford Social Innovation Review, Jyoti Sharma supports this view but makes a distinction between social enterprises and social businesses that perpetuate neo-liberal economics and those that are genuinely concerned about human welfare:

> The neoliberal model also speaks a language that donors, many of whom are supported by business funds, understand: quantifiable results that can be independently validated, sustainable revenue models, clearly quantifiable impact

5 Chik Ho Ning, not dated.
6 Ibid.
7 Greener, 2014.
8 JooHwan Kim, 2016.
9 Ibid.

> (such as the number of products sold), market-driven change, and a lack of need for conscious stewardship. Moreover, neoliberal social entrepreneurship is not an activist social movement and so does not threaten the powers that be, to which most donors are tied. Businessperson donors also connect with social entrepreneurship at an emotional level because it celebrates the power of an individual to win influence and change the 'system', much as they see themselves doing. Neoliberal social entrepreneurship also lends itself well to feel-good communication and storytelling – a just cause with young, idealistic, self-reliant protagonists ready to solve the problem on their own. All these, I think, have contributed to the popular image of social entrepreneurship with strong neoliberal overtones, rather than the hybrid reality that actually works on ground. [10]

It is obvious that Sharma is focusing her critique on the concept of social enterprises that operate within the neo-liberal development model, and not on social businesses that promote transformational change.[11] By contrast, she explains that:

> ... the focus of social entrepreneurship should be not the 'enterprise' but the beneficiary. Its design should flow from, and be anchored to, the needs and capacities of the beneficiaries. Profit-making should be secondary to making impact. Hence, charitable donations and non-profit capability that can add value to the beneficiary should be a welcome part of the solutions set... Social entrepreneurship does seem to work, however, in an 'outsourcing' capacity, where it partners with a government or donor to implement programs and perform outreach. Examples include non-profits working through Medicare as a part of the United States' Program of All-Inclusive Care (PACE) for the elderly and NGOs providing skilled staff for government schemes, such as Anganwadi, a health and nutrition program for pre-school children, pregnant women, and lactating mothers in India. In these cases, the social entrepreneur works as an efficient vendor for the welfare provider and does not depend on collections from the community for survival.[12]

According to Marxists then, there is nothing transformative about social enterprises or social businesses because there is no difference between them and the traditional capitalist mode of production on one side, and, at the other end of the spectrum, the altruism of charitable and voluntary organisations that have been around since capitalism itself.

Marxist views on change processes

With these divergent views, let us return to the question above: is social business a viable alternative to capitalism? Marx was the first to sketch a world view of capitalism, which is characterised by private ownership of the means of production, extraction of surplus value by the owning class for the purpose of capital accumulation, wage-based labour and — at least as far as commodities are concerned — which is market-

10 Sharma, 2016.

11 The differences between a social enterprise and a social business are explained in Chapter II of this volume.

12 Sharma, 2016.

based. He views it as a system that is antithetical to the human essence. Marx was also the first to prognosticate its demise and so it is useful to visit his idea of what would lead to its breakdown. In the Communist Manifesto, capitalism is seen as advancing to higher stages leading to the centralisation and concentration of capital.[13] Its collapse, however, comes with the growing immiseration of the working class. This is what we have come to know as the under-consumption thesis: capital drives wages down to increase the rate of profit, but it is these same wages that are needed to buy the goods that capitalists produce and which yields profit for them.[14]

Marx might have been wrong on the impoverishment of the working class (at least in the advanced capitalist countries) to the point that it ignites revolutionary upheaval. While exploitation of workers has not eased, there are four factors that can be cited as having extended the life of capitalism: one, the accommodation of the demands of working classes through their formal, representative organisations and their modes of struggle; two, the introduction of technology to substantially raise productivity; three, the extension of credit; four, the role of culture in manufacturing consent. We might also add a fifth, which is the role of the judicial and police force to contain workers' demands.

The much-heralded clash between capitalists and workers presaged by Marxists did not, of course, materialise in the core capitalist countries. (That it happened in a few countries in the periphery challenged the orthodox Marxist view.) The explanation came from neo-Marxists who introduced other dimensions to the analysis of the capitalist system which, they argue, bolster its staying power. The World Systems and Global Systems theorists, along with the Dependency School, contended that, for the first time in world history, a veritable World System has emerged in which all countries of the world are integrated into the capitalist order and have little or no choice to opt out. Whatever differences may exist in national systems and cultures, each submits to the iron law of capital. Any deviation is punishable by, either the multilateral institutions, or the international banking system, or the imposition of trade restrictions, and/or an assault on their currencies.

The narrowing of the space in which countries – and especially workers and their allies – forge paths towards liberation from the grip of capitalism, raises several important issues about what is possible under the given status quo. This closing of the universe, if you like, begs questions about the course that subordinate classes and subaltern groups should chart to alter the current social and economic arrangement of capitalist societies, both advanced and less developed.

---

13 Marx & Engels, 1848. Ref. the data provided by Piketty and his team in the Introduction and Chapter II. (The challenge is of course to elaborate Piketty's data in terms of the relation between the profit and labour rates, which would express (if one transports Piketty's data in Marxist equations) trends indicating strengths and/or weaknesses of the present capitalist system.

14 Marx deals with this subject in several of his publications. A succinct introduction and overview is presented in his publication Wages, Price and Profit which is the report of the address he delivered on June 20 and 27, 1865 at two sittings of the General Council of the International Working Men's Association. Marx, 1974 (original 1898).

In the Marxist scheme, the state is the principal site of struggle. Either the state is seized through revolution, or a party with strong electoral support from workers, the poor, various civil society formations and some strata of the professional and middle classes, comes to power through the ballot box. The former is now a remote prospect and the latter, where this has happened, has been disappointing in what it was expected to deliver. Thus, even where state power has been successfully wrenched from conservative hands, or a war of liberation has dislodged settler colonial regimes, the systemic and structural change that was hoped for has been left wanting. India and South Africa are a case in point. Liberation from colonialism or an oppressive apartheid regime has taken place; however, the capitalist system has not been overthrown.[15] A notable exception is Brazil, but the gains of Lula da Silva's period in office are now being reversed with the administrative coup of Dilma Rousseff. Zimbabwe, Egypt and Venezuela have been disappointing for very different reasons which cannot be dealt with here. In many cases where there has been a transfer of power to progressive forces, what is likely to be found is big capital (domestic and international) setting in motion a strategy of containment to undermine or sabotage any attempt to experiment with non-capitalist programmes of development. Domestic capital does this by withholding investment (going on strike) while international capital employs any number of other means – freezing assets, imposing sanctions, restricting travel and engineering a coup or military invasion.

Following Marx, Antonio Gramsci[16] sketched a conceptual framework to illustrate how power is organised in capitalist societies. Ownership of resources is vested in either domestic or international corporations. They basically dictate what the state (the executive and legislative branches, the judiciary, police and military) and ideological structures (schools, religious institutions and media) must do to keep the system of production operating. Neither Gramsci's model nor the orthodox Marxist view envisaged a change in the relations of production without societies first undergoing a radical transformation of political power. This political transformation then begins the process of transferring the ownership of resources. Without the transfer of ownership of resources and the subsequent change in the relations of production, there is no change in the status quo. The class structure of capitalist society – essentially a class of owners and a class of workers - remains intact, whatever else may change. For Marxists, no theory of change has any validity if it does not have this as its objective.

Profit and change in the mode of production

Would the way profit is made and accumulated make any difference to the class struggle? If the profit motive is removed or is not privately appropriated, would that change the essence of capitalism? There is no answer to this that does not generate a great deal of controversy. We should be reminded here of what profit has done to sustain

15 See for India among others Omvedt, 1973; for South Africa McKinley, 2017.

16 Gramsci, 1991.

capitalism. It is profit that gave birth to a new dominant class in Europe in the 16th and 17th centuries and it is profit – and the way it has been appropriated, accumulated and used – that has entrenched class power ever since. From very early on in the history of capitalism, though, this class power has been challenged by alternative modes of production. The co-operatives that emerged in the wake of the industrial revolution can be said to be among the first forms of organisational change to meet basic human needs. Leandro Sepulveda states that:

> [T]he roots of the social economy can be found in the French tradition where organizations were established to improve the living conditions of the most vulnerable individuals in society and to promote the redistribution of wealth and social justice (Defourny 2001; Moulert and Ailenei 2005). The social economy comprises a family of organizations including co-operatives, associations, mutual aid/benefit societies and foundations whose primary aim is organizing production and consumption as well as providing access to credit, healthcare and other welfare services (Moulert and Ailenei 2005). Social economy organizations share similar principles, including the aim of serving their members and the community; the priority of people and labour over capital in the distribution of income; independence from the state; and democratic governance (Borzaga and Defourny 2001).[17]

Sepulveda adds more detail on the motivations of the founders of the social economy: The origin of non-state/non-private enterprising organizational forms can be largely traced back to the 19th century. As capitalism advanced, groups of people linked to religious, political-ideological and other interests established organizations such as voluntary associations, charities and co-operatives in order to combat growing social and economic needs and to pacify the increasing public unrest associated with the intensification of capitalist social relations of production which followed industrialization. Broadly speaking, these developments gave origin to the 'social economy', within the continental European tradition, and 'non-profits' and the 'voluntary' and 'charity' sector within the US and UK traditions, respectively.[18]

Seeing social business in this historical context, it is clear that it emerged in response to both state and market failure some 300 years ago. The same is happening in the contemporary world.[19] The ubiquitous effects of neo-liberalism in advanced industrialised and less-industrialised countries is visible in the reduced role of the state in relation to the provision of basic services (water, electricity, transport and health care) – and the commodification of these services – and in larger interventions in the economy. Market failure has exacerbated this, either because it is not deemed 'sufficiently' profitable to provide these services at all, or because access is limited to the few who can afford to pay (private health care is the best-known example of this). In

17 Sepulveda, 2015; 846. Dr Leandro Sepulveda is an Associate Professor at the Centre for Enterprise and Economic Development Research (CEEDR), Middlesex University Business School in the United Kingdom.

18 Ibid.

19 Ref. as well Black and Nicholls, 2004: 49

the era of liberalism, when market failure was identified, it was regular practice for the state to step in. Under neo-liberalism, the state has retreated or withdrawn from the economy, leaving the burden of failure to fall squarely on the shoulders of individuals, communities and charitable organisations. Social business, with its emphasis on creating blended value for society, is seen as filling this vital gap.

Filling the gap, however, would still leave the rest of the productive economy – which is the primary source of profit in a capitalist economy – untouched by this change in the mode of production. The financial system, the secondary tier of capitalism, is also not affected. Associated with this are the stock exchange and shareholders. We can also include owners of large landholdings. It is important to mention these constituents because they make up the three great forms of income that accrue to owners of capital: rent, profit and interest. Anything which does not threaten one or all of these sources of income is not likely to be considered a major adversary of the system of private ownership of the productive resources of a country.

Before social business is dismissed as a mere daydream of change, let us pause to consider what is already happening in this field. Especially the UK, which is generally viewed as the pioneer of social enterprise and social business, has seen an explosive growth in social enterprises from 5,300 in 2003 to 62,000 in 2007; government statistics from 2015 identified around 70,000 social enterprises in the UK, contributing £24 billion to the economy and employing nearly a million people.[20] Balandina Jaquier quotes the Monitor Institute, which has 'projected the market to grow from $50 bn in 2009 to $500 bn by 2019'. This is however still less than 1% of all the global financial assets.[21] Although the market for investments in social entrepreneurs and social business is a new, fast growing market, it remains a relatively small – some would even say marginal – section of the overall economy.

Available data on social businesses in other countries show a growth trend in the following elements of the economy: the number of businesses, the sectors in which they operate, the jobs they have created, the amount of funds invested and the value generated. Only an empirical study that models this trend with several variables could help to say with any certainty what impact the growing social economy is likely to have on any of these elements. For now, that is only speculation.

More important than these figures, however, is the trend of an emerging change in culture that can be observed. As indicated in Chapter II, increasingly, more people inside and outside of the business world, civil society and public sector are longing for

20 https://www.socialenterprise.org.uk/state-of-social-enterprise-report-2015. These data should be taken as an indication of a trend and not as exact figures as both data referring to social enterprises and social business are included.

21 Balandina Jaquier, 2011: 14. Other sources, such as the Global Impact Investing Network Annual Survey 2018 and Deloitte's 2018 Deloitte Global Human Capital Trends also indicate that this market is growing, however without providing detailed global date and an indication of the percentage of the global financial assets. (GIIN, 2018; Kaji et al, 2018)

a change in economic development model – and more and more are acting on it. This can be in the form of starting a social business, or in attempting to change the existing business culture within an organisation and move towards (more) social business principles and practices.[22]

Some critics (Marxists especially) would say that this growth of social businesses does not translate into transformative power. The point is valid because the state has not been transformed and is quite amenable to having organisations from civil society take on social welfare provision. If, however, the state is not primarily functioning as an instrument of the ruling classes and is not controlled by multinational corporations, but is seen as a relation, as a battlefield, in which multinational corporations' interests sometimes overtake other social and economic interests but not per se, changes can be transformational. This is possible only when businesses no longer make profit their sole objective, but include other values. So, the site of struggle now shifts from labour to capital, to the state and to corporate culture, ethos, values and behaviour. Sepulveda and others call this historical institutionalism which looks at how 'institutions, policy ideas and values, and no particular single grand theory or societal interest ... take central stage in political and economic analysis'.[23] Institutional change comes about when economic and socio-political actors have the motivation and ability to change institutions and the existing status quo in favour of new ideas.[24] In the capitalist setting, corporations use their profits to buy power and influence which they use to make more profits. A change in values of corporate entities could end this merry-go-round.

As for what will bring about this change in values? In initial analyses, according to Sepulveda, it was thought there was 'a counter-cyclical causal relationship between the economic cycle and the growth of social enterprise, namely that social enterprise grows when the overall economy slows down.'[25] Between the early 1990s and 2000s, analysts found the opposite occurred: social enterprises emerged in the upward phase of the economic cycle. One explanation offered is that:

> ... social enterprises as hybrid organizations seem to better reflect the general spirit of an epoch as characterized by both the supremacy of the free enterprise ideology and marketization of different spheres of public and private life, on the one hand, and the subsequent resurgence of critical economic thinking that questions the core values of laissez faire by placing social and environmental principles at the heart of sustainable economic development paths ....[26]

22 This is called social intrapreneurship: social entrepreneurship in entrenched organisations. (Grayson et al., 2014). See also Chapter IX for an example of this approach.

23 Ibid.

24 Hall and Taylor, 1996.

25 Ibid page 849.

26 Ibid.

This spirit of the epoch and the critical voices that it spurred is also echoed by Stiglitz:

> ... since the 1980s (and particularly in light of the recent crisis of 'casino capitalism' [Sinn 2010], together with the state's failure to regulate markets thus allowing speculation to take place and the subsequent economic downturn), previously idealized values of free market economics such as (irresponsible) risk-taking, (extreme) individualism and consumerism have come under increased public and government scrutiny.[27]

A changed mode of production, then what?

Now the differentiation between corporate social responsibility (strong and weak), shared value creation and social entrepreneurship on the one side and the concept of social business on the other once again becomes relevant. Corporate social responsibility and shared value creation are basically 'business as usual' with the focus on shareholder value and profit. A social enterprise (a combination of a charity with a mainstream business) is also a business model within the existing capitalist framework. A social business, however, is not. Its primary focus is not on profit, but on blended value. This makes it a radical new entity in the economy and society at large.[28] Social businesses represent a change in the mode of production, but will not be able to replace the existing mode in the near future, since for-profit production shows no sign of being flung into the dustbin of history. It is therefore to be expected that a dual system will operate for some time to come. It is nevertheless useful to think about what changes are possible in the larger, profit-driven economic system as a dual mode of production develops. This should be considered for the following elements of the mainstream economy:

- the banking system;
- publicly traded companies;
- capital markets; and
- skills formation and employment.

As with all other businesses, social businesses will have to borrow from banks to get started and pay off their loans with interest. In the second and subsequent rounds, though, the amount of borrowing could fall as profits are ploughed back into the businesses in accordance with social business practice. The impact of the self-financing credo of social businesses could have far-reaching effects on private, mainstream financial institutions and, if state-owned banks and social impact investment funds were to be established, the effects would be even greater. The expansion of businesses without bank finance could mark a major change in finance capitalism.

The banking system is not likely to bite the hand that feeds it, so we should not expect its business-lending practices to make a 360 degree turn in favour of social businesses.

---

27 Stiglitz, 2010.

28 Ref. the Diagram II.3 about the typology of businesses in Chapter II.

Banks, of course, like to lend money because interest payments make up a large and lucrative part of their income. They are also focused solely on the financial 'bottom line' while ignoring the social and the environmental bottom lines. This opens the question of the need for policies to provide start-up (patient) capital or whether social businesses will have to continue to depend on private (social) investors, foundations, government-owned social investment funds and grants (from philanthropists). On interest rates, one possible scenario, as social businesses make their presence felt, is a lower demand for loans. Over time, this could bring about a fall in interest rates which could stimulate new investment and lead to improved growth in the economy. This, however, is not necessarily a predictable outcome, as we see in Europe where negative real interest rates have been in place for almost a decade but growth in investment has not followed suit. Ultimately, investment is a response to perceived changes in demand. Thus, while social businesses cannot directly influence monetary policy, they can indirectly affect interest rates which are an important pillar of that policy.

Since social businesses will not be publicly traded companies, the casino economy could lose its lustre in due course. In a social and solidarity economy there is no need for share offerings, as neither are profits distributed nor dividends paid, as is the practice under capitalism. This effectively puts an end to the derivatives market and just about every other speculative instrument that has been dreamed up. The futures market on commodities may still operate unless or until a number of primary commodity-producing countries de-link from the global marketing system.

A final question that has to be posed here has to do with capital markets, the handmaidens (or 'caddy boys') of corporations. What will happen to all the capital that has been accumulated by finance houses? Here special reference is made particularly to investment firms, asset management companies and other financial institutions which have and move stupendous amounts of money, facilitating, in the process, the continuous reproduction of capitalist relations of production. A social economy reverses the trend towards 'financialisation' and returns society to the production of real goods that do not destroy the natural world (i.e. blended value). Marx said that in the development of the capitalist system there is a tendency for the rate of profit to fall and that this leads to the eventual demise of the system. He argued that capital is continuously seeking its own expansion and so it moves in and out of industries as profits rise (usually the result of new technologies being introduced) and then fall as competition intensifies. In a social economy, profit is expected to behave very differently. It would not seek its expansion in response to the impulse of greed and avarice but rather to satisfy real societal needs. Financial services would exist to pool capital and facilitate money transfers. The transformation of this industry is vital to the success of the social economy.

As mentioned earlier, capitalism has time and again proved to be more 'resilient' than Marxists anticipated. The emergence and growth of social business may not lead to a direct crisis or final collapse of the capitalist system, but rather to the provision of a better alternative and a gradual emergence of a new mode of production. In this context the relationship between base and superstructure becomes relevant.

Base and superstructure

In the Marxian conception, the base determines the overall character of a society. This is the site where the relations of production are cast which then have a decisive effect on how society develops. In the superstructure, the power of the owning classes comes to bear on the rest of society through the state by way of legislation and coercion. The state is aided in its functions by a plethora of ideological institutions that become powerful in their own right as social and economic relations develop. These are comprised mainly of the media, schools, religious institutions, and art and cultural organisations. There is a vast body of literature which argues that the superstructure (particularly mass media) in advanced capitalism has become more influential in shaping people's ideas of themselves and the society in which they live, however precarious their conditions of life may be in the economic sphere. Ideological hegemony is maintained largely by corporatist media, whose interests are not only identical with the profit-making system, they are also highly profitable enterprises that generate good returns for their owners and shareholders. In authoritarian systems the state and the media are generally a Janus figure – two heads attached to the same body. The few independent entities that may be allowed to operate, do so with restrictions imposed on the extent to which they may offer an alternative view on social, economic and political life. The rationale offered reflects the marketisation of ideas: 'this is what our readers/viewers want or this is what sells.'

The base and superstructure act on one another in several ways: the superstructure reinforces the base by portraying the profit-based system as the best of all possible worlds and the captains of industry as paragons of success whose achievements should be emulated; the base demands that the superstructure controls the flow of information and deflects consciousness away from the class dimension of the relations of production. We naturally locate the concept of social business in the base. A theory of change would then say that this is a step towards transformation as the accumulation of profit gives way to satisfying the social needs of society. But without the necessary ideological support the transformation would be a still birth, since changes in the base can only be sustained when the set of ruling ideas (or the ideas of the ruling class) is replaced by alternative voices expressing how society should be arranged. There is nothing to indicate that this will come from the institutions that currently make up the ideological apparatus in most countries. Among and within these institutions there may be voices of dissatisfaction with the political and business establishment, but few produce a critical analysis of the need for transformation of the base.[29]

29 Those who perceive the state and big multinational corporations not as monolithic entities, but primarily as a battleground, speak, in the context of fostering social entrepreneurship and social business, of 'social intrapreneurism': bringing about change in entrenched organisations. (Grayson et al., 2014; Koleva & Azam Roomi, 2015.)

Without warm applause for its way of doing things, social business will be swimming against the tide for many years to come, if not decades. Yes, there may be some adulation expressed to show a 'kinder, gentler capitalism or creative capitalism', but anything that hits at the heart of the system of private accumulation will not be made to feel welcome. Social business cannot rely on mainstream media to give it the stamp of saviour of humankind for a world run amok by the insatiable appetite for profits. We have to then ask what should be done to spread the message of 'blended value'. An effective alternative would be to create a dedicated corps of social business practitioners who actively advocate influencing the superstructure.

Given the inhospitable environment in which social business finds itself, it would be best to start small-scale activities with communities that suffer serious material deprivation. But the relatively well-off communities can play a crucial role as well. The idea here is for a cross-fertilisation of practical experience with businesses that are better resourced in the areas of skills, knowledge and technology. The use of social media can be particularly effective in getting these initiatives off the ground and spreading the message of breaking with the status quo. Hosting forums, community markets and festivals are other potential methods of growing this movement to create interest in social business. Newsletters, electronic and hard copy, can stimulate interest especially if they profile success stories in the country and throughout the world.

This may not be a simple task. The ideological institutions of capitalism have developed sophisticated methods of 'persuasion' which cannot be easily countered. Social media, which was expected to become a source for alternative ideas, has, unfortunately, also become a platform for toxic social and political views. Social business thus finds itself operating in difficult circumstances. Fear and insecurity, which springs from the instability in economic systems through globalisation and the dramatic shift from production of physical goods to financialisation, plague societies across the globe. A message of a just social and economic order will be resisted by the established business and political elite, but other segments of society can also be expected to reject such initiatives. Cynicism has permeated the lives of many and in many countries traditional forces on the left are either in disarray or fragmented and disorganised. There is at present no organised political entity capable of harnessing mass support for a new, fairer and more just, economic agenda. The battle of ideas may prove just as formidable as the battle against capital itself.

Social and solidarity economy

As indicated earlier the concepts of social business and social and solidarity economy are still a 'work in progress'. It is far too early to picture a detailed and definite image, but the broad contours of an ideal type of social and solidarity economy and differences with the predominant economic paradigm can already be indicated (see Table X.1).

Table X.1: Schematic comparison capitalist economy – social and solidarity economy

#	Subjects/criteria	Classical capitalist economy	Ideal type of social and solidarity economy
1	Ethics	Free market as the guiding principle. Assumption that individual rationality leads to collective rationality.	Economy is a moral system with rational ethical principles.
2	Primary driver	Capital accumulation (shareholders value) through profit maximisation.	Sustainable inclusive development which is environmentally sound and enhances participation of citizens at all levels in all spheres of life: financially, environmentally and socially sustainable development. (The concept of 'blended value'.)
3	Dominant mode of production	Means of production in the hands of few using wage labour. Supported by the state and finance capital.	Profit is not privately appropriated. Labour is focused on socially useful labour. More limited divide between labour and capital and nature.
4	Mode of accumulation	Extracting surplus from labour value and exploitation of nature.	Surplus value is being created but not transformed into profit for private appropriation but used for financial sustainability of businesses.
5	Ownership	Private either in the form of an individual or corporation.	Collective. A social business may be started by an individual, but over a period of time ownership is transferred to those who are functionally involved and associated with the social business.
6	Dominant value produced	Exchange value that is transformed into financial value.	User value related to blended value is central. Satisfying needs as a social relation, not merely the consumption of a commodity.
7	Exchange	Free market extending from local to global.	Free market, barter networks, social money.
8	Relationships among actors	Asymmetric (power) relationships, with high levels of alienation.	Reciprocal in nature based on complementarity, non-alienating.
9	Relationship between work and natural environment	Extractive, unlimited growth. Disembeddedness society, economy and nature. 'Deterriorisation'.	Growth and well-being. Connected to society, community and nature.
10	Principles of consumption	Individual, according to income; status oriented.	Primarily satisfaction of need.
11	Principles of coordination	Self-regulating market with corrections by the state of market failures.	Active citizens' involvement to harmonise financial and social and environmental sustainability.
12	Business performance measurement	Return on Investment.	Social Return on Investment, ESG, et cetera.
13	Major challenges	Down turns in the business cycle. Crisis triggered by financial speculation.	Non-conducive external environment; external actors and factors are not conducive. Scaling up. Mission drift – pressure of investors for quick returns.

Source: Moolla & Van der Velden, inspired by José Luis Coraggio, 2018: 22 - 23

Conclusion

Our examination of a social and solidarity economy leads us to conclude with a discussion that Marx started on the concept of use value (the utility of a commodity) and exchange value (other commodities it will be exchanged for, often reflected in the price of a commodity). Capitalism marked a break with previous modes of production in the way it separated the products of human labour from the utility (use value, value in use) it was meant to have. In this transition, commodities assumed a power over human beings, which inverted the moral and ethical foundations of society. Commodities were given personalities; they offered comfort for woes, lifted spirits and bought love. The commodification of life has so distorted the human essence, that in the advanced stages of capitalism we are scarcely able to differentiate between natural and artificial needs. The outcome is evident all around us: often our relationship with nature and with fellow human beings is one of disposability.

Exchange value was a logical step in the transition from feudalism to capitalism. As production for profit developed, a calculus for determining the exchange of commodities had to be formulated. The common denominator in production was labour time. Nature did not feature at all – it was there to be used and when depleted, it would be turned into a wasteland. Once labour time was accounted for in production, a selling price could be set. The difference, of course, was profit. What this profit should be was at first up to the whim of the owner, but later came to be determined by the 'market' – that amorphous institution that brings buyer and seller together. The onset of competition put pressure on costs which led to the increasing immiseration of workers that continues to the present day.

The devaluation of people and nature over the past 300 years now manifests itself in multi-dimensional ways. Our natural environments suffer excessive pollution and diminishing biodiversity, degraded soil conditions and erratic weather patterns, which scientists say are the results of global warming. On the social level, health care and education are still out of reach for millions of people; homelessness grows even in high-income countries; and drug abuse and its associated ills of trafficking, gangsterism and violence plagues communities in many countries. Economic conditions show continued deterioration in the form of high rates of unemployment and poverty in non-industrialised countries, increasing inequality, high levels of indebtedness of consumers and farmers, and a fragile financial system that is prone to crises every few years caused in large part by speculation. Moreover, in many countries democracy is in crisis. Through the concept and practice of a social and solidarity economy we can possibly find a way back to use value, an economic system where human beings act out of need for the satisfaction of primary needs and with ethical norms that guide production, exchange and distribution of goods and services.

In the era of liberalism, the state was the main provider of social welfare. With neo-liberalism the market became the supreme institution to take societies to the zenith of economic and social development. In an ironic turn of history, the massive failures of neo-liberalism have placed the levers of change and transformation in the hands of communities and their associations. Between state and market there have always been the people. It is now a question of how they position themselves as agents of change. Social businesses could be one of the main vehicles towards a fair and just economy.

References

Balandina Jaquier, J. (2011), *Guide to impact investing for family offices and high net worth individuals – managing wealth for impact and profit*, Winkel/Zürich (www.guidetoimpactinvesting.org)

Black, L. & Nicholls, J. (2004), There is no business like social business – how to be socially enterprising, London, the Cat's Pyjamas.

Coraggio, J.L. (2017), Towards a new economics: concepts and experiences from Latin America, in: North, P. & Scott Cato, M. (eds.) (2017), *Towards just and sustainable economies; The social and solidarity economy North and South*, Bristol, Policy Press, pp. 15 – 35.

Chik Ho Ning (not dated), A Third Way Out?—On Adam Smith, Karl Marx and Social Enterprise, in: *In Dialogue with Humanity*, Center for Intercultural dialogue (https://www5.cuhk.edu.hk/oge/oge_media/gef/doc/best_works/4th_bestwork/HuChikHoNing.pdf).

Chomsky, Noam & Polychroniou, C.J. (2014), *Optimism over Despair; On Capitalism, Empire and Social Change*, UK, Penguin Books.

GIIN Research Team (Mudaliar, A. et al.,) (2018), 2018 Annual Impact Investor Survey, no place ,GINN. (https://thegiin.org/assets/2018_GIIN_Annual_Impact_Investor_Survey_webfile.pdf)

Gramsci, A. (1991), *Prison Notebooks*, New York, NY, Columbia University Press.

Grayson D., McLaren, M. & Spitzeck, H. (2014), *Social intrapreneurism and all that jazz: How business innovators are helping to build a more sustainable world*, London, Routledge.

Greener, D. (2014), *The rise of the social enterprise*, October 2. (www.klceconomics.com)

Hall P. & Taylor, R. (1996), Political Science and the Three New Institutionalisms, in: *Political Studies*, Volume 44, Issue 5, December, pp. 936 – 957.

Kaji. J. et al, (2018), *The rise of the social enterprise*, 2018 Deloitte Global Human Capital Trends, Deloitte Insights.

Kim, J., (2016) *Neoliberalism and the Politics of Social Enterprises in South Korea: The Dynamics of Neoliberal Governmentality and Hegemony*. Dissertation, Georgia State University, 2016. http://scholarworks.gsu.edu/sociology_diss/84

Koleva, P. & Azam Roomi, M. (2015), Social Intrapreneurism and All That Jazz, How business innovators are helping to build a more sustainable world, *Society and Business Review*, Vol. 10, No. 2, 2015 pp. 194 – 199.

Marx, K. (1898), *Wages, Price and Profit* (Report of the address delivered on June 20 and 27, 1865 at two sittings of the General Council of the International Working Men's Association), Moscow, Progress Publishers, 1974 (original 1898).

Marx K. & Engels, F., (1848) *Manifesto of the Communist Party*, various editions. https://www.marxists.org/archive/marx/works/download/pdf/Manifesto.pdf

Dale McKinley, D. (2017), *South Africa's Corporatised Liberation: A Critical Analysis of the ANC in Power*, Auckland Park, Jacana.

Omvedt, G. (1973), Gandhi and the pacification of the Indian national revolution, in: *Bulletin of Concerned Asian Scholars*, Vol. 5, No 1, pp. 2 – 9.

Piketty, T. (2017), *Capital in the Twenty-First Century*, Cambridge, The Belknap Press of Harvard University Press.

Sharma J. (2016), A Neoliberal Takeover of Social Entrepreneurship? *Stanford Social Innovation Review*, September 19.

(https://ssir.org/articles/entry/a_neoliberal_takeover_of_social_entrepreneurship)

Stiglitz, J. (2010), *Freefall: Free Markets and the Sinking of the Global*, London: Penguin

Sepulveda, Leandro (2015), Social Enterprise – A New Phenomenon in the Field of Economic and Social Welfare, *Social Policy & Administration*, Vol. 49, No. 7, December 2015, pp. 842 – 861.

Websites

www.guidetoimpactinvesting.org

www.socialenterprise.org.uk

https://neweconomics.org/

https://ssir.org/

About the authors

Worku Behonegne is one of the longest serving employees of SNV. His undergraduate study was in Management at Addis Ababa University. His graduate study was at Maastricht School of Management. He served in different senior positions within SNV, both at international and national levels. He also assumed different global roles for SNV, e.g. he coordinated the implementation of the LEAP+ programme, which is described in the volume. Currently he is back in his country, Ethiopia, as SNV Country Director.

Betteke de Gaay Fortman is, since its inception in 2007, the director of the Karuna Foundation and one of the key-persons in building a new organisation and in developing the vision and model. With her support and leadership, Karuna Nepal has grown into a strong local entrepreneurial organisation. She has been working in international development for the last 18 years. Before, she was director and owner of Servicio (a Spanish language company). She is a board member of the Plastic Soup Foundation, Action Aid and the Dutch Coalition for Disability and Development.

Pol De Greve is a development practitioner with extensive experience in different institutional environments, i.e. multilateral agencies (FAO), academic institutions (Wageningen), INGOs and as a consultant with Context, international cooperation, and since June 2018 as owner and manager with I&S Consulting. Throughout his career he has been focusing on challenges in the agricultural and rural sector. Pol has a long track record in many countries in Africa and Asia.

Jack van Dokkum studied International Development Studies in the Netherlands and worked mainly in the field of International Development. In 2013 he joined the Pactics Group to co-design and implement the Pactics Corporate Responsibility programme in its two Cambodian factories in Siem Reap (eyewear accessories) and Phnom Penh (sportswear). Currently, he is an independent consultant advising companies on enhancing sustainability in their operations and supply chains.

Eric Roetman used to coordinate the planning, monitoring and evaluation of international programmes (at ICS). Currently, he is an all-round researcher at Windesheim University of Applied Sciences in the Netherlands. He manages several research projects on innovations by small and medium enterprises. In the past two years he has focused on the circular economy. As a researcher he collaborates with fellow researchers, students, companies and other stakeholders to identify relevant topics for future research.

David Katzlinger is the Head of Institutional Partnership Development at the Head Office of SOS Children's Villages International (CVI). Acquainted with overseas commodity trade during the early 2000s, he works with SOS CVI since 2005. Over the years he has contributed to introducing and mainstreaming modern development cooperation methods into the organisation. Since 2012 he is President of the International Staff Council, which has been formed as a direct outcome of the civic driven change training drive within the Together4Change programme at headquarter level. David is an alumnus of the Ashoka CEE Visionary Program 2016/17.

Zunaid Moolla is a South African economist who specialises in economic literacy and research on alternative economics. He is a facilitator with Training for Transformation, an organisation that runs training programmes for community workers and social activists. Among the previous positions he held, was that of Executive Director of the National Institute for Economic Policy where he trained the first Members of Parliament of South Africa after its transition to democracy in 1994. He also worked for government departments in Canada. He is currently Deputy Editor of New Agenda magazine published by the Institute for African Alternatives.

Laxmi Prakash Semwal grew up in a family of farmers in a mountain village in the Indian Himalayas. He started his career as finance manager in the corporate sector and went on to set up Shri Jagdamba Samiti in 1991. This organisation aims to introduce citizen driven change to farmers, and to strike a balance between financial and socio-political objectives. In 2003 he began the conceptualisation of a business-driven partnership model in the agricultural space of the state of Uttarakhand, focusing on the apple value chain in particular. Finally, in 2007 the Apple Project was launched, with Mr. Semwal as Chairman of the Board and Managing Director. He has led the company to quickly show profitability, while never compromising on its commitment to the prosperity of the local apple growers.

Uday Thakkar is a social change activist and entrepreneur. Having started and successfully grown several businesses, a charity and a social enterprise he launched Red Ochre a social business that supports the ethical and social economy globally. Uday uses his experience and knowledge to successfully improve the performance and achievements of individuals and organisations. Uday has been voted UK Social Enterprise Mentor of the Year.

Fons van der Velden is the founder and director of Context, international cooperation, a social business that provides business development support to social businesses and development organisations. Over the past four decades he has commuted between the academic community, policy formulation and change practice. He published earlier about the international division of labour, labour conditions in multinational corporations, development cooperation and social business.

About the text editor

Hilde Bakker works as independent researcher, evaluator, writer and editor. After her studies in history and philosophy of psychology, she worked for many years as researcher and journalist of (mental health) care. Gradually, she shifted her focus to evaluation support, specialising in co-conceptualising approaches and designs, and content editing of evaluation reports. Her editing work includes supporting activists who have limited formal education to share their work with a broader, professional audience and synthesising key insights of in-depth evaluation reports into more readable formats. Hilde lives and works in Amsterdam, the Netherlands and Port Elizabeth, South Africa.

Index

There is a [illegible] going programme operated by Business in the Community[illegible] where social [illegible] ies receive workshops from specialists, but mentoring from managers [illegible] ety of large business such as BP (energy company), Freshfields (legal compa[illegible] erve (design and construction), ASDA (supermarket chain) and ExetionMe[illegible] ort published in 2015[illegible] gave considerable commentary on the benefits to [illegible] enterprises but it was difficult to ascertain which benefits can be directly att[illegible] e mentoring part of the programme. The main benefits that the [illegible]

- improve[illegible] ding of risk management
- busines[illegible] nd
- marke[illegible] develop[illegible]

All of these [illegible] part of [illegible] workshop [illegible] and it may well be that the mentoring [illegible] these skills development. The [illegible] seem to [illegible] developing their soft skills from the [illegible]

[illegible]